FIRST OF
THE MANY

*A Journal of Action with
the Men of the Eighth Air Force*

By
Captain JOHN R. (Tex) McCRARY
and
DAVID E. SCHERMAN

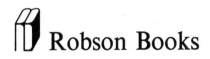 Robson Books

FIRST EDITION COPYRIGHT © 1944 JOHN R. McCRARY
AND DAVID E. SCHERMAN. THIS EDITION FIRST
PUBLISHED IN 1981 BY ROBSON BOOKS LTD., 28 POLAND
STREET, LONDON W1V 3DB.

McCrary, John R
    First of the many.
    1. World War, 1939-1945 – Aerial operations,
    American
    2. United States. *Army Air Force. 8th Air Force* –
    History
    I. Title   II. Scherman, E David
    940.54′49′73   D790

    ISBN 0-86051-129-4

Printed and bound in Hungary.

TO THE COMBAT CREWS, *the fighting teams of the 8th U.S. Army Air Force—to the "first of the many" who fought and won the fierce opening rounds of America's part of the Battle of Germany, this book is dedicated.*

To military strategists, these men proved the case for high altitude, daylight, precision bombing. But more than that, they proved the resilience and resourcefulness and leathery courage and buckskin cheerfulness that is the inherited strength of Americans, as it met its most severe test on the sky-fronts over Germany.

And if you should stop a young airman of the 8th and confront him with such high praise, he would first look back over his shoulder, then look at you, and then ask, "Who, me?"

ACKNOWLEDGMENTS

The authors hereby acknowledge their immense debt to Sgt. James Dugan, formerly of the AAF, without whose patience, persistence, and editorial know-how this book never would have been much more than a good idea. They also wish to thank the Editors of LIFE Magazine for having granted permission to use certain photographs by David E. Scherman which have previously appeared in LIFE's pages.

Those photographs in FIRST OF THE MANY which are of an operational nature, such as shots of bomb destruction, air-sea rescue, and the like, should be credited to official USAAF sources.

CONTENTS

IT MUST HAVE BEEN nearly 35 years ago that a friend let me read his prized copy of *First Of The Many*. I found the book fascinating – and still do. 'Tex' McCrary tells of the young men who were the vanguard of the thousands that served with the 8th Air Force, particularly the bomber crews with whom he flew and had an affinity. His narrative uses the racy American journalese of those times, which for me has always been part of the book's attraction. With hindsight, perhaps McCrary's reporting is too laudatory, yet it does not veil the grim reality of those dangerous daylight missions over Hitler's Europe. The account of how he missed a date with death on the first Schweinfurt mission is an example.

McCrary, an experienced journalist and war reporter, served in 8th Air Force Public Relations during the early operational period of this, the most famous, Second World War American air formation. Much of his work involved photography giving him opportunities to visit airfields and meet the men about whom he was to write. His simple prose captured and held something of the flavour of those times, with the result that *First Of The Many* is probably the best contemporary study of USAAF airmen in England.

1981   ROGER A. FREEMAN

FOREWORD

A BEACHHEAD *is the testing time of an invasion. Headlines and wirephotos and newsreels have made this clear to all Americans.*

In the air, back in 1942, the task of taking a beachhead in enemy territory and holding it by day was the assignment of the U.S. 8th Army Air Force.

The first American "invaders" of Germany were the combat crews of the Flying Fortresses who found and smashed their targets, for many months attacking without fighter escort. Not once was any mission of the 8th, escorted or not, ever beaten back by German flak or fighters. That is the keynote of this story of the daylight air invasion of Germany and the men who carried it out.

The first-priority target of the 8th was always the Luftwaffe. Gunners and fighter pilots of the 8th beat the Hun fighters in the air; our bombers sought out the factories that built the Luftwaffe and smashed them on the ground. The 8th paid high in casualties. But, wing-tip to wing-tip with the RAF, they brought the end of the war in Europe closer by many months. On D-Day of the second front, Hitler's first air-line of defense was a beaten air force. The invaders of the 8th had fought and died to beat it—and to shrink the cost of that second front.

The 8th did more than fight its own battles. It split itself to send battle-tested groups of fighters and bombers to form the 12th Air Force for the North African invasion. Out of the 12th grew the 15th, first air force to link the Allied and Russian fronts, by the mission to Russian bases in June, 1944.

And one of the Fortress groups that went on that historic shuttle mission was one of the "first of the many"—the same group that made the first heavy bomber attack on a German-held target, the rail yards at Rouen, France, on August 17th, 1942.

IRA C. EAKER
Lieutenant General, USA
Commanding General, 8th Bomber Command,
Feb. 20, 1942–Nov. 30, 1942, and of the
8th Air Force, Dec. 1, 1942–Jan. 6, 1944

CAST OF CHARACTERS

BELOW are the names of the men and women who appear in this book. Among them are some—but not all, by any means—of the "first of the many." Some of them are still fighting in the skies over enemy lands. Some have come home to inspire and to teach others to fly and fight. Some are known prisoners of war. Some—well, "parachutes were seen to open." Some have given their lives for the Allied cause.

So that not only their friends and families and neighbors shall know them, but so that all their fellow-Americans shall know them, they are named here. They are the airmen of the Eighth Air Force who were in mind when the dedication to this book was written.

An asterisk after a name indicates that the home town is not known.

Pilot Officer HUGH CHARLES ADAMS, England

Sgt. ART ADRIAN, Milwaukee, Wisc.

Lt. GERALD AHLQUEST *

Pfc. DOUGLAS ALEXANDER *

Maj. ALFORD, Rising Star, Texas

Col. FRANK ALLEN, Chicago

Capt. ANDY ANDERSON, Long Beach, Cal.

Sgt. FRED ANDERSON *

RAF Flying Officer KOMING ANDERSON *

Capt. ANDREWS, Costa Mesa, Cal.

Lt. Gen. FRANK ANDREWS, Nashville, Tenn.

Lt. DON ARNS, Algona, Iowa

Gen. HENRY H. ARNOLD, Gladwyne, Pa.

Sgt. MICHAEL AROOTH, Springfield, Mass.

Capt. ATWELL *

Major HALEY AYCOCK, Midland, Texas

2nd Lt. H. L. AYRES, Indianapolis, Ind.

Lt. DON BADER, Addison, Ohio

Lt. BAIRD *

Lt. Col. ADDISON E. BAKER, Akron, Ohio

Capt. IRL BALDWIN, Yakima, Wash.

Lt. DAN BARBERIS, Bergen, N.J.

M/Sgt. BARNHILL *

2nd Lt. E. D. BEATTIE, Albany, Ga.

JACQUELINE BEAUVAIS, London

Capt. WALTER BECKHAM, DeFuniak Springs, Fla.

Capt. BOB ("SPOOK") BENDER, Pollockville, N.C.

2nd Lt. J. L. BENNETT, Tucumcari, N.M.

Lt. LOUIS BIANCHI, Bakersfield, Cal.

Capt. GEORGE BIRDSONG, Miss.

Lt. GEORGE BLACK, Monterey, Cal.

Maj. NAT BLANTON, Okla.

2nd Lt. V. A. BOEHLE, Indianapolis, Ind.

S/Sgt. HARRY BOHNEMAN, Pittsburgh, Pa.

2nd Lt. R. A. BOOCK *

Lt. D. E. BOOTH, New York, N.Y.

Sgt. BENNY BOROSTOWSKI, La Salle, Ill.

Sgt. FRED BOYLE, Reno. Nev.

AUDREY BOYLES, South Africa

Lt. F. R. BOYLES, Mt. Vernon, N.Y.

Sgt. JOHNNY BRADSHAW, Ft. Worth, Texas

2nd Lt. R. C. BRALEY, Lemoore, Cal.

Sgt. RUSS BROOKS, Gooding, Idaho

BILLY BROWN, Hollywood, Cal.

Sgt. BEN BUCHANAN, Ft. Worth, Texas

Flt. Lt. ROBERT A. BUCKHAM, Canada

Chaplain JIM BURRIS, Mo.

Lt. ED BUSH, Hollywood, Cal.

Maj. ROBERT CAMPBELL, Marshall, Texas

Lt. ROBERT L. CAMPBELL, Liberty, Miss.

Lt. TONY CARCIONE, Bethlehem, Pa.

2nd Lt. R. G. CARE, Angola, Ind.

Lt. ED M. CARMICHAEL, Maryville, Mo.

Lt. GEORGE CARPENTER, Oil City, Pa.

Lt. JOHN CARROLL, Chicago, Ill.

2nd Lt. V. R. CASTLE, Bluffs, Ill.

LADY CAVENDISH (ADELE ASTAIRE), London

M/Sgt. CHARLES CHAMBERS, Mechanicsburg, Pa.

2nd Lt. A. W. CHATTERLEY *

Lt. J. A. CLARK, Long Island, N.Y.

Maj. GALE CLEVEN, Odessa, Texas

Capt. CHARLES E. ("RED") CLIBURN, Hazlehurst, Miss.

S/Sgt. CLARENCE CLUCK, Chicago, Ill.

T/Sgt. JIM COBB, Freemont, N.C.

Maj. OSCAR COHEN, Carbondale, Ill.

Lt. KEITH CONNOLLY, Portage, Utah

Capt. WALLY COOK, Cincinnati, Ohio

THELMA COUGHENOUR, New Bethlehem, Pa.

Lt. L. R. COVER, San Carlos, Cal.

Maj. W. S. COWART *

Maj. "PAPPY" CRANDALL, Detroit, Mich.

Lt. Col. BILL CUMMINGS, Lawrence, Kans.

S/Sgt. WALTER G. DAGER, Monroeville, Ind.

M/Sgt. BOB DALTON *

Sgt. JIM DARRALL, Springfield, Pa.

Maj. GUS DAYMOND, Burbank, Cal.

Lt. CLYDE DE BAUN, Buchnell, Ind.

Lt. AUGUST V. DE GENARO, Conn.

"HENRI DERAIN," France

Lt. Gen. JACOB L. DEVERS, York, Pa.

Sgt. DEVINE, Jersey City, N.J.

Lt. Col. KENNETH O. DESSERT *

Lt. BILL DICKSON, Selma, Ark.

Maj. GERALD ("DIXIE") DIX, Sullivan, Ind.

Capt. DUFOUR, Ford, Essex, England

Sgt. "BULL" DURHAM, Chattanooga, Tenn.

Lt. Gen. IRA C. EAKER, Llano, Texas

Lt. BILL EANES *

2nd Lt. P. M. ELLINGTON, Tulsa, Okla.

Lt. COY ELLISON, McLean, Texas

2nd Lt. MORRY ELSTUN, Ross, Ohio

Lt. "BABE" EMMONS *

Capt. JACOB C. EPTING, Tupelo, Miss.

Lt. JOHNNY EVANS, Edmond, Okla.

Sgt. FARENHOLD *

Sgt. FERRORGIARRO, San Francisco, Cal.

Capt. FETROW, Upland, Cal.

2nd Lt. J. M. FINK, Philadelphia, Pa.

RAF Pilot Officer WILLIAM MEADE LINDSEY FISKE, Chicago, Ill.

S/Sgt. ELMER FJOSNE, Cornell, Wisc.

M/Sgt. WILLIAM W. FLEMING, Jenkins, Ky.

HUGH FLETCHER, Cleveland, Ohio

S/Sgt. JOHN FOLEY, Portland, Ore.

S/Sgt. FABIAN FOLMER, Mansfield, Ohio

S/Sgt. JAMES FORD, Chicago, Ill.

"FRANZ FORZMANN," Vienna, Austria

Lt. JUSTUS FOSTER, Junction City, Ky.

2nd Lt. F. J. FRANCE, Oklahoma City, Okla.

Lt. "BOB" FREIHOFER, Troy, N.Y.

Sgt. WAYNE FRYE *

Capt. CLARK GABLE, Hollywood, Cal.

Sgt. JACK GAFFNEY, San Bernardino, Cal.

Capt. DON GENTILE, Piqua, Ohio

MRS. HARVEY GIBSON, London

Lt. JIM GILL, Puckett, Miss.

S/Sgt. ROY GILLET, Stockton, Cal.

Sgt. HARRIS BENJAMIN GOLDBERG, Brookline, Mass.

T/Sgt. HARRY GOLDSTEIN, New York, N.Y.

Sgt. JOHN GOODGION, Ruston, La.

M/Sgt. BOB GRANT *

Sgt. WAYNE GRAY, Coraopolis, Pa.

Warrant Officer WILLIAM GREENFIELD, England

Capt. LEE HALL, St. Louis, Mo.

Capt. HALSEY, Chickasha, Okla.

Brig. Gen. HANSELL, San Antonio, Texas

Col. "CHICK" HARDING, W.Va.

Sgt. ARIZONA HARRIS, Tempe, Arizona

Air Chief Marshal SIR ARTHUR TRAVERS ("GINGER") HARRIS, London

Sgt. RAY HARRIS, Walled Lake, Mich.

Wing Commander GRAEME HARRISON, England

Flt. Lt. GEORGE H. T. HATTON, England

S/Sgt. HERBERT G. HAYS, Parkersburg, W.Va.

TRIS HENDERSON, London

WAYNE HENDRICKS, Salt Lake City, Utah

Lt. Col. TOMMY HITCHCOCK, New York, N.Y.

Lt. H. D. HIVELY, Athens, Ohio

Capt. TEX HOLLAND *

Capt. HOLLANDER, Hawaii

PAUL HOLT, San Francisco, Cal.

Lt. A. H. HOPSON, Dallas, Texas

Lt. RALPH HOUSMAN *

Lt. Col. TOM ("SPEED") HUBBARD, Ft. Worth, Texas

Lt. BOB HUDSPETH *

FATHER HUNT *

Maj. Gen. FRANK O'D. ("MONK") HUNTER, Savannah, Ga.

S/Sgt. PAUL HURLES, Columbus, Ohio

Lt. WILL HURST, Homer, Ill.

2nd Lt. ASA IRWIN, Portland, Ore.

Capt. JAY *

Maj. JOHN JERSTAD, Davenport, Ia.

Capt. GERRY JOHN, Owenton, Ky.

Sgt. HUGH JOHNSON, Ill.

Wing Commander JOHNNY JOHNSON, England

Col. LEON JOHNSON, Moline, Kans.

Lt. ROBERT S. JOHNSON, Lawton, Okla.

Lt. JACK JONES, Franklinton, La.

Lt. JIM JONES, Columbia, La.

Flying Officer N. M. O. JONES, Wales

Sgt. BOB JUNGBLUTH, Arlington, Neb.

Col. JOHN RILEY KANE, La.

Capt. FRED KAPPELER, Alameda, Cal.

Sgt. KEN KATE, Manchester, N.H.

Capt. CHARLES KEGELMAN *

Capt. HARRY KENDALL, Charlton, Iowa

Col. BILL KENNEDY *

Sgt. WILLIAM T. KENT, Beverly Hills, Cal.

Sgt. JOHN W. KERN, Newcastle, Ind.

Brig. Gen. ALFRED A. KESSLER, Sacramento, Cal.

Sgt. DON KING, Imperial, Texas

Sgt. KISS, Jersey City, N.J.

S/Sgt. LOUIS KLIMCHAK, Josephine, Pa.

Capt. BENNY KLOSE, South Dakota

2nd Lt. KEITH KOSKE, Milwaukee, Wisc.

T/Sgt. BEN KUROKI, Neb.

Lt. R. Y. KURTZ, JR., Bellerose, N.Y.

Sgt. BILLY LAMB, Belton, Texas

CAROLE LANDIS, Hollywood, Cal.

Sgt. ELDON R. LAPP, Ft. Wayne, Ind.

Lt. PHIL LARSON, Quincy, Ill.

Lt. ED LAWLER, Camden, Ark.

Col. LAWRENCE *

Col. BEIRNE LAY, Hollywood, Cal.

Capt. HARRY LAY *

2nd Lt. PHIL LECHRONE, Salem, Ill.

Sgt. COLIN LEE, Sun River, Mont.

Flt. Sgt. GEORGE LEIGHTON, England

Maj. Gen. CURTIS LE MAY, Ohio

SGT. JAKE LEVINE, East Nassau, L.I.

2nd Lt. HELEN LIEB, Minneapolis, Minn.

Sgt. ARLEY LINDSEY, Ada, Okla.

Capt. CHARLEY LONDON, Long Beach, Cal.

S/Sgt. MARSHALL R. LORD, Providence, R.I.

Lt. J. E. LUTZ, Fulton, Miss.

Sgt. FLOYD MABEE, Lafayette, N.J.

Lt. KENTON D. MACFARLAND, Galt, Cal.

Capt. WALKER MAHURIN, Ft. Wayne, Ind.

Col. LESTER MAINTLAND, Boerne, Texas

S/Sgt. FRANK MALONE, Hones Bath, S.C.

Capt. MARTIN *

Lt. JACK MATHIS, San Angelo, Texas

Lt. MARK MATHIS, San Angelo, Texas

S/Sgt. DICK MCALLISTER, Patterson, Mo.

JIM MCBRIDE, Akron, Ohio

Lt. BOB MCCALLUM, Omaha, Neb.

T/Sgt. JOHN MCCLURE, Atlanta, Ga.

Maj. D. B. MCGOVERN, Providence, R.I.

S/Sgt. JIM MCGOVERN, New Haven, Conn.

Cpl. JAMES MCLOUGHLIN, Broughty Ferry, Dundee, Scotland

Capt. MCMINN, Salt Lake City, Utah

Maj. JOHN J. MCNABOE, New York, N.Y.

Squadron Leader BUCK MCNAIR, Canada

Lt. Col. MCNICKLE *

Capt. MCPARTLIN *

Sgt. CHARLES J. MELCHIONDO, Medford, Mass.

Sgt. BILL MERCER, Zanesville, Ohio

Lt. ALPHONSE MARESH, Ennis, Texas

2nd Lt. R. K. MERRITT, Rockland, Me.

Lt. E. L. MILLER, Oakland Cal.

2nd Lt. H. L. MILLS, Leonia, N.Y.

M/Sgt. MISHMASH *

T/Sgt. RAYMOND T. MOORE, Corbett, Ore.

Capt. BOB MORGAN *

2nd Lt. JOHN C. ("RED") MORGAN, New York, N.Y.

Capt. JOHNNY MURPHY, San Diego, Cal.

2nd Lt. D. D. NEE, Long Beach, Cal.

Lt. LOUIS NELSON, Minneapolis, Minn.

Lt. JOE NEWBERRY, Crookston, Minn.

Sgt. JIM NOLAN, Cleveland, Ohio

Sgt. VINCENT NOVACEK, Max, Neb.

Col. GLENN C. NYE, Raleigh, N.C.

Maj. JACK OBERHANSLY, Spanish Fork, Utah

Capt. OSCAR D. O'NEILL, Rio de Janeiro, Brazil

Col. ORDWAY *

Lt. W. T. O'REGAN, Los Angeles, Cal.

FRANK OWEN, Wales

Lt. C. V. PADGETT, Bethesda, Md.

Lt. PHILIP T. PALMER, Wellington, Kans.

Lt. JOE PELLEGRINI, Philadelphia, Pa.

Lt. JOHNNY PERKINS, Chicago, Ill.

Col. ARMAN PETERSON, Flagstaff, Ariz.

Lt. Col. CHESLEY G. PETERSON, Santaquin, Utah

2nd Lt. K. D. PETERSON, Mesa, Ariz.

Lt. AL PEZZELLA, Newton, Mass.

Capt. MICHAEL G. PHIPPS, Westbury, L.I.

2nd Lt. S. H. PISSANOS, New York, N.Y.

Lt. PETER G. POMPETTI, Philadelphia, Pa.

Sgt. EUGENE PONTE, St. Louis, Mo.

Lt. Col. RAMSAY D. POTTS, JR., Memphis, Tenn.

Lt. R. L. PRISER, Troy, N.Y.

Col. "PUT" PUTNAM, Texas

Maj. Gen. ELWOOD M. ("PETE") QUESADA, Washington, D.C.

Maj. BOB RIORDAN, El Paso, Texas

Lt. WALT RIVERS, Paducah, Ky.

Maj. GENE ROBERTS, Spokane, Wash.

Maj. JOHN R. ROCHE, Davenport, Iowa

Congressman WILL ROGERS, JR., Cal.

2nd Lt. D. H. ROSS, Huntington Park, Cal.

Capt. "DOC" ROSS *

Col. BARTON RUSSELL, Montana

JOYCE SAMSON, England

T/Sgt. NEGELY SAPPER, Noblesville, Ind.

Warrant Officer ALLISTER SAUNDERS, New Zealand

Maj. DAVE SCHILLING, Detroit, Mich.

Lt. GLEN SCHLITZ, North Camden, Ohio

Lt. SCHOOLFIELD, Baltimore, Md.

SAMMY SCHULMAN, AP photographer, New York

Capt. DONALD SCHYLER, New York, N.Y.

T/Sgt. BAYNE SCURLOCK, Gladewater, Texas

Capt. ROBERT SHANNON, Washington, Ia.

Capt. DON SHEELER *

S/Sgt. PAUL J. SHOOK, Akron, Ohio

Lt. C. W. SILSBY, Dothan, Ala.

JO SIPPY, St. Louis, Mo.

Lt. W. C. SLADE, Draham, Okla.

Lt. G. J. SMART, Sedan, Kans.

Col. JACOB E. SMART, Jessup, Ga.

Lt. SMITH, Austin, Texas

1st Lt. SMITH, Molokoff, Texas

Lt. BOB SMITH, La Mesa, Texas

2nd Lt. K. G. SMITH, Boise, Idaho

Sgt. MAYNARD ("SNUFFY") SMITH, Caro, Mich.

Marine 2nd Lt. PAUL SMITH, San Francisco, Cal.

2nd Lt. F. J. SMOLINSKY, New York, N.Y.

Sgt. STAN SOLOMAN, Scranton, Pa.

Col. BUD SPRAGUE *

2nd Lt. A. J. STEPHANSON, Los Angeles, Cal.

Capt. STEPP, Ketchikan, Alaska

Lt. Col. JIMMY STEWART, Hollywood, Cal.

Capt. WALTER STEWART, Benjamin, Utah

Col. EARL STORRIE, Denton, Texas

Lt. HAROLD STOUSE, Seattle, Wash.

Lt. MALVERN SWEET, Livermore, Cal.

Lt. CALVIN SWOFFER, Memphis, Tenn.

Sgt. ALONZO SWOPE, Harlington, Texas

Lt. BILL TANNER, Canastota, N.Y.

Lt. Col. JOSEPH S. TATE, JR., St. Augustine, Fla.

Lt. BOY TAYLOR, Ontario, Cal.

Col. H. B. THATCHER, Chevy Chase, Md.

S/Sgt. LLOYD THOMAS, Larussell, Mo.

Sgt. FLOYD THOMPSON, Durant, Okla.

DIXIE TIGHE, London, England

Brig. Gen. EDWARD J. TIMBERLAKE, San Antonio, Texas

Lt. BOB TREDINNICK, North Caldwell, N.J.

2nd Lt. FRED W. TUCKER, Milton, Mass.

Lt. DAVID A. TYLER, JR., Hartford, Conn.

Lt. Col. ELIOTT VANDEVANTER, Baltimore, Md.

M/Sgt. PETER VERVERIS, Norwich, Conn.

Capt. "BUZZ" WAGNER *

Lt. DICK WALKER, Albany, Ga.

Capt. TOMMY WALLACE *

Sgt. REECE WALTON, Joplin, Mo.

Sgt. AYGMUND WARMINSKI, Hamtramck, Mich.

STAN WASHBURN *

Wing Commander RICHARD H. WATERHOUSE, England

T/Sgt. JOHN WEATHERS, New York, N.Y.

S/Sgt. TYRE C. WEAVER, River View, Ala.

S/Sgt. WEIDEMANN *

Capt. WEITZENFELD *

Lt. BILL WHEELER, Scarsdale, N.Y.

Lt. J. A. WILKINSON, Swarthmore, Pa.

Capt. DON K. WILLIS, Ft. Leavenworth, Ind.

Ambassador JOHN G. WINANT, Concord, N.H.

Capt. JOHN G. WINANT, JR., Concord, N.H.

S/Sgt. WIRTZ *

Lt. CLIVE WOODBURY, Fresno, Cal.

Lt. DENVER WOODWARD, Portsmouth, Ohio

Maj. JIM WRIGHT, Cleveland, Ohio

Lt. Col. WURZBACH *

Maj. WILLIAM WYLER, Hollywood, Cal.

Lt. ANTHONY C. YENALAVAGE, Kingston, Pa.

S/Sgt. "PAPPY" YOUELL, Boomer, W.Va.

Lt. D. A. YOUNG, Buffalo, Kans.

Col. HUBERT ZEMKE, Montana

Pilot Officer ALEKSY ZUKOWSKI, Vilna, Poland

1. In the bearded, haggard face of Pilot Harold Stouse, Seattle, in the tired lines of his Mae West and leather jacket, in the grimy lumpiness of the canvas bag that holds a wet oxygen mask—in this single picture is the story of all the physical and mental and spiritual strain of a daylight raid on Germany—and the relief, too, that another "rugged deal" is ended. Stouse fills out his flight report on the first 8th Air Force mission to Germany. Date: January 27, 1943.

2. In the beginning there were 4 Fortresses. The RAF combat-tested them over Germany in daylight in 1941—minus the Norden bombsight, more than a year before Americans flew them to Germany. RAF verdict on the early Forts like this one was: "Maybe."

3. We didn't get along too well with the English weather. "They oughta cut the cables on them barrage balloons and let the Island sink," was the shopworn gag in every fogbound GI's letter home. No joke to the 8th Air Force was weather like the cloud-cramped horizon above.

4. "The Boss," Ira Eaker, Texan, Commanding General 8th Air Force. A general is first an executive. Gen. Arnold, commanding all U.S. Army Air Forces, runs an organization bigger than the U.S. automobile industry. Eaker's share of the job is bigger than General Motors. First boss of the 8th was Lt. Gen. Spaatz. He once said, "I never saw a happy general." Eaker is no exception. When a Fortress gunner dies over Germany, before that gunner's family knows, Eaker knows and feels it first.

5. Among the first of the "first of the many" to be decorated was Capt. Charles Kegelman. Flying with RAF Bostons a half-dozen 8th Air Force crews celebrated the 4th of July, 1942, by bombing Nazi targets in Holland. For bouncing home on one engine from this first mission, Kegelman was awarded the Distinguished Service Cross by Maj. Gen. "Tooey" Spaatz, then commanding the 8th.

6. Comes John Henry. Negro engineering battalions, camped in the mud and greenery of England, were the first to begin bulldozing taxi strips, hard-standings, dispersal areas, and perimeter tracks; digging bomb dumps in the rich earth. At the beginning, all-American 'dromes were being built night and day for bombers still "on order."

7. The men of Negro aviation ordnance units now help handle the bombs for the bombers. Crew of this unit, here picking up three 250-lb. bombs with special crane, is under supervision of T/Sgt. John Weathers, New York (in foreground).

8. Deep penetration. On March 4, 1943, a force of Flying Fortresses hit the railroad yards at Hamm, beyond the Ruhr Valley, Germany. This was then the deepest penetration by the smallest force of American heavy bombers.

9. Rendezvous four miles over England. Before bombers cross the Channel they form their battle ranks in the flying wedges that fight through Focke-Wulfs, Messerschmitts, and Junkers, to their daylight target.

10. Sweetest moment of every mission: the instant when the wheels touch down in a tiny puff of white smoke. This is the instant when all strain and chilling fear is ended and forgotten. Be it ever so muddy, damp, chilly and miserable, there's no place like home-station at the end of another rough mission.

11. Through a 20-mm. shellhole the ground crew chief of "Jersey Bounce" cusses and grumbles about his pilot's carelessness in stopping a Nazi bullet, as he takes out the guns to put the ship to bed.

12. "Early American." Somewhere in England, this Nissen hut was first headquarters of an Air Force that began in 1942 with seven officers and one general. Now, in 1944, it numbers thousands of men, hundreds of planes, and dozens of targets.

13. In his RAF uniform Britain's King and his Queen study the bombers that do by day what Britain's bombers do by night.

14. We get along with the British. Orphaned by the Blitz, by British campaigns in Norway, Greece, Dunkirk, Singapore, Tobruk, these British kids went to Thanksgiving and Christmas parties in Yank mess-halls throughout the British Isles, raised their voices, timidly at first and then loudly in "Silent Night, Holy Night."

15. American pilgrimage to Westminster Abbey. For the first time the ancient stones of England's most famous Cathedral rang with the hymns and prayers of another nation. Thanksgiving Day Services, 1942.

16. Anglo-American relations: Six-year-old Jackie Harris, whose father is Air Chief Marshal "Ginger" Harris, comes into the garden to say goodnight to two visiting generals, U.S. Air Forces' first four-star general, "Hap" Arnold, and Eaker of the 8th. Harris and Eaker fathered "round-the-clock" bombing of German Europe.

17. John G. Winant, World War I airman, father of a B-17 pilot (now a prisoner of war in Germany), Ambassador to the Court of St. James, saw from the first that Gen. Eaker and his 8th Air Force were America's "best ambassadors to Nazi Germany," plugged for more planes.

Chapter 1

LOW EBB

"...they fought through to bomb the target
...but sixteen Forts were so few..."

SQUINTING through the ring sight of a calibre-.50 gun, down the spine of a giant Flying Fortress, right smack into the teeth of every kind of Nazi fighter plane that you can find in the recognition charts—that's when you realize why the skies of Germany's industrial targets have come to be known as "The Big League."

Our Fortress—"Invasion II"—was one of the planes that fought through to the railroad yards at Hamm, Ruhr Valley, Germany. The others went to Rotterdam. Weather over our target was the best this side of Cahuenga Boulevard, Hollywood.

Our bombs plastered the target. Five of our bombers didn't come back. That's about all the official communiqué said about the Eighth Air Force's deepest penetration so far into Nazi Germany. But there was a story between the lines.

My reason for being there at all was newsreel photography. My mission was to get some good pictures of fighter attacks.

It seemed so placid up there, in the radio hatch of a target-bound Fortress. Far less belligerent than it used to be at the ringside, Madison Square Garden, where I used to slip in among the professional news photogs and click a furtive amateur camera at the weaving fighters inside the ropes.

Then the radio gunner lurched against my back, knocking me through the passageway, down onto the curved top of the revolving ball turret. My foot caught in the turret gears. A little panicky, I tried to yank it loose. But looking at my hands, I saw blood washing down the rubber-matted floor and curling over my fingers.

3

I had never seen so much blood before. I didn't know where it could have come from. It was strangely impersonal—just so much red paint.

And then I looked beyond my hands, slowly. Crumpled on the floor was the radio gunner—the strong-legged boy who had just snapped on my oxygen mask for me not ten seconds ago. I saw his face. It was twisted in pain. The red that was sogging my gloves and flying boots was burbling out of a wound in his back. A slug had crashed down through the bomb bays and struck him squarely.

There was nothing impersonal, nothing detached about this war now. Not any more.

I didn't know this boy's name. I had reached the plane just in time for the take-off. No time to swap names. But seconds ago he had been offering me chewing gum to relax the popping in my ears. Now he had fallen across my oxygen lines—that's serious five miles up. Without oxygen, you can't help anybody else; you become a liability to the others.

But there was no time to fix the lines. Time only to rip off my parachute, dive for the first aid kit, claw at the unfamiliar dressings and scissors, start hacking at his clothes.

This job needed the help of fingers more skilled than mine. I grabbed two spare film packs, took careful aim, and threw them at one of the waist gunners down inside the bomber. I was afraid I might never make it back that far without oxygen.

One film pack hit its target. The gunner looked around. His wits were as quick as my fingers were slow. He grabbed a walk-around oxygen bottle, came back, and helped administer the pathetically inadequate first aid. Two hypos eased the boy's pain.

All I could do was wish I had paid more attention to the flight surgeon's lectures at gunnery school—or that I had been a doctor instead of a newspaperman.

And then the war muscled in again. We were over the target now. Not until then did I realize that we were alone—just our group. Having missed the briefing, I didn't know that the other groups had turned off for another target.

A group is about 20 planes. That's bush league, deep in the heart of the Ruhr. What we needed here was the 1,000 bombers the RAF had pitched at Cologne the year before.

Suddenly our bombs were away. I didn't even know when ours let go. But I knew they were away because I saw the big eggs being laid from another bomber in our group. A bomber looks funny with its bays hanging open— like a little boy with his pants down. I knew we were on the way back. I was just hanging onto the radio-hatch gun, trying not to look too silly as a "qualified air gunner" in the wrong shooting gallery. The real gunner was lying there beneath his gun, between my feet. My camera? The gun seemed more important. I kept trying to remember what a veteran had preached to me once:

"Just keep the lead in his eyes, bud, keep the hot lead in his eyes, and Jerry won't knock on your door."

And then the Jerries really piled into us. I tried desperately to remember the rest of the gunner rules for deflection firing, the stuff about wing spans and recognition and the number of ring sights to lead your target. I filled the sights with 17 enemy planes during the next crowded half hour. Did I hit anything? Of course not. All I tried or hoped to do was to "keep the lead in their eyes." It does make you more comfortable to pull triggers than just to stand there doing nothing useful, hoping that they're after another plane, not the one you're in.

The gunners talk about "sweating out the Jerries," tossing tracers at them as they swing into position for a swooping pass at your nose. Most of the sweating over the Ruhr that day was done by this reporter. I would watch the grey-bellied JU-88's crawl up from the rear, overhead, out of range. On and on. Then I couldn't see them any more. They were ahead of us, and I could look only to the sides and the rear. All I could see was their vapor trails. That told me they were getting cocked for another frontal attack from somewhere on up ahead. And then my sweating would start. I would pull my neck in like a turtle, wishing I had brought a tin hat, waiting for the screaming zoom of the Jerry as he made his pass overhead or below us. Each time he went by I would scramble frantically to toss a necklace of slugs at him. Wasted? Sure.

But a lucky hit had scored on our gunner; maybe it would work for us. Our top turreteer creased one Jerry proper, and our right waist gunner tattooed the shark belly of another.

Outside, beyond my ring sight, one of the Forts was falling back out of formation. That's what the Jerries love. You know how the buzzards gang up in the sky over the desert when a horse goes down in the hot sand. That's the way the Jerries ganged up over that limping Fortress. They seemed almost to queue up to take passes at it. Down and down and down they hammered it. I didn't see it hit the deck. A JU-88 was paging us from the other side.

I swung my gun, squeezed the trigger, and silently prayed that one of the Lord's MP's would point the gun right for me. Foooof—foooof—foooof—little hot balls of tracer were dancing out along the trajectory—still hitting nothing but the place where Jerry had just been.

But just the sound of a gun can be as good for your morale as a slug of bourbon—when the gun is your own. Blitzed London must have felt like that when the ack-ack guns were tossing noise and flak up at the Jerries during the Battle of Britain.

Before I went to England, in December 1940, I had gone first to the one man who knew more about war than any other American, and had asked him, "What do you need to know about England before you can know whether she will stand or fall?"

He said, "Tell me how the pilots of the Hurricanes and Spitfires are standing the strain of fighting against such great odds. And tell me what German bombing is doing to the ports in the West of England. Never mind what is happening to the factories and to London and the other cities. If the fighter pilots and the ports hold out, we can send enough stuff to Britain to keep her going until the tide turns and runs the other way."

Those were the critical questions in the mind of an American who got this grudging praise from Hindenburg after Germany was beaten the last time: "He understood war." The man was Bernard Baruch, head of the War Industries Board in 1918.

The RAF and the people of Britain gave him the right answers in 1941.

The second time I went to England, I brought two more questions, to gauge our own contribution to the destruction of Germany.

"Could the combat crews of the Flying Fortresses and Liberators stand the strain of heavy casualties until the case for daylight bombing was proved and the Eighth AAF got the bombers it needed to finish the job? And could precision daylight bombing crack through the flak and fighter defenses of Germany and, with the RAF, concentrate enough bombs onto production and transportation targets so that, when invasion came, the Huns would be unable to move fast enough to meet it?"

In March, 1943, I was out there getting part of the answer, in "Invasion II," one of sixteen Fortresses whose target was the railroad yards at Hamm, beyond the Ruhr Valley. It was the first "DP," deep penetration, by the U.S. Eighth Air Force.

The skipper of our Fort was Captain Oscar O'Neill, a dark, handsome boy from Latin America. He looked like George Raft. He was as steely as Raft acts. The whole Fortress throbbed with O'Neill's confidence, which pulsed back through the ribs and muscles of the bomber, transfused from his hands on the controls. He made "Invasion II" buck and dive the way Tommy Hitchcock used to handle a polo pony.

My knees buttered later—when it was all over. I wasn't really scared while the show was on. There wasn't any room for terror on O'Neill's ship. And besides, there was that boy on the floor.

"Could our combat crews stand the strain of heavy casualties?" I got the answer later. When you try to translate one actual casualty right before your eyes into terms of icy logic, you can't.

What had seemed like creaking hours had in fact been minutes. I expected it to be at least 5 P. M., when we finally raced to a landing. Captain O'Neill had poured on the coal to get our wounded gunner back to the base. The take-off had been an early one—8 A. M. I was several hours wrong on the elapsed time.

We got down fast and hard and taxied quickly off the runway, toward a waiting ambulance. No sooner were we off than I saw another Fort steam down where we had just been. Steam is the right word. No brakes—it boiled right over the end of the runway, into the barbed wire and brush.

The medicos raced out to our bomber from the ambulance. Men swarmed inside. Our gunner was stretchered out through the side entry, as gently as men who admire courage can lift a mortally wounded boy. He died a few minutes later. He never had a chance. His spine was severed.

Chapter 2

THE INVADER

". . . his wing men followed him down . . ."

Lt. Douglas Adoue McCrary,
Torpedo Squadron X, Aircraft Carrier Y,
℅ Postmaster, San Francisco.

Dear Douglas:

Got a good letter from Mother yesterday, gave me latest news of you, said you had made the 2,000th landing on your carrier. That ought to make you and your carrier veterans by now. By the way, think you'll find that the skipper of your ship is the brother-in-law of the pilot who flew me to England in a Catalina two years ago—"Small World Dept." Saw a book reviewed in *Time* the other day that is supposed to tell all about what you guys in the Torpedo Squadron do. No picnic, the way the review read. I'd like to know a lot more about your job; trouble is, the different services never do get to know about other jobs. Remember how you were kidding me when I met you in Florida, about the way the Navy pilots say t ey ought to take the oxygen away from the Fortresses so they'll come down to where they can hit something? Well, chum, the Forts are doing pretty good over here now, at least the fellows who fly and fight in the Forts are. Never saw such kids.

Reckon every way of fighting this war, from filling teeth to firing a bazooka, places a special strain on the fellow doing the fighting. But I'd like to argue the case to prove that the boys in the Forts over Germany have the toughest time of all—with the possible exception of the guys who go down in submarines. There are so damn many ways to get killed in a Fortress, special ways:

Your oxygen mask can freeze up and you'll keel over before you can get help or yell for it, and you're a stiff in ten minutes;

You can get fragments of flak or 20 mm. shells, chunks the size of brass knuckles to stuff the size of gravel—both will make a mess of you, and that doesn't count direct hits;

You can get hit by rocket projectiles or air-to-air bombing; or you can crash head-on with a Focke-Wulf carrying a dead pilot, or one of your own Forts going down;

Any one of four engines or several gas tanks can stop an explosive slug, and that spells curtains;

Or maybe a couple of your engines go out, and you lag behind the formation, and then the fighters cut you to pieces.

And all this happens about five miles above the earth—which is maybe a little more unnatural place for men to be than down under the Pacific in a submarine. And that's the thing that doubles the strain on your nerves—the environment in which your guts have to digest danger is *unnatural*.

But damned if the kids in the Forts don't seem to get used to it. Take the crew of "Invasion II," the outfit that took me to Hamm. I've had three trips with them since then, got to know them pretty well.

Captain Oscar O'Neill was the pilot. (See Illus. 18.) He looked like a cross between something out of the Ballet Russe and a bullfighter—should have flown his Fortress in red and green velvet tights, with gold braid all over them, and his black hair in a braid down his back. His was the old South American story—mother Spanish, father Irish. Comes from Brazil, educated at Colgate. And here's the funny thing:

Before he came back to the States and went into the Air Forces, he was selling *dental supplies* down in Brazil. Get that! A guy who looks like a bullfighter, selling dental supplies. Too bad it takes a war to turn up a job worthy of a man's strength and courage and genius for action.

Riding up in the nose of "Invasion II" was one of the finest kids I've ever met—Lt. Ed Bush, from Hollywood, but preferred to say he came from Los Angeles. (See Illus. 20.) Got into the war early, enlisted, had a crack at pilot training, flunked, and then went into a school for bombardiers. He was the best bombardier in the Group. Enlisted men worshipped him because he used to be a GI. He rode herd on them and they loved it. Make them check their guns double and double again. Always cleaned his own guns. Before take-off, he would run an inspection worthy of the toughest top sergeant—on oxygen masks, heated clothing, guns, ammunition, gloves, Mae Wests, escape kits, "ditching drill"—the whole works.

You know, when a fortress crew reach "Mission X," they get grounded, because medicos figure that a certain number of missions is all you can stand. Bush, because he never wanted to miss a mission, even came back from a pass when one was scheduled; he had piled up three more missions than anybody else in "Invasion II." But Bush wasn't going to quit when he hit his "X"— he was going to take three extras until the whole crew wound up.

"As long as O'Neill will take me over the target, I'll be in the nose."

The nose of a Fort is as vulnerable as a fishbowl in a shooting gallery. Guess you know how a bombardier sits out there in front, with one eye on the bombsight as the Forts go into their bombing run. That's the time when all the thousands of people who build bombers and make bombs and refine gasoline and do all the other things that get a bomber into the air—when all the kids who have trained to fill their jobs in a combat crew—when the whole vast effort behind an air offensive hangs upon the judgment of a bombardier during those scant seconds when his skilled fingers twist the knobs that put the cross hairs of a bombsight across a target some 25,000 feet below.

I watched little Bush on three runs, watched him only, for signs of nervous strain. There were none. He crouched up there in the nose, with the belts of ammunition flopped down his back; red, black, and blue noses of the shells looking like an Indian chieftain's feathered headdress. Every time he yelled "bombs away" into the intercom, he would whip his arm and snap his gloved fingers like a crap shooter trying to roll a seven with a million dollars in the pot.

And then he would jump up and man his nose guns—because the Jerries pile in on you in the bombing run; they get cocked when they see your bomb bays open, and they throw the works at you. Bushy loved his guns better than he loved his bombsight. You could get so much more "personal" with a gun. There was a fighter out there blazing at you, and you had a gun in your fists to blaze back—it was kill or die in split seconds.

Over the target, everything was frontal attack; but as you were going home, sometimes over the Channel, the JU-88's would hammer away with rear attacks, especially if there were crippled Forts. Bushy used to leave his guns in the nose and come back to the waist guns to work on the JU-88's. His mask covered his face right up to his eyes, but, even when the lids were frosted, in his eyes you could see that he was laughing behind his mask when he had a

.50-calibre gun in his fists. I don't want you to get the idea that Bushy was a husky, ham-fisted lunk who loved to kill—anything but. He looked like the trap drummer in a college orchestra, and he played on his guns that way.

The navigator shares the bombardier's cramped quarters in the nose. He sometimes gets a chance to use one of the side nose guns. It's a relief for him to get at the guns. The boys tell me that navigators are under the worst strain of all. They've got to keep thinking and thinking and thinking all the time; nothing to do with their hands but push a pencil. That makes the big differ-ence, having something to do with your hands. The only time I've ever seen real, naked terror was in a navigator's eyes—on the ground. He had been grounded, but the terror was still echoing in his eyes.

I was sprawled out on the grass in the sun, still in my flying clothes, cussing. Col. Ordway had called up and ordered me yanked out of a bomber. It was shaming as hell; they were already lined up for take-off when the Operations Officer came bouncing across the field in a jeep and hauled me out by the scruff, complaining. Then this navigator came over—he's a kid you know very well:

"Listen, McCrary, you goddamn fool. What're you griping for? Why do you have to have somebody order you to get out of those things? Don't you know people get *killed* up there?"

That was the first and only time I ever heard anybody use that phrase to describe what happens. To this boy, it wasn't "written off," or "gone West," or "he's had it"—none of those insulated evasions. It was raw and bloody death.

The navigator of "Invasion II," Lt. Carmichael from Maryville, Missouri, was the quietest man of the crew. (See Illus. 21.) He came home from the roughest raids looking very bored and a little sleepy, as unruffled as the radio voice that says "when you hear the musical note, the ti-yum will be ex-actly . . ."

I guess you know how you get pretty close to guys—I mean you learn a lot about them quick, in war. I was always slow to ask questions and slow to answer questions, but in the two hours or so between briefing and take-off, in the half hour after you cross the Channel on the way home,—in the hour of the interrogation, as your stomach wriggles happily against hot chocolate and spam sandwiches, that's when you get to know a lot about people. Must be even more true in the little community of an aircraft carrier.

Take a kid like "The Little Horror," spark plug of the whole ship from his all-seeing post in the top turret. His name was Harry Goldstein, and he was from the Bronx. (See Illus. 22 and 196.) In his recent civil life, he had been a lace salesman. No kidding—sold lace to lingerie manufacturers. First time I was aware of his great skill and of his special value to "Invasion II" was on the way home from Hamm.

We were being pounded down out of formation. Three Forts had been shot down already, another was on fire; we were scattered all over the sky. Oscar was duelling with frontal attacks. Both waist gunners and I were working over the dying radio gunner. Suddenly the tail gunner yelled:

"Coming at us . . . high . . . 6 o'clock . . ."

I stood up, grabbed a gun, looked through the ring sight and saw an ME-110 screaming down onto the spine of "Invasion II." I couldn't squeeze the triggers—couldn't move, paralyzed by the certainty that in one-tenth of a second we would be split in half. And then there was the vibration of the top turret behind me, like thumping a washtub with a stick. The ME-110 seemed suddenly to get sick at the stomach. It half-rolled over, then looped up and spun crazily down, vomiting black smoke and debris. One-time lace salesman Harry Goldstein had hemstitched himself another Jerry.

That was his third. Put him in line for a DFC. You want to find out more about a joe like "The Little Horror"—that was the nickname that had been affectionately hung on him by the girls in the Red Cross Rainbow Corner. Harry once made a crack to Jim Dugan that was the most revealing lie I ever heard:

"Listen, Jim, about this medal racket. I guess you know I just want the DFC because it will help me in my business, that's all. Maybe some day I'll be the lace king of America, and the medals won't hurt."

Now Harry Goldstein was a very smart boy. He could add and subtract, and he knew all about percentages. For instance, he knew that if losses run to 5%, then after you make 20 raids, you are living on borrowed time.

There are two ways to get a DFC if you are a gunner. You can shoot down several German planes, or you can go on flying until you've finished the required number of missions. Both ways, you run a pretty good risk of getting your top blown off. And without a top, you cannot be the lace king of America, DFC or no DFC. Harry knew that, but never once did the Little Horror fake a cold or sinus trouble or a bellyache to duck a mission.

I remember how guys used to kid Harry and say, "If you get shot down over Germany, we don't have to worry about you. In a week you'll be running the Black Market in Berlin."

The truth is that if "Invasion II" were shot down and the crew had a chance to escape by somebody walking straight into a Hun with a tommy gun, the first guy to tackle the tommy-gunner would be Harry—first, because he thinks quicker than anybody else in the crew, and second, because Sgt. Harry Goldstein, from the Bronx, U.S.A., liked all the guys in "Invasion II" more than he loved life.

He was fresh and tough and tried to sound cynical. But he probably respected and understood the Distinguished Flying Cross a lot better than the man who thought it up. Harry was the only guy in "Invasion II" who really understood what this war is all about, but still he would talk like this:

"Sometimes I say to myself, on the way over the Channel: 'Goldstein, you are a dumb palooka. What are you doing up here in this thing?'

"But back on the ground, all I want is to get back up in the air again. Don't get me wrong—I don't claim any noble reasons. Sure I got plenty of grudge against Hitler, but I got no noble reasons for fighting.

"Sure, I could get taken off combat. Anybody can. But I like fighting."

"Flak-happy" is what they call you when you talk like that and mean it. Harry was talking half-truth when he said he "liked fighting." What he meant was:

The biggest kick that a man's primitive instincts can find is to feel the paralysis of fear, and then to beat it off until it leaves him strong-fingered and clear-brained and leather-nerved for mortal combat.

Harry Goldstein had whipped fear, and superstition, too—all except the one that the whole crew of "Invasion II" shared with him.

The tail gunner, thirty-one year old "Pappy" Youell, from West Virginia, one-time welder (See Illus. 22), wore the same suit of long underwear all through training, across the Atlantic, and on every mission. The crew would rather take off without oxygen than without Pappy's underwear.

Pappy was no talker—and he frequently punctuated with a sharp period the exciting narrative of one of the other gunners' claims for an enemy aircraft destroyed. A gunner would tell how his bursts brought fire and black smoke from an onrushing fighter, and then the Intelligence Officer would look at Pappy Youell for confirmation. Pappy would be back there in the tail where he could see everything that happened, after it happened. If a fighter was knocked down, Pappy knew it, but his standard comment was:

"Me, I didn't see nothing."

He has been top scorer on the skeet range—his guns have never frozen—he was always the one who made the other gunners clean their .50's after a mission, no matter how rough it was, no matter how late they got home. He was a good and dependable gunner—but he never claimed a fighter destroyed.

Charley Melchiondo was another of the crew who always flew backward, when he was on his gun. (See Illus. 22.) He was the radio operator—the *new* one. Remember, the other one got it going into Hamm.

Oscar O'Neill was funny about the battle scars on his ship. The time the Major went along as co-pilot, ranking the regular—Bob Freihofer, from Troy, New York—out of his seat, he got a 20 mm. smack in the chest. It killed him instantly, splattering the cockpit with shell fragments. One fragment cut a notch in the half-wheel that controls the ship, but Oscar never would get a new wheel. His fingers always wrapped around that notch.

The ragged hole in the door to the bomb bay through which the slug had crashed that cut the first radio operator's spine in two . . . that hole was still there too. I couldn't take my eyes off it. It always made me feel like somebody had poked a chunk of ice down my neck. So I was watching the hole the first time we went out after Hamm. All the gunners were packed into the radio compartment to get the weight forward for the take-off. Charley Melchiondo (See Illus. 22 and 25), one-time woodworker from Medford, Massachusetts, hot as Fats Waller on the piano, was busy with the gadgets of his radio. I looked at him and then I looked at the hole. The Little Horror saw me. He laughed, and slapped me right where my back was coldest, and then he said, very loud:

"Listen, Captain, this radio operator is new. It's his first mission—he's never even fired a .50 at altitude before. If things get hot, you better take over the gun again."

The Little Horror was treating me like a veteran—I felt like the President had hung a Congressional Medal of Honor under my Adam's apple.

The kid I knew least well in "Invasion II" was the ball-turret gunner, Benny Borostowski, from LaSalle, Illinois. (See Illus. 22.) Guess his job is about the loneliest in the war, riding down there like a baby kangaroo in his mamma's pouch. You get a feeling of complete detachment from everything and everybody in that position. The Fort you belong to may be flying east, but you can turn around from east to north to south to west, or look down or out or almost

up. You can follow the bombs as they string down and walk across the target—
that's fun.

Or you can watch a Focke-Wulf roaring in for his frontal attack, watch
the leading edge of his wings snap flame at you as he rolls over on his back,
watch the slugs rip into the belly of your own Fort and wonder if things are
burning up inside, watch the Jerry rip into his pull-out and roll away as your
own tracer starts reaching out to snag him before he drops beyond your range
—that's pretty good fun, too.

And if there is trouble inside that knocks out the controls, you must wait
and wonder if there is anybody left to wind up your turret so that you can
scramble out inside and grab your 'chute. The ball-turret gunner is the only
one who flies without his 'chute ready for a quick bail-out. That's not fun.

I never could get Benny Borostowski to talk about his job, and I didn't
push him—you don't like to make a guy talk about a tough job coming
up.

The waist gunners had the coldest job in the ship—wonderful pair of kids,
the "Hind-End Kids." They called themselves that because they always stood
end-to-end as they manned their guns out opposite windows. They got the full
blast of 40-below-zero air that curled around the waist deflectors, plus the
gale that blew down through the radio hatch.

The left waist gunner was the baby of the ship, good-looking kid named
Don King, from Imperial, Texas. (See Illus. 19.) Only nineteen. Joined up
about forty-eight hours after Pearl Harbor—two of his best friends were
killed out there in the Navy.

"My Dad, he was over the last time. This time, when I told him I was
a-joinin' up, he laughed and said to me, 'Son, I was just waitin' to see if I was
gonna have to chase you roun' to a recruitin' office.'

"And then doggone if he didn't go and double-cross me. He went and joined
up with the Navy."

And the other waist gunner, his name was Eldon Lapp, of Fort Wayne,
Indiana. (See Illus. 22.) Know what he used to be before he was a waist
gunner? An optician.

An optician, a lace salesman, a dental supplies salesman—all those most
unwarlike professions were represented in the combat crew of "Invasion II."
Talk about your "citizens' army."

Each, typical American. But each typically different.

And "Invasion II," she was just another Fortress, built to specification—but she was somehow different, too.

You know, they say that all mules look alike—but the man who works them knows that no two mules *are* alike. It's the same with Forts. "Invasion II" was by common acclaim the best Fort in the Group. She was faster—she handled better—and somehow she seemed to be blessed with good luck.

Inside, after a mission, she was usually full of the same stuff that any Fortress collects—empty shells, hundreds of them clanking underfoot, chewing gum wrappers, cookie boxes, crusts of sandwiches, and caramel wrappers, and, after long trips, the waxed containers of emergency rations. On her hardstanding, resting after a mission—and Fortresses actually do "rest"—she looked exactly like all the other Forts in the half-light of a winter afternoon. And the ground crew looked like any other ground crew. But even the ground crew of "Invasion II" was different.

When she came back from her 17th mission, Capt. O'Neill pointed to the 14 bombs painted on her nose and said to the crew chief, Master Sgt. Bob Dalton:

"Listen, we got three more bombs coming to us up there—I checked this morning with S-2 and they give us credit for 17 missions. That's official."

Crew chief Bob Dalton rubbed a greasy hand against the stubble on his stubborn chin and looked Capt. O'Neill very straight in the eye—and that is not easy to do:

"Listen, Captain, I don't give a damn how many missions those S-2 guys up there give us, see? That airplane has dropped bombs only 15 times on the target, see, just 15 times. And them's the only kind that count as missions on my airplane, see?"

Capt. O'Neill just grinned and said "okay." Such pride in the record of a ship among her ground crew would increase the chances that she would come home from many more missions. But—

It was a Saturday night. I was in town, laid up with sinus—thank God. The boys had gone to Bremen that morning. Target was the Focke-Wulf factory; the boys cheered at the briefing. I was damned anxious to find out what had happened—for several reasons. Col. Ordway, boss of the Eighth Air Force Intelligence Section, was to have made his first mission that morning. I had told him:

"Go with Oscar O'Neill. That guy will bring you back if he has to get out and carry 'Invasion II' home."

I called up the station about eight o'clock, and got Col. Lawrence, operations officer, on the phone. There was a lot of music, very loud laughter in the background.

"Listen, Colonel—can you hear me? How's Oscar? Did he get back okay—and the crew?"

Before he answered, I knew what the answer would be. It came, awkward, slow: "Oscar? Well—guess he didn't make it. Yes, he went down. Col. Ordway? No, he's okay. He decided to go with somebody else. Well, it was pretty rough—we lost 6. Oscar was leading the low flight. Flak must have hit him. The boys say his wing men followed him down. You know how they always followed Oscar because they always figured he knew what was best. And then the fighters must have got them, wiped out the whole flight. Last anybody saw of Oscar, he was still going down. But he seemed to have his ship under control. . . ."

The Jerries have quite a bunch of our Forts now—we lost more than 400 during the first year of operation. They're even flying some of the Forts, coming up and joining our formations. Bet you if they ever get "Invasion II" up into one of our formations, she'll bring them right on back to England and land them here. The boys always used to say:

"You know that ship of ours, by God, she must have some homing pigeon blood in her somewhere. She always gets home."

Yours,
Tex

Chapter 3

"THE BAD PENNY"

"...kinda beat up, but she always brought us back..."

I've always had a pretty cramped view of Southerners. Went straight from a little Texas cotton town to school in the East as a kid, and eight years on the New York *Mirror* didn't stretch my knowledge much. Afraid I always had the idea that Southerners were pretty slow and lazy in more ways than just their talk. I had to come to England to find out how wrong I was. I learned about Southerners from a boy named Red Cliburn. (See Illus. 27, 28, and 29.) He was the most decorated pilot in the Eighth Air Force when he finished up his "ops."

Red comes from a town named Hazlehurst, Mississippi. About 6,000 people there. Folks were farmers ever since he can remember—not cotton, truck farming. Red's father was in the last war. He was a cook, in the infantry. Red showed me a snapshot of his mother and father—fine, strong-faced people. She wore a stiff-starched Sunday gingham and he was squinting in the sun. His hands were big, hands that have spent a lifetime making things grow.

Red went to high school in Hazlehurst. Then to a Junior College near his home—played football and basketball, and then, along with ten other kids, he took the Civilian Pilot Training program.

Red Cliburn never had been outside of Mississippi before he learned to fly. But between the time he passed his cadet exams in May, 1941, and the day in September, 1942, when his group got their Forts for the flight to England, Red Cliburn had trained in Arkansas, Florida, Washington, and Maine. He had looked down from a four-engined bomber on States that before had been only pink or green or brown or red places on a map.

And he saw England first from a bomber, the same as other Americans first

18

saw China and Australia and Germany and France and Italy and Africa and India and a hundred other places that American fighting men never saw when mobility was geared to the slogging march of a doughboy.

Red has a Mickey Rooney grin. You should have seen him after he finished "Mission X," wound up his combat career, and had his first real drink to celebrate. His grin met at the back of his head. He moves slow, talks slow, his eyes blink slow, he chews his food slow, he even shoots pool with a slow poke.

That's all on the *ground*. In the *air* things change—not on the outside of him but on the inside. Things happen inside Red Cliburn that are translated through the controls of the Fortress, transfused into the crew. I've been on the other end of an intercom and I've felt it. I've balanced on the catwalk inside a bomb bay going into the target run, looked down between the bombs and seen two yellow-nosed Focke-Wulfs boring up at us, stalling to get their sights on our belly. They were down where Red couldn't see them, but he seemed to "feel" them there. At exactly the right instant, he flipped into evasive action, and the flinting lines of the fighters' fire missed their mark.

I don't suppose you'd say that Cliburn "thought fast"—he just reacted. Maybe he does drawl—but not with the controls of "The Bad Penny."

He's flown several ships. His first was one called "Kwityerbitchin." That one got shot out from under him on an "experimental."

Somebo   up top got the idea that we ought to try bombing from a little less altitude. The U-boat base at St. Nazaire, where flak is more accurate than any I've seen over here, was picked for the test—altitude 10,000 feet, less than half normal height. This was Red's second mission. The description in his diary was brief: "Went to St. Nazaire today. A little rough."

Cross-examined after I had loosened his tongue with two straight Coca-Colas, Red told me what happened.

"Yep, that one was pretty rugged, I reckon, seein' it was our second show. Sure, I remember it—every detail. Well, we got a direct hit from flak. Yep, they're pretty good with the flak down there. Knocked out two engines, wounded both the waist gunners. Didn't hurt the radio operator—we had a borrowed one that day; our regular radioman went with another ship and got shot down. Reckon some of us thought *we* wouldn't get home. Doggone near blew us in two. We crash-landed in the south of England. Couldn't fly home for a week. Took that long to patch her up."

For that ride to St. Nazaire, Red was recommended for the DFC, and was awarded the Air Medal. Two weeks later, they went back to the same target, this time at 23,000 feet. The entry in Red's diary for that date read: "Back to St. Nazaire. Rough again."

Everybody in his own Group turned back before they got to the target—bad weather. That is, they all went home except Red and four other Forts. Two of those were shot down. Another crashed and didn't get home; another crash-landed in the south of England. Only Red came back with his ship. The navigator did some pretty good work. Yep, pretty rough, I guess.

For his work on that one Red was awarded the Distinguished Flying Cross. The citation reads: "During the course of repeated fighter attacks, Lt. Cliburn was painfully wounded, three other crew members were severely wounded, the plane seriously damaged, the electrical and hydraulic controls shot away, the right elevator disabled. Displaying great courage, and extraordinary flying skill, thinking only of the safety of his crew and the valuable airplane in his charge, and with complete disregard for his own safety, Lt. Cliburn . . . completed his mission. . . . The courage, coolness, and skill displayed upon this occasion reflect highest credit upon this officer and the Armed Forces of the United States."

After that, they had to give him still another Fortress—"The Bad Penny." "A fellow who was shot down on the St. Nazaire raid in another ship, he named it. Seems like it was always having trouble or getting shot up or something and nobody much wanted to fly it. But there wasn't any other ships around so I said give it to me. I've had her ever since. Don't go much for superstitions and jinxes."

There was another jinx ship on the field, too, "Taurus." Everybody simply refused to fly her. So Red took her to Wilhelmshaven on March 22. He had been there in "The Bad Penny" on our first raid into Germany back in January. Near got shot down then, all the control cables shot away except one elevator and the ailerons. But he went back to Wilhelmshaven in "Taurus," the jinx ship. Again the diary: "Flew a new ship to Wilhelmshaven today. Second trip there. Rugged."

Here's what happened: One engine blew up, damn near blew right out of the wing, over the target. He started home on three, the dead one spewing out a huge smoke-signal invitation to every Jerry in the sky. Red nursed "Taurus" out over the North Sea. Slowly he lost altitude, fell behind his group. Five watching, trailing JU-88's screamed down on him, closing for the kill. Just then, another engine, on the same side as the first, exploded. "Taurus" should have been cold meat.

The crew was huddled in the radio compartment. Guns and ammunition had been thrown out to lighten the load, to help her stay up with her group—but she couldn't. As the JU-88's closed, Red turned and dived back into the next Fortress group that was following the leader. That scraped two of the JU-88's off his tail: they were shot down by the guns of the other Forts. And then Red nudged the crippled "Taurus" into the cover of that group's fire-power. Again he lost altitude. He used about 15-degree flaps to keep her in the air. Her air speed dropped to 125 mph. One squadron of Forts hung back and circled "Taurus" until she limped home to the coast. Red had brought her home to base on two engines—both on the same side.

"They tried to tell me she was a jinx ship, but I still don't believe in jinxes. She's a hangar queen now—just stands there and the engineers strip her down to patch up other Forts—she was a good ship."

Red flew on every mission they'd let him fly, and on some they wouldn't let him go on. For instance, he wasn't supposed to fly to Vegesack. That was the first great air battle fought by our Forts, and they knocked down more than 50 Jerries. That was the show which finally proved the case for daylight bombing, proved that we could fight through to a target and bomb without uneconomic losses. Everybody knew it would be tough. Red's roommate, Don Bader, from Addison, Ohio, was along on that show. It was his first raid since he got out of the hospital with a Purple Heart. Red sneaked out and went as Don's co-pilot.

"Ever'body got pretty mad at me—said I shoulda asked somebody. Shucks, if I hadda asked, they'da made me stay home. We had a lot of fun."

Red and Bader were pretty close. On Red's last raid, the one to the air-frame factories at Meaulte, the tail gunner croaked an obituary into the intercom: "One of ours—busted wide open—going down—no 'chutes opening—"

That was going into the bomb run, and Red was too busy to ask questions then. But later, when the Spits showed up to cover us on the way home, and our own P-47's were sweeping the skies between us and the coast, he started:

"What was the number of that Fort that went down? Where was she flying? You sure nobody bailed out?"

There was no definite answer to any of his questions. He kept twisting in his seat, trying to check over the ships that were left in the formation, hunting. "I wonder if Bader is okay?"

Red Cliburn's career covers a significant and bloody span in the operation of the Eighth Air Force; he flew on most of the tough missions the First Wing handled. He went to Hamm, and on the first raid on Germany, and to Vegesack, and he wound up at Meaulte.

Meaulte was a landmark. That was the first time that the new groups from his wing went along, and it was the first time that the Thunderbolts went into the target in force with the Forts. That was May 13. The "first of the many" were no longer so few.

But the show was over for Red, for a while. It worked like this at that time: if you got through a required number of missions, and then volunteered for five more, and got through those, you were grounded for the duration. If you didn't take the extra five, you got a long rest and then maybe you would go back on combat, as a squadron commander. Red and I sat on the grass and talked, that evening after he had completed his tour of combat missions.

"Nope, I'm not gonna take that extra five, for two reasons: First place, I want to fly some more, after I get home and get a rest. And second place, I want to come through this war without getting any Oak Leaf Clusters on my Purple Heart, or any posthumous decorations. Along about this time you start feeling kinda posthumous."

Red didn't get to go home, not the last time I saw him. He was moved up to a Combat Wing job, where they needed his experience. Morning after morning he would get up and go to the briefing, watch them take off, and ache to go with them. Not bellyache, just ache.

"I reckon I was nervous just once, and scared just once, real bad. But I never got real mad.

"The time I was most nervous was on my first one. You're most nervous going over the Channel. All of a sudden, I saw a lot of pretty fighters sitting out there on my wing. Boy, I sure felt comfortable to see those Spits with us, when, all of a sudden, they banked and turned toward us, firing as they came in. I was just telling the boys on the intercom not to shoot because they were Spits when they opened fire. Reckon that's the only time I ever cussed into the intercom—it's not good for the pilot to get excited out loud. But I sure cussed then, and I yelled to our gunners to let 'em have it."

"And the time you were scared, Red. When was that?"

"That was on the second Wilhelmshaven deal. An FW was boring into us, firing to beat hell, when our ball turret man got him cold. He stopped firing, but he kept coming. Reckon he was dead, coming head-on. This all took about three seconds, but that was plenty of time for me to get sort of frozen. And then I just snapped out of it and rammed the controls forward, and down we went, and he went right over us. I swear he missed us by not more'n four feet."

"But you *did* know what to do. You *did* do it, scared or no scared. You say you never got real mad, Red?"

"Never really. You see, I never got any of my real good friends killed. That mighta made a difference. Yeah, I guess that would have made a difference. Kurtz, he's my navigator (See Illus. 28), he got pretty mad once. That was on the St. Nazaire job, when we were the only one in our outfit that got back to base. We were pretty badly shot up, trying to make it out to sea and duck into the cloud. The Jerries turned back to the French coast, but doggone if Kurtz didn't jump up and down in the nose, hanging onto his gun, and yelling at them, 'Come on back here and fight, you yellow sons-of-bitches! Come on back here!'

"I told him he better not hope they come back because we were in pretty bad shape for fighting. He was mad, all right. But me, I never did get real mad. It seems kind of impersonal up there. You don't see the faces of the guys in the planes you are shooting at. You don't really think of there being guys in those German fighters at all. You just call them FW's and let it go at that. I've been a lot madder at fellows on another football team I was playing against.

"But then, like I say, nobody I ever liked a lot got killed. Reckon it would have been different if they got somebody I liked, somebody like Bader."

I got Red's crew together after his last mission; asked each of them to write me a letter, telling me exactly what he thought of Red. I wanted to make it easy for them to be emotional by letting them put it in a letter. Best one came from his co-pilot, who went on flying "The Bad Penny" after Red left:

"He was one of those men who simply don't know how to give up. Four times he had every reason to make a landing on enemy territory, to save his neck by losing his ship and winding up the war safe as a prisoner. But he always brought his ship home, no matter what the odds were against him. His crew would have flown through hell with him, because they knew he would always bring them home."

Chapter 4

TWO FROM TEXAS

". . . if you come from California,
why don't they call you Cal?"

AT Exeter Academy in New Hampshire there were four boys from Texas. I was one. We were all called "Tex." And ever since then, I've tried to figure out just why it is that if you come from Texas, you get called "Tex"—but you don't get called "Cal" if you come from California and it's never "George" for Georgians, or "Minnie" if you come from Minnesota. I still wonder what the difference is between Texans and other Americans.

Clare Boothe Luce got a great kick out of telling me this story she brought home from her trip through Africa to India. It's about Texans:

A bunch of RAF guys were making dirty cracks about Americans, at an air station out in the Egyptian desert. Clare turned Tom Dewey on them and started a hard-hitting cross examination: "Okay, so you don't like Americans. Why? What have Americans ever done that the British don't do? Don't generalize. Be specific. Why don't you like Americans? Why? Why?"

Pinned down, the RAF boys couldn't really pile up much evidence against us. Finally, one of them, cornered by Clare's fierce attack, took this evasive action:

"Well, as a matter of fact, you know, it isn't really the Americans that are bad, it's just these bloody *Texans* who are so insufferable!"

I've met a bunch of Texans over here. Haley Aycock, a major, he's the one I got to know best. (See Illus. 42.) Met him first when his leg was in a cast up to the knee. He got shot up on his second mission—a 20 mm. explosive shell hit him. Blew all the lining out of his boot, splintered the bone in his leg. That was last November; he's gone home now to get it fixed up right. He spent about

24

three months in a hospital after he got hit, and then he couldn't take it any longer. He got up and flew again, five missions with his leg in a cast, once as a bombardier, four times as a co-pilot.

"It's like getting thrown from a horse. If you wait a whole day before you crawl on another horse, you're a little nervous. If you wait two days, you're scared. If you wait a week, you'll probably be so damn scared, you can't even pull up in the saddle. It was like that with me. The longer I stayed in that hospital, the worse I knew it was going to be when I finally tried to fly again."

Aycock is a pretty husky guy, six foot three, big bones, strong face. He was born near Midland, Texas—folks on both sides were ranchers. There were three boys, but one of them died—not from getting run over by a street car or from drinking bad gin or from infantile paralysis; not from any of the things that happen to you in the city. He was killed by the bite of a rattlesnake.

"The first time I went out on a raid after I got hit was straight hell. I never was bothered much with imagination, but it sure was working that day. Ever' time the top turrets fired, there was a helluva vibration in the nose of the ship. Dust and shreds of insulation would fly around, and the plexiglass would crack. Each time, I knew damn well we were hit. Just nerves."

Haley went into flying after a year of working in the oilfields—"that was too rough." So he went into the Army Air Forces—"I just wanted to get into the airlines, but after I got out of Kelly in 1940, they decided they wanted to keep us in the Army."

He was sent to Florida, trained in the old B-17's—"those were the ones they gave the British. Reckon they didn't make out so good." And then he went to Newfoundland, then back to the States on anti-submarine patrol.

"Bob Campbell and me, we were a two-man Task Force with two B-17's, flying around the Gulf of Mexico, hunting subs. Just found out the other day that an Air Medal for scoring a probable hit on a sub caught up with me finally. We lived in Houston and had a damn good life."

And then both of them were dumped into one of the first Fortress Groups that came to England, the one that's flown more missions than any other. Haley was the first squadron commander of Oscar O'Neill's old outfit.

"I was the first man wounded in the group. It was something new to all of us, the idea of being hit. The whole Eighth Air Force had lost only two ships then. They had made eight missions without a loss. We all had the feeling that the Jerries just couldn't knock us down. And then I got hit.

"First thing I thought was—I'm going to be a goddamn cripple the rest of my life! The pain hurt me up high, all the way up to the hip. Thought I had my whole leg blown off. Bill Eanes was flying co-pilot. He was white as cigarette paper. The shock kept me from hurting too much. There wasn't any hypo in the ship in those days. I made a tourniquet out of the wires of my headset. Don't know how I did it, but I managed to land the ship—overshot the field and had to circle it short and slip it in. Damn near fainted when they took me out. Loss of blood, maybe . . . or maybe because it was just that the tension was over and I knew it wouldn't matter if I did faint."

On his third raid after he got out of the hospital—"it takes about six to get over being scared"—they went to St. Nazaire and lost eight ships. Haley's Fort got an engine knocked out over the target:

"They were just starting their frontal attacks then. Listen, those guys were damn hot—if all the fighter pilots we've had to go through were as good as the ones we met over French targets, they'd have wiped us out before now. The best of them were down there to work us over. It was a pushover in Germany for the first few raids. The ones down in France were the ones you read about. They'd do a little stunting just to show off before they hit us. Listen, you've got to *fly* a fighter to be able to hold those guns onto a Fort while you're doing a slow roll. They used to fly through the group for three or four passes—never go through more than once or twice now."

For a long time after that St. Nazaire job, he used to wrestle with the same bad dream night after night—a ball-turret gunner falling out of his cocoon, without a 'chute, just waving his arms like a singed beetle.

It was more than just a dream. It was rooted in what Haley had actually seen. You never forget it when you see a man falling without a 'chute.

I got to know Haley best after a raid we went on together, not in the same ship. We sat around and talked out on the grass after lunch. The sun bored in and untied all the knots that keep you from talking. He just rambled on.

"Only time I ever get really mad is when I see one of my gunners not leading his target. I'll yell at him through the intercom, 'GODDAMN IT, LEAD HIM, LEAD HIM, HEAR ME, LEAD HIM,' but by the time I've said that, the shot is gone.

"Funny thing about getting mad, I mean fighting mad. It's the same with everybody, most of us just don't get mad. Maybe we'll cuss a little under attack, but you'd say the same thing if you were on the losing side in a rough football game. It's pretty hard to feel very personal about bombing a target 25,000 feet down below, so far away you can't see people or even make out houses and buildings very clear. And besides, it doesn't help your reflexes much to get mad. Of course, there are exceptions.

"The best damn gunner I ever knew was mad all the time. Not mad at the Germans, he was just mad—because once he came to town on a forty-eight hour pass and caught syphilis. He was mad at everybody after that, and it sort of made him feel better to go up there and shoot at somebody.

"Another boy I knew was all the time mad. His brother got killed in a very messy way down in Africa—burned up in a tank.

"These reporters are always asking me if the Germans are yellow, or if they are getting any easier. That's a tough one to answer—there's all kinds of groups of German fighters, like there's all kinds of groups of Fortresses, some green, some old hands. When you bump into the green ones, it looks like you've got Jerry on the ropes; then along will come a tough outfit and knock the be-jeesus out of you.

"But one thing you can tell, when you go back again and again to the same target, or even to the same area, you can tell you are softening them up a little. They don't bore in so far. They lay off and lob cannon shells at you, hoping to nail an engine. And lately they been trying dropping bombs on us. Hasn't scared anybody much."

I don't really know what makes a good pilot; but I always felt that I'd go anywhere with Haley.

"There's just one thing that makes or breaks a pilot—*responsibility*. That's the whole thing about command, anywhere—responsibility.

"It's tough to watch a guy wilt when he first realizes he hasn't got the guts to carry the responsibility of other lives. He wants to go on, but his guts are gone. When he admits it and pulls out, the boys really admire that, and they feel sorry for him, too. Not too many fellows crack—not so many as you'd think, the way things were around here for a while. And when they do crack, nobody calls them yellow. Maybe they'll say a fellow is chicken, if he's just an all-round bad guy. But you see, ever'body has been too near cracking himself to start making jokes about somebody else cracking.

"I knew a navigator who lost twenty pounds before he got through ten missions. Just watch around the big room when there's an alert on. Watch the boys that stay around reading the same-old magazines all over again, or hang in a poker game long after they ought to be in bed. Those are the boys who don't want to go to their rooms and turn off the lights and find out they can't sleep.

"About the saddest case I know was a pilot who thought he was bad luck for everybody, because every time he went out somebody else on his ship got killed. That pilot just had to stop flying.

"Some of the boys are downright battle-happy, flak-happy. Some of them really love it. It's good to have a couple of guys like that in the crew. They'll sing and cuss and crack jokes going over the enemy coast—the time the sweat is the worst—and that bucks up everybody else."

(It's always like this—when you get a pilot to talking, he'll tell you more about fighting the war than the best reporter could learn by going on a dozen missions.)

"I know a pilot who would duck behind his instrument panel ever' time a fighter would come in on him. He had real guts: went on and finished his missions, but then shifted and went as a co-pilot. He knew he didn't have the guts to handle the plane and be responsible for everybody else in it, but, by God, he was going to share the risks with everybody else. He came through okay.

"One thing I do believe, and that is that if you figure out fear, you can cure it.

"When you stay around a station and watch some fellows getting shot down, and watch the others go out day after day, you get to where even when you aren't supposed to go, you sort of want to go along and help out.

"By God, you may not believe it, but I know damn well that most of these fellows around here really have down deep in them that old stuff about Duty, Honor, and Country. I don't mean it's been drilled into them in the Army. It's just *there*. I swear it is. Reckon we're just a proud people."

The other Texan I got to know real well was Lt. Smith, from Austin, Texas. He had a special significance among the "first of the many"—you see, he didn't come over with a whole group; he came over with thirteen other crews as replacements. And brother, we were needing them plenty about the time he showed up.

He got to the Group over here on a Saturday night, and on Monday morning he went on his first raid.

"I didn't really have time to figure out what this war was like over here in the Big League. Didn't really have time even to ask anybody what to expect. Before I was moved in real good, I was gettin' briefed for my first mission—to Wilhelmshaven."

He went as co-pilot that day—they try to send you out as a co-pilot with a veteran first pilot on your first mission. Smitty picked a good one—Red Cliburn.

"But I picked a lousy mission for my first raid. That was the one that Cliburn came back from with two engines shot out, *both on the same side.* Neither one of them would feather. So many of our controls were shot out that she kept wanting to loop, as if it wasn't enough hell that we couldn't keep altitude. I didn't really have time to ask what the fighting was like over here before the take-off, but I sure found out before we got home."

That was on March 22; Smitty made damn near every raid after that, straight through, and finished up on a long but easy one, to Heroya in Norway, on July 25. He had twenty-five missions in four months—that's better than six missions a month, and mister, that's rugged. I wanted to take the last with him, because I took the toughest with him in "Our Gang." He had promised to let me know when it was coming up, but he didn't.

"I didn't want to take you along any more. Every time you go along we get the hell shot out of us. I don't mean you're exactly a jinx, but—"

So he took his dog, Skippy, along with him instead. Skippy was Windy's brother, and Windy belonged to the top-turret gunner, Sgt. Devine, wonderful guy, used to read the *Daily Mirror* regularly, not for the editorials, but for "L'il Abner." Sgt. Devine picked up Windy during training out in Wyoming; Smitty liked the pup, drove all night to get one like him—hence Skippy. Windy and Skippy flew over with Smitty's crew. Skippy attended every briefing, waited on the hard-standing after every mission until "Our Gang" came home. At mess, Skippy would sit under Smitty's hat, and wait patiently for his master.

Smitty flew his second mission as a co-pilot, too—with Capt. Morgan of the "Memphis Belle." And on his third, he flew as first pilot, leading the group— the co-pilot was Major Haley Aycock, group leader that day.

"There's a helluva big difference between being pilot and co-pilot. It's all in that same old thing—responsibility. The pilot takes off and lands usually, and generally takes the ship over the target. But the co-pilot flies about half the total time. Formation flying is a big strain. And there's sure 'nough a lot of responsibility on the group leader when the target is heavily protected by flak. He's got to know how to get his whole group through flak. He's got to be careful he doesn't zig when he oughta zag. You can really get a group chewed up by flak if you figure wrong."

Smitty was born on a farm down in Texas, outside Austin, but his folks moved to town when he was a kid. His Dad was a barber. Smitty played football in high school—he's husky as a bull. And he played freshman year at the University of Texas, but not after that—got hurt. He worked his way through college, cleaning the gymnasium and as part time janitor in his dormitory. You can often tell when a boy has worked his way through college. He's matured a lot earlier than those whose parents pay the bills. Smitty majored in Physical Education.

"I was a WPA supervisor for a year after I got out of school, and then I coached football at Crystal City. Afraid our team was pretty pore."

He got married in November, 1940, to a girl who went through college with him. That kept him from going into the Air Forces until they lifted the marriage ban.

"I always wanted to be in the Air Force. I was 'bout ready to lie about being married when they made it okay to go in even if you were married. We haven't got a kid yet, but one is on the way. We already got him named—Michael. Got a Father's Day card from him the other day—I mean from his mother for him. I was scared about her having a child, with the war on and everything. But she was sure I would be okay and come home. You know, I believe women have got more guts than guys have in this war, no kiddin'."

Smitty got his Air Medal and the Oak Leaf Clusters and the DFC—but he said something to me one day that would have sounded pretty Dale Carnegie from anybody but Smitty.

"You know—you know what the greatest feeling in the world is? I'll tell you. It's just knowing you did a good job up there today."

Sure, I know how it sounds, but Smitty *meant* it. I know Smitty pretty well. I was in "Our Gang" with him when we all thought we'd have to bail out, going in to bomb a target beyond the Ruhr.

Chapter 5

427 TONS ON HULS

"...this is where I came in..."

I'M a Paddlefoot. My business is photography. When I fly, I am a passenger. At first, I tried to tell the story of the Eighth in words. Impossible. That's why I drifted into pictures. On a tabloid paper, I never learned the words you need to tell the story of the Eighth.

A lot of war correspondents take the attitude that the story of one raid is just like another. They're wrong. Every raid, like every plane and every pilot, is different. But every pilot will tell you that one certain raid was "the best."

My candidate for the "best" raid was the job the Eighth did on the synthetic rubber plants at Huls. We got 183 Forts through to the target, and 427 bombs onto the target, about as much as the Jerries ever scattered over the whole of London in any one night.

This was a good example of what "strategic precision bombing" means—the searching out of small and vital targets that will cripple the whole war machine of the Hun when you smash them. At night, the RAF worked on whole cities; by day, we struck at precision targets like Huls.

True, we lost 18 planes on the Huls job, and that's too close to 10%. But the Eighth never expected low losses; the investment of men and bombers would be heavy, the dividends would have to come from accurate bombing and enemy aircraft shot down. We claimed 49 Jerries knocked down on the Huls job. It was the first time I ever really saw many fighters go down. I went along to get pictures again; and, once more, missed. But this time I got more of the whole story of a mission than ever before—the suspense, the tension, the actual, visible sweating that oozes not from your flesh but from your nerves. It was a rich experience to see so much of the full impact of air war on the combat crews.

The real story of any mission begins hours before the take-off. The story
of Huls began thirty-six hours before. At midnight, Sunday, June 20, I was
still on the scrambler phone, trying to work out a deal for getting a B-24 down
to a Fortress station to take Dave Scherman out to photograph the rendezvous
of the bombers that were taking off for some target early Monday morning.
Nobody has ever managed to catch more than a dozen Forts in one picture.
Here was a chance to get a picture of more than a hundred, maybe two hundred. We had tried for weeks to get this shot; this was just one more try.

There was another job on for Monday morning—Sammy Schulman, hero
of the book, *Where's Sammy?* and American Pool Photographer over here,
wanted to get some color shots of the new 4,000 pound bomb. The request had
been sent in by OWI, accompanied by a sketch to show what they wanted—
trick camera angles to distort the size of the bomb, and make the bomb look
enormous. I nixed the distortion, but arranged for the shot. Scherman, Schulman, and I left London about 2:30 in the morning, and got to the bomber station about an hour later. The earliest grey light predicted a clear day. RAF
heavy bombers were thrumming back home to their flarepaths from another
night over the Ruhr. Outside of swallowing hot chocolate after a long, cold
mission, there is no more warming and satisfying feeling in this war than the
sound of bombers on their way to work, or coming home from another job. You
don't hear it with your ears, but with your stomach.

We pulled into the station, past the guardhouse, Schulman and Scherman
sleeping soundly. I piled out and stumbled through the half-light into the Ops
room. Strangely ominous atmosphere. The cold I felt was more than atmos-
pheric, the tension more than fatigue. Somehow the Ops room is always grim
and businesslike. On one wall are the names of all the combat crews available,
with special little marks after those names that are missing in action. On another wall are charts to show how many missions each pilot, navigator, and
bombardier has had; which are missing, and how far the rest have to go before
they reach their coveted "Mission X" and the long lay-off. And looming over
the whole room is the blackboard with the numbers of the ships for the day's
job, and the names of their pilots, with a big "C" after the numbers of four
ships. "C" means they carry cameras. The criss-crossed board was hard and
impersonal, but behind those numbers you knew there were ships like "Our
Gang" and "Piccadilly Commando" and "Mizpah" and "Delta Rebel" and
"Eagle's Wrath" and "Dame Satan" and "Royal Flush" and "Big Dick" and

"Little Joe" and "Slide Kelly" and "Careful Virgin" and "Bomb Boogie" and the rest.

Across the tilted-top table with the huge map on it, I could see the red-eyed, alert officers behind long desks, and the phones that linked this bomb group with a dozen others, with wing headquarters, with Bomber Command, with the whole complex operation of a mission. The Ops officers sat with their elbows on the table. Dented old peanut tins full of cigarette stubs, still burning, sent up lines of mystic smoke. At one end of the table, oblivious, two officers sat and smoked and drank coffee and ate steak sandwiches that drooled grease over their fingers, and, with their free right hands, solemnly played checkers. One of those boys was due to go on the mission today.

Other Ops officers were trying to figure out the carbon-backed attack order, trying to translate terse orders into flight plans which would wisely consider very human factors like the fact that "Joe needs a rest—better let him fly in the second element today."

I looked at these leather-jacketed young men and the sign on the door of the Ops room had more meaning than ever—"Strictly Out of Bounds For All Except Authorized Personnel." Major Alford, from Rising Star, Texas (I never heard of his home town and he never heard of mine, so we always figured we were even), looked up and saw me:

"Hey, what are you doing up here? Come up for a ride, or just for some fresh eggs?"

"What's the target, Boss, what's the target? Answer me that, and I'll answer your question." He walked over and pointed to the red wool string, wound around the yellow-headed pins that marked the check points on the attack order. I saw the string go deep into Germany, after it sliced down from the North Sea, feinting at the Bremen area. That was to draw the fighters up there, away from the target the Forts were after. Down and down the red string went, toward that area that is crayoned in red, red for heavy flak. Red for the Ruhr Valley, "Happy Valley," heaviest flak area in Germany. The guys at the Ops desk were watching me, waiting for me to start inventing an excuse.

A knot the size of a hangman's noose grew inside my throat. This is what happens inside every kid in the Eighth Air Force, morning after morning. Some of them learn to swallow the knot, swallow fear, swallow even nervousness, but no other form of warfare has placed such a long drawn out strain upon the nerves of combat men as this lofty fighting in Fortresses over Germany. It begins with the alert on the day before one mission and does not really end until the mission is over, and night of the next day passes without another alert to rob you of sleep.

I moved closer to the map to study the fine type that named the target. There it was, H-u-l-s—Huls, beyond Hamm—the target this Group had hit alone, with 16 planes, four months before. Back to Hamm and beyond. This was where I came in!

The guys at the Ops desk started kidding me. "Yeah, thought that would make you lose your appetite for combat eggs. What's the matter, chicken?"

It was all good-natured—nobody who *has* to go on missions ever really blames you for ducking the tough ones if you don't have to go. But for a lot of reasons that defy explanation, I did have to go on this one. I knew what they were after at Huls, even before I read the attack order—synthetic rubber. This was a show that I *had* to see. Very quietly, because he understood that I was scared, Major Alford asked: "How about it? Want to go?"

It was one thing to say to myself that I would go; quite another thing to say it out loud to these guys. Too difficult to back out once I got all tangled up in bravado. So we ducked the question, cracked an unfunny joke, and went on back to take Scherman and Schulman over for a combat breakfast before the briefing.

Briefing was scheduled for 4:30, take-off at 8. It was 4 now. Number One Mess, or the House of Lords as they call it, was full of sleepy men in leather jackets, half of them unshaven. Those going on the mission were standing in line with their fresh eggs, or sitting and eating them, in silence. The mess at this station is rather elegant—it was a permanent RAF station before the war, far more comfortable than the new stations we have scratched out of the English fields and covered with tin shacks. A lot of the bigshots we bring up for a look at the Eighth Air Force visit this station, because a large percentage of them want to get as close to the war as they can without being too uncomfortable.

I don't agree. I believe it's a lot easier to fight after you've been living where there is no shaving, bathing, or Claridge's, no show girls and plush-seat movies to make you love life and loathe death. Plentiful comforts don't help make killers out of young Americans.

Sammy Schulman was being enormously funny on the subject of eggs, only nobody laughed. Nobody knew what the target would be for today's job, but they all seemed to sense that it would be tough. Right way to let the kids find

18. O'Neill from Rio. Capt. Oscar D. O'Neill (Chapter 2), who had an Irish father and a Spanish mother, was the pilot of the Fortress, "Invasion II," shot down on its 24th mission, over Bremen.

19. The kid from Texas. Nineteen-year-old Don King, of Imperial, Tex., was a waist gunner on "Invasion II." (See also Chapter 33 and Illus. 110) Youngest combat crew member, he bumped bottoms with his "hind-end buddy" at the opposite gun, Eldon R. Lapp, Fort Wayne, Ind.

20. The bombardier from Hollywood. Slender Eddie Bush rode the bombsight in "Invasion II." He was due to finish his tour of duty before the rest of his crew, but volunteered to go on with them—and went down with them.

21. Pathfinder of "Invasion II"—the coolest man in the crew, Navigator Lt. Ed. M Carmichael of Maryville, Mo. He found the targets that Bush bombed from Lorient to Hamm to Bremen.

22. Praise the Lord and swab your guns, so they'll pass your ammunition. Doing so, left to right, are T/Sgt. Benny Borostowski, La Salle, Ill., ball-turret; T/Sgt. Harry Goldstein, New York, top-turret; S/Sgt. Pappy Youell, Boomer, W. Va., tail gunner; Sgt. Charles J. Melchiondo, Medford, Mass., radio operator; S/Sgt. Eldon R. Lapp, Fort Wayne, Ind., waist gunner—all of the "Invasion II."

23. No. 4 engine was Jack Gaffney's sweetheart, named Judith after his best girl back in San Bernardino, Cal. He helped groom "Invasion II's" horsepower and tap-danced to amuse the crew.

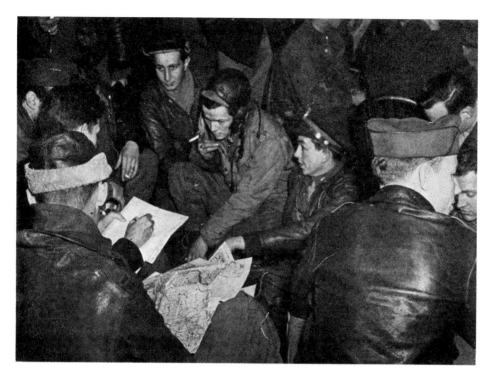

24. Back from Vegesack. Interrogation: "Going into the bombing run, two FW's hit us . . . we got our bombs away . . . the target was already smoked up by the bombs from the group ahead of us. . . ."

25. Boogie-woogie. Gunner Charlie Melchiondo, onetime woodworker, beats out the jive that massages a gunner's nerves.

26. Target: Bremen. One-way trip for the "Invasion II." They followed their bombs down, by parachute. For "where they are now," see Chapter 33.

27. He talked to his crew through the throat mike and intercom; his calm was always an antidote for anybody's nervousness. From bombardier to tail gunner, the verdict was always the same: "Listen, I'd fly to hell in a Piper Cub with Red Cliburn." (Chapter 3) The 10 men in Red's combat crew came from 8 states (see opposite page). One of the original "first of the many," Red made the famous Mission to Moscow in June, 1944. (Chapter 34)

28. The crew of "The Bad Penny": Top row, Lt. R. Y. Kurtz, Jr., Bellerose, N.Y., navigator; Lt. Philip T. Palmer, Wellington, Kan., bombardier; Capt. Charles E. Cliburn, Hazlehurst, Miss., pilot; Lt. Clyde DeBaun, Buchnell, Ind., co-pilot; S/Sgt. Herbert G. Hays, Parkersburg, W.Va., waist gunner. Bottom row, T/Sgt. Raymond T. Moore, Corbett, Ore., engineer; S/Sgt. Clarence Cluck, Chicago, ball-turret; S/Sgt. Paul J. Shook, Akron, Ohio, waist gunner; S/Sgt. Walter G. Dager, Monroeville, Ind., tail gunner. (Chapter 3)

29. Last interrogation, first laugh. Maj. John J. McNaboe, onetime New York State Senator, quizzes Cliburn's crew at the end of "Mission X." Until the last mission, an interrogation is almost as grim as a briefing. But when "Mission X" and all combat is ended, the cue is "Laughter."

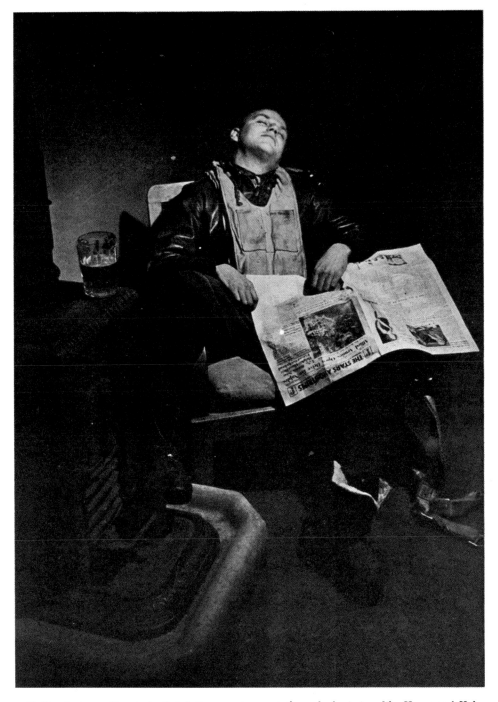

30. Knocked out. The strain that flattens an airman at the end of missions like Hamm and Huls and Schweinfurt begins hours before the takeoff. (Chapter 4) This is 2nd Lt. Fred W. Tucker, 27, Milton, Mass., veteran of 19 raids. Name of his ship: "The Vicious Virgin."

31. No debutante ever dressed more carefully for a first dance than a gunner dresses for a Fortress mission. "Buckle it carefully now, because your hands will be too cold later. Don't forget the knife, in case you hit the drink and have to cut loose from your harness." S/Sgt. William W. Fleming, Jenkins, Ky.

32. "In forty seconds . . . the time will be . . . Oh-two-thirty-two hours . . ."

33. First: Stations time. Then: Taxi time. Then: Takeoff time!

34. Rendezvous: Toward the target . . . Over the target . . . Interception . . . And then . . .

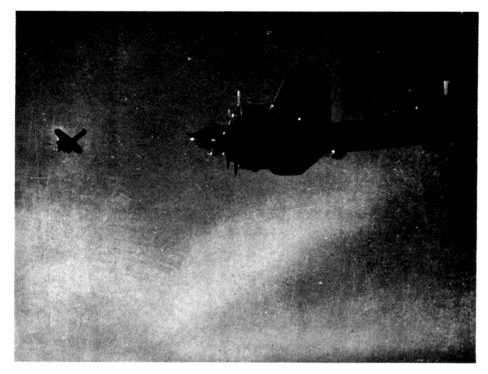

35. "Almost worse than getting hit yourself is seeing another Fort going down."

36. Throwing shadows on each other, the Fortresses fly in tight formation to mass their firepower against fighter attacks.

37. "Hello, trunks? . . . I want to put through a personal call . . . yeah, to London . . . Golder's Green 4463 . . . I want to speak to Miss . . ." Sgt. Jake Levine, East Nassau, L.I., top-turret gunner of "Our Gang," gets home from Huls.

38. What's wrong with this picture? Answer: There are *ten* men in a B-17 crew.

39. Some were hit, but walked away from their ships . . . and some had to be carried.

40. No alert for tomorrow . . . Some slept . . . Some who could not sleep played poker.

out they're in for a rugged ride is to sock them with the news while they're huddled together at briefing. That way, the tough ones transfuse their courage into the nervous ones. I went over to the briefing early, for I wanted to watch the others do what I had done—follow the red thread to the target. I wanted to watch their faces as their eyes digested the target. Already this morning, I had learned again that I was fundamentally yellow, and cowards love company—at least I do. But though I searched every face as it changed with full realization of the dangers that would ambush this mission, I could find no fear. Nervousness in some form in all of them, but no fear. Tremendous strain in many of them, but no fear. Faces did change, deeply. They got older, and, in the pinkest and youngest face, there came a kind of greyness, but still no fear. In the faces of those who had not slept làst night, you could see anxiety, but no fear. Damn it, somewhere a writer with the right words, a photographer with the special genius, an artist with the necessary keenness of perception must be found to capture the courage that is in these boys. The real test begins at briefing. I don't think prose can handle the job of painting the scene. Words must be airborne to do the job. It takes poetry, strong poetry, and maybe music.

(I remember the day Marc Blitzstein came to me and said he wanted to write a symphony about the Eighth Air Force. He wanted to tell the story of how aviation was born so that man might shrink the earth for the benefit of man; of how man through airplanes could now reach a little further and a little faster toward the horizon of man's dreams and aspirations; of how evil men had misused air power, and the story of how the good men were now using air power to beat down ihe evil ones. He wanted to call his symphony *The Airborne!* That's what this story needs—powerful poetry, magnificent music.)

The doors were locked now—the briefing was about to begin. I sat beside Smitty, whom I just told you about—a pilot whose flying time would cover much of the story of *The Airborne*. At twenty-six, this boy was already gnarled and weathered and toughened. His strong fingers were laced in the coat of his dog Skippy, sprawled on the table before him. Skippy seemed to sense from the stiffness in his master's fingers that this was to be a **special** mission. Usually, Skippy's head rested still but wary between his fore**paws**. Not this briefing. His head was up, his ears cocked, his eyes snapping with interest. You know how dogs are supposed to howl when somebody has died. There was first a whine and then a growl in Skip's throat today.

Off in the hut where the gunners were being briefed for this same mission,

Skippy's brother, Windy, squirmed in the arms of "Our Gang's" top-turret gunner, Sgt. Devine, from Jersey City. The only time Skippy and Windy really got together was out at the hard-standing after the take-off, where they waited for their bosses, and muzzled old .50-calibre shell cases across the cement, fascinated by the tinkle of the metal as it rolled. Or they would pull on opposite ends of a greasy rag that had been used to clean a gun an hour or so before. The single most pathetic sight on a Fortress station is to watch a dog wait for a Fortress that will not come back. Dogs show what people hide.

The A-2 officer, one-time New York State Senator John McNaboe, now Major Mac, pushed on with the briefing. Sleepy lids opened no wider, chins hung on chests—until he came to that part about the number of fighters that could be expected to try to stop this mission today—250 single-engined and around 160 twin-engined.

Instantly, there was reaction. Half the kids whistled, the special whistle that means "Jeeeee-sus-keee-rist!" Skippy jumped up and began to bark, and everybody laughed. There wasn't anything really funny, but everybody laughed, very loud. Too loud. Some groaned. "I quit!" "Let's form a union and picket Bomber Command!" "I'm going to write a letter to my Congressman!" "Where's the doctor? I need an operation!"

The Chaplain, Father Hunt, stood by the door. Solemn, tight-lipped, he clutched the silver cup that was a tool of his profession, somehow strange, and yet welcome in this scene. The purple cloth stuck up from under the leather jacket he wore to keep out the chill of the morning. Some COs don't like the Chaplains to attend briefings. "Don't like my boys to be reminded that they are liable to need anything more than luck and guts to get home."

As the laughter and whistling died, the briefing went on. The CO smiled. He knew his boys were awake now, alert, listening. The lights went down, and the gadget they use to project target pictures and weather dope onto the white sheet over the blackboard sliced through the gloom. Major Mac gave a running commentary on the target. At different stations, different officers run the briefing. Major Mac does a good job. He pointed out the way the tall stacks on certain key buildings cast long shadows that would help locate the Aiming Point today. And after the route in and home was briefed, the weather officer came on. They call him "Sunshine." He used to be a football coach at Princeton, Capt. Atwell—best weather man over here. He always gives you, hurriedly, the official weather that is teletyped down to him, and then, slowly, he gives you his own dope. The official dope has often been wrong—Sunshine's, never. Literally never. The Group swears by Sunshine's weather. He was right about Hamm when the official weather was wrong.

Sunshine has a theory about daylight bombing: "You ought to take off before dawn and get over the target at sunrise. That way, you get good visibility, and you know damn well you can't stooge around over a target in the daytime, hunting for a hole in a cloud. If you wait to bomb late in the morning or afternoon, the sun has warmed the earth and driven moisture into the air, and that makes clouds and messes up another mission."

In some groups, guys are encouraged to have theories and develop them, and COs push their theories up through channels to the Big Brass. In those groups, bombing is best, losses are lowest.

The Ops Officer, Major Alford, got up and drawled out the flight plan for the day's job. Everybody is very much interested in that, damned interested. On a job like Huls, nobody likes to fly the "low flight"; they call it "Purple Heart Corner." Lately, we had been getting the brunt of the fighter attacks on that low flight. The four squadrons in a group rotate that flight.

Interesting to watch a kid who is up for his last mission, the last before he gets grounded for a long rest, and watch him sweat out one of the tough ones like Huls. Often the Squadron Commander will let a boy with all except one behind him pick an easy one for the last. All the psychological strain of the long grind is focused on that last mission. One of the boys up for his last mission today was Lt. John Carroll, from Chicago. Looked like Robert Taylor, only stronger face. Wondered what he would do—he didn't have to go, wasn't scheduled. He ended speculation by saying: "I'm going today." Made everybody feel better—if Old Johnny was going, it couldn't be so bad as it looked. Hell, if he was picking Huls to make his last one, no point in getting scared about making your 7th or 10th or 17th or 20th on the same deal.

Major Mac wound up the briefing with the usual advice about what to do if you get shot down: "Give your name, rank, and serial number, that's all. Destroy all secret papers and documents. Destroy the bombsight, and, if necessary, destroy the plane itself." Sounded especially ominous this morning.

I walked over to study the flight plan, with two things in mind: I wanted to pick a plane that would give me good camera angles for covering whatever happened to other planes in the group; I wanted to pick a crew that had experience, a crew that I felt would bring me home. Convinced there's a half-science in picking a plane that will come home, half science and half hunch. Never missed yet. Believe in it as firmly, almost as belligerently, as any gambler ever believed in his system for breaking the bank at Monte Carlo.

I picked a ship flown by a boy named Baird—name of the ship was "Picca-dilly Commando," nickname for the whores who work the streets of London in the blackout. Baird had plenty of experience with trouble. He was the boy who "rubbed the deck," coming home from St. Nazaire, went right down to the trees and fought his way all the way home across the neck of France, with six FW's on his tail. When they got cocked for frontal attacks, Baird would turn right into them and really try to ram them. Their nerve always broke before his bluff did. Seems to be tough for a fighter to nail a Fort when it's down on the deck like that. When the fighter tries to make a long, level, rear attack, the prop wash from the Fort rocks him around, and he's an easy mark for the tail gunner. If he tries to dive in for a rear or deflection shot, he's liable to "mush" into the ground.

I shook hands with Baird as the crews were piling out of the briefing room for their separate bull sessions—one for bombardiers, one for pilots, and one for navigators—to iron out their special problems. The CO's last instruction was: "All the Catholic boys who want to meet with Father Hunt will find him in the navigators' room as usual."

Two ships were down on the board as "extras" today. They would take off with the Group, assemble with them, and go out to the rendezvous—if any ship had to abort before the rendezvous, it was the job of one of the extras to fill in. A lot of the boys, including me, don't like to fly in the extra ship. You see, you never know just where you're going to fly in a Group until the Channel is under you. You can't adjust your mind to fit the flying habits of the pilots who will wind up around you in the slot that luck drops you into, until you're dropped. And in case you do get a safe spot in the formation, say up high, second ele-ment, then sometimes you feel: "Well, looks like I've had my share of today's good luck, before I get to where I'm gonna need it." Most of the kids feel very strongly that they have only an allotted "share" of good luck, like a bank account that can be overdrawn.

Smitty and Weitzenfeld were flying the extras today. Weitzy had a bad one the other day—one of his own group "bombed" him, dropped a 1,000-pounder through the left horizontal stabilizer, smashed it right to the roots. No explo-sion, damn lucky. That kind of experience leaves you a little shaky about the whole idea of formation flying for weeks afterwards. People don't realize the special strain of formation flying. Look at it like this:

You're driving one of 24 fifty-ton trucks down Broadway, fender-to-fender at 275 miles per hour, while the whole New York police force is blazing away at you with tommy guns. That will give you a rough idea of what the Forts do on a mission.

Because it is so damn nerve-wracking, you do like to know before the take-off who your neighbors are going to be in the formation. Smitty and Weitzy were kidding about who would be the first man to fill in for an aborting ship. There was plenty of kidding, but none of this grandstand stuff about: "Let me do it—I'll go first." They said, "Let's flip a nickel"—they hadn't been over here long enough yet to say, "Let's flip a shilling." And Weitzy lost.

Walked back to the Ops Room, got on the phone again, and tried to double-talk to the Ops Officer of the B-24 outfit that was going to lend us a ship to go out and photograph the rendezvous today. Scherman had really sweated this shot—and today looked like the day. Weather was to be good; we could go out over the rendezvous at a low altitude, no oxygen needed, perfect for a picture that would show the Forts streaming out across the Channel like migrant blackbirds in the fall. The Lib outfit promised to get one of their ships down for the job. I slumped into a big chair, pulled yesterday's newspaper over my face, wrestled with nervousness, tried to sleep, and gave up.

The struggle for sleep is a never ending battle in the Eighth Air Force, a battle in which there are countless slow casualties and no medals.

Take-off was to be at eight. Always the low-ebb hour for me. I watched the clock for five minutes, finally ended the debate about going today, went down the hall to my room, and started crawling into the bright blue "zoot suit" that feeds electric heat to your body when the temperature hits forty below. That is another of those "points of no return"—when you start dressing for a mission, then it's too late to turn back. Especially if anybody sees you getting into all the junk. Scherman was there, watching with eyes as sharp as a candid camera, making a lot of salty cracks, such as: "Well, well, well, lookit our Junior Commando, all dressed up for war!"

We all went out to the ship together. Timed my arrival for five minutes before taxi time—it's a bad half hour, those thirty minutes between Stations and Take-off. Wanted to shrink it to a minimum. No point in lying around on the ground, feeling your nerves crack, like pulling adhesive tape off places where you've got lots of hair.

What followed had happened sixty times to most of the combat crews over here. This was mission 60, and besides the shows that had come off, there were about that many more that had been scrubbed. I want to try to tell you something of the quiet torture of the hours before you get over a target, or into the first combat that releases all your knotted nerves with the blessed intoxication of action. If I were a skilled psychiatrist, I could probably tell this story in terms of somebody else—but I can't. I've got to project what happened onto the reflecting surface of my own emotions, like a movie, to make you see it.

The pilot yelled, "All clear!"—the putt-putt pumped the juice in for the starter. A protesting whine—a sudden explosive cough—a cloud of blue-white smoke—and the props caught and the steady roar grew. One after the other, four engines. I walked toward the rear entry door. Clothes that weighed perhaps thirty-five pounds felt like sixty—camera equipment that weighed about sixty pounds felt like two hundred. Just as I opened the rear entry door to climb in, the Signal Corps photographer I had brought up to work on the job with Dave yelled, "Hold it." He got a picture, and laughed. I was standing right beside a rough-painted sign on the door: "Is Your Journey Really Necessary?" That's the sign that is over every railroad ticket window over here. Very grim humor on the door of the "Piccadilly Commando," destination, Huls.

Don Sheeler, the tall blond boy who always used to be behind the Ops Desk, was going along as co-pilot today. First time they put him back on combat, he flew as the tail gunner, as a special observer, in the lead ship of the group. Good idea—keeps the pilot of the lead ship informed about what's happening to his group. I always thought you could settle this whole argument about the number of German fighters we really shoot down by permitting no more claims to be made by a group than an officer observer in the tail of the lead ship sees go down. From his experience in the tail position, Sheeler agrees. He was riding up front today.

Never could figure out where I get the most nervous—riding in the nose with the bombardier, or in the radio hatch, where you can see only to the rear. In the nose, you see what is about to happen to your own ship—fighters boring in, bursts of flak working toward you; in the radio hatch, looking back, you see what has just happened to other ships—see them go down in flames, or into lazy spirals that accelerate to wild spins.

I was on one trip when a ship went into a spin—flak got it, there were no fighters in sight. Our tail gunner, two waist gunners, ball-turret gunner, and radio gunner were watching it go down, and, over the intercom, they were making bets as to when the tail would snap off—in the second, third, fourth, or fifth whirl. It's okay for combat men to get a "death pool" on each other—

but you should have seen the hell raised over here when a newspaper printed a story about a bunch of civilians who ran a pool in a pub, based on the number of RAF bombers that would be lost on the next raid. It would have made me a little sore to find out that a bunch of brass-railers were running a pool on how many Forts would not get home from Huls today.

The plane was already rumbling its readiness. The gunners who fight in the rear of the ship were hauling on their clothes, and then huddling together in the radio compartment to get the weight forward for the take-off. My cameras were piled over in a corner; I was riding here today—hoped to shoot the bomb-fall from the high flight. I would be looking to the rear.

We were taxiing out now—another "point of no return." There is such a lumbering awkwardness about a Fortress taxiing. It leaves the moment its tail wheel pushes away from the earth, in the seconds before "Airborne!"

Suddenly, the engines spluttered, choked, and died. I wasn't on intercom; nobody was but the radio ops. We all looked at him. In the itching silence that followed the roar of the engines, he grinned, and shrugged, "Postponed five hours."

Nobody knew whether to be fed up or happy. I was fed up. Making a decision was always what scared me—now my decision was unmade. We all piled out on the grass to wait for transport to take us back to quarters. Quickly, good humors shook off the tension. There were bets that the mission would be scrubbed, and no takers. A sharp-witted kid from Jersey City, Sgt. Kiss, top turret gunner, was the target for a barrage of wisecracks; this was to be his last mission. After he had finished his career as a gunner, what then?

"So you wanna be a pilot? Wotta dope! Why don't you shoot yourself now and save the Government all the expense of pushing you through flying training so you can come back over here and lose a whole crew!"

Kiss was glad this trip had been postponed, and hoped it would be scrubbed: "Listen, I gotta take the rest of my physicals today. I'm scared of that depth perception test, where you line up them pointers by moving a couple of gadgets up and down. If I can't do that, it means they figure I won't be able ever to land a plane."

Baird told him a secret: "Listen, all you gotta do is to look at the weights at the ends of the strings. When they're even, your gadgets are lined up. It's simple!"

"Hell, I'll tell 'em I can already land a Fort better'n my skipper can and he's supposed to be a hot pilot!"

Everybody agreed that Baird always landed a plane four times to get it down once, three bounces and a skid. He howled rebuttal, but nine men howled louder. Then the tail gunner said: "Say, why do you always wear that ol' huntin' cap? You know we never get off a the ground when you wear that ol' cap."

"The hell we don't! I wore this cap to Hamm. We sure got off the ground then."

So Baird had been to Hamm, too. There was a lot of reminiscing about Hamm. I listened with keen interest. Some day, a psychiatrist is going to dig into my head and find scars rooted in that ride to Hamm. Said the tail gunner:

"Hot damn, do you remember how you buzzed me and asked how many Forts was back behind us, and I said there wasn't none and asked you how many was up front. And you said there wasn't none up front neither. And then botha us said, 'JEEEEESUS, WHERE IN HELL ARE THEY?'"

I remembered to myself that I had been looking back for Fortresses that day, too. But where the Forts should have been, there were fighters. German.

It was fun being a part of this bull session, fun being treated as a "veteran." Interruption: A truck pulled in and we piled on, back to mess. Scherman's B-24 was in. We all sat around and talked with the Lib crew about how they ought to fly to get the best pictures of the rendezvous of Forts going out over the Channel.

And then, five hours later, we all went back to the "Commando" again. I was so sure it would be scrubbed that I wasn't nervous now. Same as everybody else. You get feeling like that. Seldom wrong. We went all through the same deal again. Taxied out, got off the hard-standing this time, nervousness had just begun bulking up in my throat, when the engines died again. Radio ops gave us the news again, with this addition: "Not just postponed. Scrubbed!"

Then there *was* cussing. Everybody pretended he really wanted to go. Maybe they did. There's a saying that "You die before take-off—not after you're hit."

And besides, for a deal like this one, everybody felt certain that it would be on again, the next day, or the first day the weather opened. It doesn't help to go to bed with a briefing for Huls, riding a team of nightmares through your dreams. All the kids who had had more than 20 would sleep damn little tonight.

We all flopped on the now dry grass; sun was out. We were talking about the name of the plane. One of the gunners complained:

"Never did like that name, 'Piccadilly Commando.' Hanging the nickname of them London bags on your ship don't make Lady Luck like you no better. I tell you, boy, I get pretty damn religious when I'm over Germany. I say my prayers when we go over the enemy coast, and I carry this Bible with me every time, damn right I do. My Dad, he carried it all through the Argonne in the last war and he come out okay."

A folded ten-dollar bill fell out of the pages of the Bible as he held it out. What's the ten bucks for?

"Oh, that. That's for gittin' drunk as hell after I wind up my last mission. Never been drunk in my life, but man, when I wind up my missions, look out!"

The truck pulled up to take us back once more. Piled in, rumbled off. Interesting clue to the route by which these kids arrive Somewhere in England: Our gunner looked at the funny yellow boots that another gunner was wearing —sort of like cowpuncher's boots, only with low heels. "Where'd you get them purty yaller boots, boy?"

"Brazil, when we came through."

Back at mess once more, ate lunch with Davey. Seconds and thirds of everything. Biggest damn meal I had eaten since I landed in Portugal after a winter in blitz-weary England two years ago. Fear really gives you an appetite— after you stop being scared. After chow, we all went out to watch the Lib boys take off for home. Bunch of the Fort boys were around the Lib, kidding the crew. "How in the hell do you guys fly that pregnant cow, anyhow?"

Back-cracked the Lib crew: "Better'n that Glamour Gal you fly in. Hell, don't you know a Fortress is just a four-engined medium bomber?"

But there were too many of the Fortress boys and this was their home ground; they won by volume. The Lib outfit were a little hot around the ears as they pulled out down the perimeter, and took off. We ambled back toward the mess. Suddenly there was a thundering roar and the Lib buzzed the field, right down on the deck. This was prophetic. They would do this one day to the refineries at Ploesti, but today it was a Lib's way of thumbing its nose at a Fortress. At the end of the run, the Lib climbed, banked, and turned for another buzz, even lower, this time. The Fortress boys watched, and scorn turned to admiration. "Good show, good show."

We walked back to mess, and stopped by to kibitz on a tennis game between two medicos and two WAAFs. At change of sets, one of the medicos, guy named Doc Ross, came over to register a complaint:

"Did you see that picture in the London *Mirror* yesterday, of those American officers and Army cars at the Derby races—with that stinking caption, asking where Americans got gasoline to drive official cars to the Derby?"

Doc had used one of those cars to take a bunch of flak-happy veterans over to the races for relaxation; he was burned up. So was the whole Group. Little incidents like this seem trivial—but they leave scars. The combat men seemed to feel that somehow it was the fault of Headquarters PRO that the picture had been printed. No use in trying to explain in terms of "freedom of the press."

After dinner, Haley and I drove into London—wanted to pick up a still camera that had been fixed that afternoon. There was an alert on for Tuesday, probably the same job. Huls again. Passing the plant where they make Mosquito bombers, we saw a bloody accident: dispatch driver caught his head on the edge of a truck going in the opposite direction. Very shuddery sight. Didn't help my nerves. In town, stopped by the Dorchester for one drink, ran it up to three rums very quickly. We were joined by the wife of an Irish peer, friend of many Americans. She had known Oscar O'Neill very well, liked him —the Brazilian rearing made the difference. She was bored by Aycock. He knew it, but ignored it.

We went back to my diggings and turned in, tired, warm inside with rum. I couldn't sleep. This was the first time I felt the sweat of fear gather first in the small of my back, and then spread, itching, up my spine and over my shoulders, until my scalp was first hot, then icy cold.

We woke up at three, drove through the night, got lost, and finally pulled into the last quaint English village—they all look like movie sets—just before you get to the station. As we turned the corner, we saw the first Fortress climb into the sky. It was the take-off. The driver speeded up; we slithered through the gates of the station, tore through the still sleeping grounds, and out onto the perimeter track. Only four planes left to take off. Haley was studying the numbers. "There's Smitty's plane! Want to make it? You can."

The driver took the cue; we drove alongside Smitty's plane—"Our Gang." Three left to take off now. I grabbed all the gear I could carry, dropped my tin hat—ill omen—and scrambled through the rear entry door as the plane swung into the runway and braked while the engines roared for the sprinting take-off.

Collapsed in the rear of the plane, I was suddenly and forcibly reminded that I had had only tomato juice for breakfast and that it was down there swearing at last night's rum. None of the kids train half so hard for a Fortress raid as they would for a football game—but one rule that is seldom broken is: Lay off the hard liquor before a raid.

I walked up to the radio compartment where the gunners were huddled to get the weight forward for the take-off. We were rumbling down the runway now—the tail was lifting—now! Airborne! I knew all these gunners, and grinned "hello" to them. Their reply was formal, cold. In the grey half-light of dawn, their hostility was sharp as ice. I was an albatross, an ill omen on this trip, and they did not try to conceal their feelings.

Haley once told me: "When a crew decide that they don't like a pilot, they'll freeze him out, and if he's smart, he'll quit, because you can't lick it once they turn against you."

I went back to my duds, began to dress. Very carefully. I wasn't sure where we were going today, but from the grim tension of the gunners, I knew it would be rough. Probably Huls again. That meant oxygen for perhaps five hours. There must be no constriction of clothing to stop circulation or make movements consume more energy and oxygen. I put on the heavy hunting underwear I wore the first time I flew to England in a bomber, two years ago. Then the blue electrically heated suit. Then the coveralls, the heated shoes, and the leather boots, then the throat mike for the intercom, then a silk scarf tight around my neck, then a wool muffler, then a wool headgear beneath the leather one—your skull damn near cracks from the cold when you stand up in the radio hatch. The silk and wool gloves I stuffed into one knee pocket, on top of the escape kits. I strapped a knife and bail-out bottle around my right leg. Then into the parachute harness.

Sitting on my 'chute pack, I was checking my cameras, when one of the gunners came back, suggesting I come up forward. "It's warmer up there."

They had relented. I felt better already. I scrambled up between the bombs to see Smitty—the bombs were somehow bigger and uglier today. Smitty was bigger, today, too. He turned his head, grinned, then turned back to his job of climbing into formation. I went back to the gang in the radio compartment.

They were huddled together like cattle in a gale. Eyes half closed. Faces grey through the stubble of a shave delayed two days now. Funny how crews can be so different. Take one like Mississippi George Birdsong's gang in the old "Delta Rebel." Wonderful outfit that mirrored George's gay, hell-for-leather spirit. The little ball-turret gunner always played the harmonica until the "Rebel" got over the Channel—the throat mikes on the intercom pick up

the sound of a harmonica, magnify it, and deepen the tones like a pipe organ
or a fine cello. He would play old jazz songs and Italian songs and boogie. We
would sing the songs we all knew like a gang around a bar—the barber shop
ballads. The intercom mixed the voices into close harmony. Always, going
into enemy territory, the song would be the same: "Dixie"! And the crew
would wind up with the rebel yell.

The "Rebel" had more missions than any other in the group at one time;
and after George wound up, nobody in the old gang would fly it—said George
had used up all the luck in the "Rebel." And sure enough, a new crew took it
out, and went down on the first mission. Same thing happened to "Dame Satan"
and "Mizpah" and "Connecticut Yankee."

This crew of Smitty's ship reflected the spirit of the Boss, too—tough and
grim. The ball-turret gunner lay stretched out on the floor, looking as if he had
been kicked in the belly, knocked out. He pulled in great gulps of air, held it,
then let it out slowly, the way a man does the smoke of the first cigarette he's
had in months. He was "storing up oxygen."

We climbed fast today, or so it seemed. The gunners moved back to their
positions; the radio operator was twirling his gadgets—he was serious, like
the others. So different from the "Rebel's" radio operator—"Short-Burst"
Beazy. He used to read the same book going to and coming home from every
raid: *Death in the Clouds.* He always held the title page so that others could
see it.

We were on oxygen now. The cool draft of mixed air and oxygen on my
lips was as delicious as vanilla ice cream. I sucked it in and relaxed. The
electric juice in my zoot suit was on high—wherever there was a crease or
pressure on it, there was wonderful warmth, like stretching your pants tight
when you back up to a log fire. It's a good idea to hunt little comforts like that
on a mission, and cling to them as long as you can. Helps.

We were over the North Sea now. Got up, poked my head out into the slip
stream to study our place in the formation—we were an extra ship again, but
this time we would go all the way into the target. High flight, we were, closing
the diamond. Not good for pictures, fine for safety. While I was poking my
head out, the thing happened that always scares the hell out of me—and out
of anybody else who isn't battle-happy: The top turret test-fired his guns . . .
wham wham wham wham! Damn near jumped out the hatch. The radio operator laughed. You could see his grin push out from behind his mask.

We spotted the first enemy fighters a few minutes later, flying parallel to us,

out of reach of our .50's. Milk white, they were, like the ones that had been flying over the formations and dropping bombs down onto the Forts.

Then we turned South, slashed into enemy territory, and headed for the
long run down to the target. We came into Germany high to the north, like a
reverse play in football, to trick the fighters into protecting the wrong target.
Saw the first fighter get cocked for an attack, high and just in front of us. Too
close for firing at us, unless he had a new trick in his kite. He turned even
with us, then knifed back for a long dive at the following group. The whole
play was followed by our gunners—as the Jerry dived, our waist and tail
gunner cut loose on him, so did the other gunners in our group. This was good
shooting, best I ever saw. Several of the gunners gave Jerry the right lead, and
damned if somebody didn't rope him! There was a sharp flash that obscured
the midsection of the Jerry, then another lesser flash, then a crackling explo-
sion as tracer still reached out for him, then the billowing black smoke just
like you see faked in the movies. Then the wild spin as the plane screamed
down onto Germany, right in the teeth of the following group.

There was a chatter of victorious cussing on the intercom. First blood for us.
I felt confidence again. The tension was gone.

It was fifteen minutes before there was another attack. Maybe that first
lone attacker had been a green pilot, over-anxious. But now others, too many
others, were stooging along beside us, out of range, ganging up, probably
under control from the ground, sparring with us to find out what our target
would be. They seemed to be waiting for us to go into the bomb run, when
we would have to fly straight and level for about forty seconds to give the
bombardier time to work his gadgets. That's when the Jerries throw the works
at you. But their patience and their gas seemed to be running out; they piled
in earlier than usual. Smitty's "coach's drone" over the intercom was going
now; he talked to the kids in the crew like a quarterback does to a huddled
team before the next play. When the fighters started their attacks, Smitty
quickened his commanding spiel:

"Okay, okay, git set. They're linin' up out there. Lookit them bastards
gettin' ready to eat us up. Oh-ho, oh-oh-oh—heeeeeere they come. *NOW*, in
high 2:30. Reach for him, nose gun. Reeeeach! Hit 'im, top-turret. Okaaaaay,
he's gone. Tap him goodbye, tail. Look *OUT!* Another noser. Okay, Devine,
we're handing him to you, catch him—he's *YOURS.*"

Smitty would turn into the attacks, dive into them, to make the Jerry shorten
his time of fire before he inverted and pulled out. Very seldom does a Jerry

hold his line of flight when he sees a Fort diving down on him. It's got nothing to do with being a German or a Nazi or anything else, it's just that a guy has to be nuts to try to ram a Fort. It's been tried. The Fort came home; the Jerry didn't. Smitty kept his fight talk crackling—not crackling, but more of a drone, rising in pitch only on words like "NOW!"

Wonderful for the nerves. It soothed nervousness and needled carelessness. It kept the gunners' eyes on their areas of search.

Suddenly, a Fort peeled out of the element ahead of us, right up and over and down so close we could see the cockpit, a furnace of orange flame. One 'chute opened as a man bailed out of the waist. The 'chute fouled the tail and the man was jerked right out of his harness. Another man bailed out of the nose escape hatch, on fire. His 'chute did not open. And then the whole Fort seemed to explode, as if TNT had been tucked into every cranny of it. Quick and easy for the guys still in it—but how about the two who plunged to earth without 'chutes?

"Our Gang" suddenly dived—sharp, shocking to every raw nerve end. Thought we would never pull out—we were just going down into the middle flight—no, it was the low flight. Purple Heart Corner. Suicide Flight. Fine place for pictures—if you get home. Still don't know why Smitty went down.

I got braced against the padded walls of the radio compartment, elbows against it, camera cocked against the side window for a shot at the bomb fall from the flight above us. Best place to catch that picture is out the hatch—but the gunner was busy there today. Suddenly—everything is sudden—there were clusters of white puffs off our wing, like tiny flak—20 mm. bursts. They were reaching for us. Closer. *GOT US.*

There was a sharp crackling on our left wing, like gravel thrown against a tin roof, then WHAMM, a direct hit at the roots of the wing, like the sound of flailing a tub with a rug-beater. Smitty's voice cut in:

"Okay, radio op? Okay. Okay top-turret? Okay. Okay waist gunners? Okay. Okay. Okay ball-turret? Okay. Okay navigator and bombardier? Okay. Okay. Okay tail? Okay."

Almost as an afterthought, he droned a postscript: "Okay cameraman?"
"Okay."

Everybody was nervous, but unhit. And then Smitty bawled a warning:
"WILD FORT, COMING THROUGH US. HOOOOOOOLD IT!"

Another Fort had been hit. It climbed out of the flight above and peeled down through us, scattering us like pigeons. Scattered, we were cold meat for

Jerry. This was on the bomb run too. We tried to re-form as the FW's piled in.
Smitty held her straight and level for the run-up to the target, and then,
WHAM WHAM WHAM WHAM, and we were hit again, hit hard this time.
And instantly there was a sheet of orange flame blasting by the window that I
held my camera against, brilliant orange. I swear the first thought I had was:
"Goddamnit, no color film!"

That thought lasted approximately one-thousandth of a second; hard on its
heels, came panic. The radio operator howled the report of "FIRE, LEFT
WING" to Smitty. Calmly as he would ask for a second helping of soup,
Smitty said: "Stand by. Watch it—we may have to bail out."

I looked a frantic, unspoken question at the radio operator. He had missed
the exact wording of Smitty's command, as I had. He was scrambling a little
wildly into his parachute harness. He leaned over and yelled at me: "Stand
by to bail out!"

Guys never seem to remember exactly what they thought about before they
bailed out or ditched in the Channel; I do. I was just mad. Too scared to feel
fear, which may sound crazy, but it's true. I've talked to a boy who was hit in
the neck with a 30 mm. slug—he said it hurt so much that it didn't hurt, all
feeling was simply knocked out. But he was mad, too, mad that he hadn't
ducked, or something. Mad at himself. So was I now. I thumbed over in my
memory all the stuff about what to do when you bail out in enemy territory.

The radio operator was on his gun again. I stood up, looked at him. No
more panic. He had one eye on his ring sight, glued to his area of search, and
the other eye on the flame. Both my eyes were on the flame. It would grow
in length and fierceness, then shrink back inside the wing, then belch out again.
That went on for what seemed like thirty minutes, actually was less than five.
The fighters, attracted by the smoke and flame, like flies to cake, ganged up
on us again.

Smitty's granite drone went on and on, like Ned Sparks, talking through his
cigar. And then the welcome warning came over the intercom. "BOMBS . . .
AWAY!" The bombs gone, there was no more need to fly straight and level.
Smitty handled the Fort like a Spitfire now. We would dive so steep and
sharp that the gunner and I and all the gear in the compartment would just
leave the floor, like the things floated around in *I Married a Witch*. Then we
were all chucked into one corner in a heap, ammunition boxes, odd bits of
radio equipment, parachutes, cameras, thermos jugs, sloshing hot coffee over
the pile. A case of .50's jammed a corner into my guts on the way down. That

exploded the turbulent mixture in my stomach of tomato juice and rum and fear, and I dived for the bomb bay. It's bad to vomit in your oxygen mask . . . I yanked it off and heaved. And heaved. And heaved! Then I turned around to face the radio gunner, ashamed of my performance under fire, unable to alibi it. He was roaring with laughter behind his mask—not mean laughter, but sympathetic. He rubbed his own stomach and rolled his eyes to indicate that he was about to toss the works, too. What a guy!

I stood up now, helped the gunner wrestle with a new can of ammo on his gun, then poked a camera over the edge to get a shot of the target we had left behind us. The rubber plants were bleeding black smoke up into the white cloud that had almost blanketed the objective. And then another Fort started down, but this time there were the white puffs of 'chutes opening, one, two, three, and finally ten! And still the drone of Smitty's fight talk over the intercom.

Things were quieter, suddenly. It is always like that. Suddenly there are fighters and flak. And then, suddenly, there aren't any more fighters or flak. The tail or waist gunner cut into the quiet: "THE BASTARDS ARE BACK—HIGH—11 O'CLOCK!"

I looked up into the slip stream, just over the edge of the deflector . . . yes, there were the black specks of fighters, with their white plume vapor trails streaming behind. But Smitty experted the new crisis: "Not the enemy. Spits. Don't shoot."

That was all. But the tension snapped, somebody started singing. That had made it easy, though, to see how trigger fingers instinctively contract at the sight of anything with a single engine, after a scrap with the Jerries. Afterwards, we learned that 90 FW's had taken off from the French dromes to intercept us on the way out; the Spits handled them. We were over Holland, then the Channel was below. Smitty paged me: "Come on up for a cigar."

I catwalked through the bomb bay, crawled through the top turret base, and stood up beside Smitty. He grinned, and poked a cigar at me. No thanks, said my stomach. The whole story of the hell we'd just skinned through was sure tattooed onto Smitty's face. Some day, I'm going to take a picture of a pilot before and after a tough mission. There was always calm in his voice over the intercom today, but there had been turmoil inside him. Not fear, just turmoil. We were dropping now, off oxygen. We talked about the fire. He said he was glad he hadn't known how bad it was; might have made him sound nervous. That would have been bad, said Smitty. Check.

And now England was below. We left our position for the third time today, and climbed into A flight—Smitty explained that he could land first from A flight. Sign of a veteran. We made a good landing—the crew kidded him about it, but it was good. Smitty pulled off the runway, taxied over to the hard grass by the hangars. The gangs of sweaters-in flocked over to poke curious fingers into the holes in "Our Gang." The gunners were wise-cracking with the ground crews. We piled out, and Smitty walked over and looked up at a hole in the wing, where a 20 mm. had barely missed a tank. He squinted and looked close, then spit, and walked off. We all piled into a truck and headed for the interrogation.

In the A2 shack, I looked for Baird and his crew, the outfit I was supposed to have gone with. A bunch of kids were collected around his bombardier, pounding him on the back, congratulating him on getting home from his last mission. The navigator had a flak wound in his head—not bad. Baird was holding up the stump of a 20 mm. slug that had hit his boot, exploded, blown all the fur lining out of his boot, singed the hair on his leg, and shredded his socks and pants, but had not scratched his skin. He was grinning like he had struck oil.

And then I saw John Carroll, the boy who had decided to take his last to Huls, though he wasn't slated to fly today. He looked as if somebody had cut out his heart with a rusty knife. Got the story later. His ship had exactly one hole in it—where a single .30-calibre slug had gone into the nose, and hit the navigator in the head.

I left the interrogation, and walked out into the sun, very tired, mostly in the stomach. Couldn't even drink hot chocolate and hold it down. Last thing I saw that day of the gunners of "Our Gang" was the top turret, Devine, riding off on his bicycle, balancing a stack of cake in one hand—for the dogs, Windy and Skipper.

We drifted over to Smitty's room in the afternoon—wanted to shoot some more pictures of him "at home." More than ever, a bomber station seemed like a college campus back home—the pictures on the walls, girls in bathing suits, the snapshots of girls back home, and the family, the trophies, the signs, the general litter. Could have been Texas A&M or Dartmouth or Stanford. We flopped on the beds and talked about the guys that were missing today, quite impersonally, the way you talk about guys who have graduated, so they won't be around for football next fall. Smitty's roommate had had a narrow squeak: he let his whole crew go with a kid who was making his first mission as a pilot, quiet little Irish kid called "Slats." Everybody liked him; he had had about 17 missions as co-pilot, but this was his first as Boss. That was his ship that had come roaring down through our flight and into a spin.

Another wonderful guy made his first one today as a pilot—Broadnax. Born comedian. He hated to go as Skipper—but he went and he came back, and now he was celebrating and everybody was glad for him. Three missions later, he got it, too.

This group lost 5 ships today, out of 22 over the target. About 25% loss, same as Hamm. Pretty rough. Once this group was the best; before it finished its first year of operations, it was doomed to be so shot up that its morale would go down again and again for the count of nine, but never quite for ten.

Smitty dropped off to sleep, and Haley and I went on into town. A well-known London lady was giving a dinner for several famous Americans; it was promised that there would be a crap game after coffee, real on-the-knees crap game. Sounded fun. We dropped in. Dinner talk was thickly insulated against the war. I don't mean to be critical. If people talked only of war after dark over here, Britain would have been bughouse long before now.

The crap game got started around ten, mildly at first. But as it progressed, the pressure mounted, as did the pot. Fascinating to watch character emerge under the stress of a wartime crap game, when money means so much more than usual to some people, and so much less than usual to others. Gambling in Britain has never equalled the peaks set in 1943.

One man, a celebrated figure in Hollywood and New York, noted as a plunger, folded as his losses mounted. A famous American banker lost steadily, but wisely never bet more than a pound. Haley Aycock stripped off his coat, rolled up his sleeves, and made a wonderful picture as he coaxed the dice. He won for a while; then he started losing heavily. Again and again he reached into the pocket of his jacket, the pocket under all the medal ribbons, and pulled out first five-pound notes, then three uncashed pay checks, one by one. And finally, he was writing out IOUs. There was only one man against him, a non-flying officer, tremendously wealthy, good guy. He tried every way he could to lose; made bad bets at bad odds; anything to lose. He couldn't. You know, that's how it goes sometimes. And Haley couldn't win.

And so, a day that had been full of excitement wound up sort of flat and sad. We put on our coats, said good night, and went back to my joint. Haley walked along, head down.

Pilots burn up all their luck over Germany.

Chapter 6

DOUBLE TROUBLE

"... for me, a Smith means disaster."

You've got to start training a kid at fourteen for what he's got to stand in modern air war. Take the case of a baby-faced boy named Bob McCallum. (See Illus. 45.) In a half dozen missions, he had enough things happen to him to crack the mind of a man of thirty. His youth, plus his long training, absorbed the shock.

Bob was born in Scotland, went to America with his folks when he was two, grew up all through the Middle West, and went to school in Omaha. He was in the ROTC in high school.

He was headed for medical school when the urge to fly started wrestling with him and finally won. His mother argued, and lost. He took a CPT course, and then came to England via the Clayton Knight Committee, after training with a bunch of guys that included: "a technical engineer, a radio commentator from Cleveland, a fellow with eight years in college studying chemistry, an instructor in flying, and a guy who had a rating from the Boeing School, but wanted to fly fighters. And there was a Hollywood producer, too. The Eagles were getting a lot of publicity about that time; I guess that's what decided a lot of us."

Bob had tried to get into our own Air Forces, but it seems that when he was in college, "there was a collie dog chasing a cat one morning and they both ran between my legs and I landed on my elbow and I've never been able to get my arm straight since then. Something always happens to me."

Besides that, he was born in Scotland. So he was just about to go on Ops with the Lancasters in the RAF, when everybody started transferring into the Eighth U.S. Air Force. One of his best friends went into Lancasters. Bob has seen him several times since, and compared experiences:

"There's plenty of tough things about both kinds of flying, night and day. In the Forts, we fly in formation, and formation flying is plenty tough. At night, there's one good thing: if you have to bail out, you got a pretty good chance of escaping before dawn, or at least of getting away from the spot where your 'chute landed."

Bob came over into the Eighth in January, when things were bad. He had nine missions before "the real disaster"—and nobody ever had more trouble in 20 missions than he had in 9. His first one, though, was a pushover, to Rotterdam. Made him kind of cocky.

The next one looked easy at the briefing: Antwerp. But before they got back, they lost a fourth of the bombers in their group.

And then came the famous Battle of Bremen—where Oscar O'Neill and the Invaders went down. Oscar's outfit lost 6 planes that day; Bob's lost 10 of the total 26 lost by the whole Eighth Air Force.

"We never had a name for our ship. Didn't have anything on the nose. My pilot, Johnny—I was flying co-pilot—he figured that he didn't want to put any pictures on the nose of his ship, because it might attract the attention of some Jerry fighter and make him concentrate on us."

Then they went to St. Nazaire. "This was to be my pilot's last mission. It looked easy. He went to the target, bombed, and then started home. The visibility was lousy, but we were pretty happy. There was just one little flak hole in the left wing. We were kidding each other about what an easy way this was to finish a tour of combat duty. We were over water all this time, when, all of a sudden, we saw land ahead. The whole group started letting down, because we thought it was England. And then Johnny started kidding about how he ought to ditch the plane just off the coast to make a dramatic story he could tell his children.

"We were crossing the coast, letting down all the time, when all of a sudden, there was a terrific cross fire of flak, wham wham wham wham, and we were in the middle of it. We had stumbled into a French port—navigator's error. We were right over a big city now, and all hell was coming up at us.

"I thought to myself, oh hell, here goes the whole group! First one of our wing men went down and then the other. Then we pulled up into a tight turn and got the hell out of there. We took a heading due north and poured on the coal. And then the fighters came in at about 3 o'clock, ripped in through the haze. We broke away, went right down on the deck and hedge-hopped to shake the Jerries off. It worked. They didn't know how to handle us down on the deck. Couldn't seem to get in for the kill. That's what we thought, anyway, when, all of a sudden, the tail gunner yelled out, 'Fighters at 6 o'clock!' The slugs came all through us. The whole ship shook and kind of bonged like a sound effect in a Walt Disney movie.

"Farenhold, the top-turret gunner, came down and yelled that there was a helluva fire in the back of the ship—the intercom was shot out and so were most of the controls. I looked back through the bomb bay and all I could see was bright red flames, like looking into a furnace. We gave him both our fire extinguishers and told him to go back and handle it. He came back in a minute and said it was too damn hot to get near the fire. We sent him back again, told him he *had* to put out that fire. Get help from the two guys in the nose. He went up and found out they were both hit bad, no help.

"By this time, we were out over the water. Farenhold came back up and said somebody was back on the other side, fighting the fire. He didn't know who it was. He had used up our coats and boots and everything to try to smother the fire. And then finally we saw England. Boy, did it ever look so good to us! We had to get there, because, if we had ditched, we knew the dinghies would have been burnt up. God knows how many wounded we had aboard. We landed without controls, and the tail wheel wouldn't let down. And then we checked up: The tail gunner had been hit in the belly with a 20 mm. shell; the two waist gunners and the radio operator had panicked and bailed out somewhere down the line. Johnny sure had his story to tell his children about his last mission.

"Who was the guy who fought the fire? Oh, that was the first of the fellows named Smith who meant bad luck for me. Sgt. Smith, ball-turret gunner, the one that got the Congressional Medal of Honor. He saved the ship, no doubt about that." (See Illus. 57, 58, and 61.)

After that ride, Bob got a week in the rest home—"Flak House." And then he came back to his station. First raid he went on was a tough one: to Kiel.

"Looks like they just wouldn't let me go on an easy one. It's no fun being a co-pilot. When an easy one does come along, they take a new first pilot and let him go in your place, to sort of let him see what a raid is like before he has to go on his own as a first pilot. And a lot of times, you get ranked out of a ride by a general or a colonel, so you never finish up with the pilot you started out with. For the Kiel job, I drew a seat with a fellow I knew real well, another Smith, Bob Smith, from La Mesa, Texas. We roomed next to each other in the hut. (See Illus. 45.)

"The Kiel job was the first time he went out as a first pilot; he picked me as his co-pilot. A pilot and a co-pilot pal around together a lot. They're usually closer than anybody else in the crew. They split up the flying time, about every fifteen minutes, switching generally every time the big hand on the clock hits 12, 3, 6 and 9. The big difference between the two jobs is the pilot has to decide what to do when you get in trouble."

There wasn't too much trouble on that run, though. But the next one was another German job—they started for Wilhelmshaven, but had to hit the secondary, Heligoland. That was the one that "Old Bill" got messed up on. Then they went back to Kiel again.

"Somehow or other we got a big American flag painted right up by the nose of our ship, four foot square. I felt that was gonna cause us some trouble. Some Jerry was bound to see that flag and head right for it. No use asking for trouble, I always said. I got enough without asking."

And on the next one, back to Wilhelmshaven, the trouble came, in double doses. Bob and Smitty were flying in the low element of the low squadron of the low group, the hottest spot there is. The fighters hit them before the flak did that day; and the Jerries used new tactics. They would fly alongside out of range, not singly but in 18's. They would pull on ahead and turn together and then peel off and hit the group "company front" to divide the Fortress firepower. The squadron leader went down in flames before they reached the targets. That jumbled the formation, which didn't help. Then the Forts dropped their bombs and made their turn for home—and that was when they got it.

They stopped a burst right at the roots of the left wing. Knocked out the superchargers on engines 3 and 4, put a couple of holes in the ball turret, but didn't hit the gunner. The manifold pressure dropped down and down on the left side, and the ship dropped back, out of the group. The engines weren't burning, just lack of power. Then the fighters came in again. A 20 mm. burst on the nose of engine 4. The oil pressure dropped to 0. Then she started throwing oil. Had to feather it. One gone and three to go.

The crippled Fort was just about over the German coast, at 18,000 feet. Another burst of cannon fire knocked out the oxygen system all over the ship, and scrambled the intercom, too. The cowling of engine 2 was shredded, and disappeared. The engine kept turning over, naked in the gale, but very little power. Then it was hit again and the prop ran away. And then there was fire. First in the engine, then back in the radio compartment, as another shell exploded in the bomb bay.

Smitty put the ship into a steep dive to shake off the fighters. The tail gunner had used up all his ammunition; he crawled forward for more from the nose. Then the crew forward threw out everything they could to lighten the ship— waist guns and ammunition and radio. Everything that wasn't bolted down went out the window to help the staggering Fort keep flying.

A flock of Jerry fighters were stooging alongside, watching the show, certain they could close for the kill at will. Smitty was flying like a madman, fencing with the fighters. One of them made two slow passes at the nose, and Smitty ducked him both times. Didn't leave him enough room to go between the Fort's belly and the water. The Jerry didn't fire either time; Smitty figured he was out of ammunition, just trying to trick the Fort into dipping into the North Sea. Next time, Smitty held her steady when the Jerry bored in. He guessed wrong. The Jerry raked the whole spine of the ship with all guns blazing. Smitty cussed and cried into the dead intercom. He figured all the crew had been butchered back behind him.

He told Bob to get up in the top turret and "try to swat down a couple of the black-bellied bastards." Bob climbed up, switched on his gun buttons, and swung the turret through a half circle, just in time to see a JU-88 creeping right down over the rear elevator, getting cocked for the kill. The Jerry swung wide for a raking shot. He filled the turret sights and slopped over the edges, he was in so close. Bob squeezed hard on the trigger handles and fired and fired until the guns would fire no more. The Jerry seemed to stand still in the air, then he jumped, then climbed straight up and then over, smoking like a locomotive. Bob crawled out of the turret, and back into his seat, grinned at Smitty, and yelled: "Reckon I scared him away."

They had gone over the target at 12:40; Bob fired his last shot at exactly 2:10. That was a good hour and a half of steady fighting. And the fight wasn't over yet. They had one good engine left, and that was coughing. The airspeed sank down and down. 120—115—110—100.

Smitty dropped the flaps a third to hold her off the water, trying to nurse her home. They were only thirty-five minutes from the English coast. And then the airspeed dropped to 95, and she headed for the drink. Hit with a helluva thump, threw Smitty and Bob against their safety belts, knocked out two of the crew, cold. Water spewed all over the place, rushed in through flak holes and up through the crushed bomb bay. Smitty scrambled out one window and Bob out the other—it was a tight squeeze. "Listen, if that hole had been only six inches square, I'd a-gotten out anyhow—"

They crawled up on the right wing; the rest of the crew was already there. One dinghy was out, the other one stuck. They yanked it loose and inflated it. They were all pretty happy to be alive—they had gone down in the right tradition, fighting. The gunners had knocked down 11 Jerries—a record that beat the previous high set by Capt. Martini and his "Cocktail Kids" in April. They called the roll:

Smith and McCallum were okay. Sgt. Wayne Gray, from Coraopolis, Pennsylvania, who toggled the bombs off that day, was okay. Sgt. Art Adrian, from Milwaukee, the ball-turret gunner, he hadn't been caught in the crash landing. The radio gunner, Sgt. Ken Kate from Manchester, New Hampshire—okay. Two waist gunners, Sgt. "Bull" Durham, from Chattanooga, and Sgt. Aygmund Warminski, from Hamtramck, Michigan—both okay. Navigator, Lt. Dan Barberis, from Bergen, New Jersey—okay. Tail, Sgt. Billy Lamb, from Belton, Texas—okay, but a little groggy. Top-turret gunner, Sgt. Ben Buchanan, from Ft. Worth—okay, and sore that Bob had swiped that last shot at the Jerry.

They were all out there in the two dinghies, laughing. When a Fort circled them, with the whole crew waving out the waist gun windows, they said: "Hell, this is a cinch. We'll wait out here until Air Sea Rescue picks us up, and then we'll get a week in the rest home. Pretty soft."

Wrong again. They watched their ditched Fort poke one wing into the air, then its tail, then dive out of sight. They settled down and waited to be picked up. And waited. And waited.

Darkness brought anxiety and anxiety brought fear. It was cold. This was May, in the North Sea. All of them were pretty wet by now. It rained. They heard a plane about 1:15, fired flares and yelled, but heard the plane no more. They huddled close to keep warm. Next morning, they had to comb scrambled ice out of their hair. Everything was white with frost. There was no cheerfulness now. There was dense fog. You could scarcely see from one dinghy to the other—they were tied together. They paddled. Pretty pitiful, paddling with something the size of a fly swatter, out in the middle of the North Sea.

Three times during the day, they heard the sound of engines. They fired flares wildly and blew their whistles, and yelled. But yelling only made them jumpier. And then the rain came again and their spirits touched bottom. It was night again. Nobody said—"Christ, we're finished"—but everybody felt it. Suddenly, one of the boys jumped up and yelled: "There's a boat. Look, a big goddamn boat. Right there."

And he pointed straight ahead. One of the boys started to clip him on the jaw to shut him up, thought he had gone off his nut. But another one jumped up and yelled: "Sure, he's right. There it *is!*"

This time, he pointed up, not out, and sure enough, there it was. Bob stood up and looked and gasped: "My Gawd, it's a battleship!"

But it wasn't. It was a trawler, out hunting for them. They blew their whistles and yelled, and then they were hauled over the side. Dry clothes and hot soup and brandy sent their spirits soaring again. They were ninety-two miles off England when they were picked up, drifting the wrong way.

Back at their stations, they did get sent to a rest home for a week. And after a week in the rest home—

"The first damn day we came back, we were alerted for a mission. We went to the briefing, and what do you think was the target? Bremen! Like I told you, they never give me an easy one. Smitty was scheduled to be sent home, but they sent him to Bremen instead. He was plenty mad. And the whole crew, except three of the gunners, we all went along with him. Sure it was rough—we got three flak holes in our new ship. But the fighters didn't bother us this time. We didn't have anything painted on the nose of the new Fort. Not even a name."

This was the mission where the new wing went to Kiel and the old boys hit Bremen. Coming home from Kiel, the "first of the new" got careless; the gunners all took their guns out, started cleaning them on the way back across the North Sea. Half way home, a flock of JU-88's jumped them. Total losses of the Eighth that day were 26 Forts—22 were the "new boys."

In the Battle of Germany, the fighting doesn't stop when you step out of the ring.

Chapter 7

TWO FROM HOLLYWOOD

". . . what the hell, it's all the same war . . ."

THERE was a Fortress squadron that took its battle nickname from a single miraculous ship called "The Fitin-Bitin." (See Illus. 55.)

I got its story from a boy who comes from Hollywood. He was raised in the movie business, but over here he learned that truth often makes a better movie than fiction. Tell you about him later. First comes the story of the "Fitin-Bitin" Squadron. That outfit sweated and prayed and worked and flew and fought for one thing—not God or Country, but for The Record.

For six months in the Battle of Germany, this squadron had gone out day after day on 42 missions, without the loss of a single Fort—and only one man had been killed in action. That was The Record.

Some called it luck; some simply envied and cussed it. But The Record survived until they hit the U-boat yards at Kiel on July 29. On that grim and bloody day, The Record died.

Slugging through the fighters, two ships of the "Fitin-Bitin" Squadron stopped solid bursts of flak. One ship was named "Jeiavad"—a name made up of the first letters of the names of the wives of the seven married men aboard. The "Jeiavad" went down under control, and parachutes bloomed in her wake. The name of the other ship was "The Fitin-Bitin," the flagship, the Fort that carried the fighting bug on its nose. She went down in flames.

This proud squadron entered the Battle of Germany in the Fall of 1942. The first ship to cheat the Luftwaffe out of a kill was "Wahoo"—she came home with one engine shot out, large holes chewed in her tail, and a new sixteen square foot window chopped in her side by German 20 mm. shells. Her skipper was a young lieutenant from El Paso, Texas, now the squadron CO, a boy named Bob Riordan. (See Illus. 54.) Doctored up, "Wahoo" went out again, was shot up even worse this time, and junked. "Wahoo II" got the works at Romilly in December, but Riordan brought her home for junk.

In the early rounds, before The Record started, some of this squadron's ships did not come home; but they all went down fighting. Most famous was the "Son-of-Fury." When she hit the drink on the way home from a raid, the last thing anybody saw was top-turret gunner Arizona Harris, blazing away at the German fighters that had hounded the "Fury" down into the sea. His guns were still barking and biting as the Channel closed over their muzzles.

But once The Record got going, the boys of "Fitin-Bitin" always brought their ships home, no matter how. They almost slipped once when they went deep into Germany, to Hanover. The Squadron Commander that day looked back and saw one of the "Fitin-Bitin" ships in trouble, smoking and lagging out of formation. The ship was named "Sis." He thought he saw 'chutes open. Into his intercom, he growled: "Sonofabitch! There goes The Record!" But he was wrong. Back at base, they watched the skies for stragglers, and sure enough there came "Sis," limping across the horizon. Skipper Schoolfield from Baltimore reported:

"Yep, we were in trouble. Five times I started to ring that bail-out gong, and five times I thought of The Record—so we came on home."

They almost lost another ship that day, too. The "Dixie Demo" dropped back to cover a crippled Fort—the "Fitin-Bitin's" always do that. It's not healthy, but the "Fitin-Bitin's" don't give a damn. They don't like to lose their own ships, but they don't like to see any other Forts go down either. And so the "Dixie Demo" dropped back to cover a pal.

Skipper of the "Demo" was Lt. Alphonse Maresh, from Ennis, Texas. His ship got hit hard, gas tanks drilled—but he'd done his job. The ship he covered got away okay. Then the fight began, to get his own ship back across the Channel. He had to save The Record. The crew tossed out everything they could, chopped loose the fixtures and tossed them out too. But they couldn't quite make it. The shores of England were only a few hundred yards ahead when the "Demo" had to ditch. She hit in shallow water, and when the crew piled out, they only got wet to their waists. They felt pretty silly, sitting in their rubber dinghies, paddling ashore, with a thousand and more people cheering for them. They felt silly and sad, because they'd killed The Record by not getting their ship home.

But next day an Air Service Command Mobile Repair Unit fished the "Dixie Demo" out of the drink and brought her home. Once more The Record was saved.

Now The Record is dead, though some still cling to the hope that the crew of "Fitin-Bitin" and "Jeiavad" will turn up as Prisoners of War. But when you call the extension of the squadron, you still get the same old answer: " 'Fitin-Bitin,' Major Riordan speaking."

"Fitin-Bitin" Squadron is almost a separate air force. Just by luck the radio gunner of the "Fitin-Bitin" is still very much alive. He has finished his combat tour and got his DFC in another ship. And he's a Hollywood boy. Used to be an usher out there. His name is Billy Brown.

Billy Brown was born in Minneapolis—but he lived in California for fifteen years. His father was a vocal teacher—trekked to California when the sound movies came in, sort of prospecting, because he figured a lot of silent movie stars would pay good money to learn how to sound the way they looked on the screen. Billy worked as an usher in a movie while he was going through Hollywood High—lots of the big name stars sat in the same classrooms. He remembers them by their real names.

He worked up to be manager of Warner's Theatre there; then he got fed up with that, got a job with Douglas Aircraft. After that he tried to get into the Air Force. He had a private pilot's license. Couldn't get in because he had no college education—we lost a lot of good pilots that way. He tried to get into the Canadian Air Force—was all set when Coca-Cola offered him a swell job, and he took it:

"I really got a good chance to study America going to war. The soda fountain is a damn good pulse on public opinion; and it was my job to sell Coca-Cola to soda fountains all through the West."

But after a few months of that he "got tired of having people look at me and wonder why I wasn't in a uniform." He looks like a kid—though he's thirty, not married, and doesn't want to be. Again he tried to get into the Air Forces as a gunner, and was turned down on account of his eyes; then he sneaked into combat through the back door, as a radio operator on a Fortress. That's how he wound up as the radio gunner in the flagship of the "Fitin-Bitin." On the day she went down, Billy and his whole crew were off on pass; a new crew took their ship on the trip to Kiel. "The pilot I trained with all through the States was skipper that day, Lt. Keith Connolly from Portage, Utah. I believe if I had been along the ship would have come home. A fortune teller said there wasn't anything on the Germans' side that would hurt me in this war. I believe that."

Billy would like to be a newsreel cameraman after the war is over—he's instructing at Combat Crew Replacement Center now: "Don't think I'd ever be able to settle down and be a salesman again when this war is over. As for the movie business, well, I've had too much of the real thing.

"Or maybe I'll stay in the Air Force. I've got one good friend in the Air Forces who's done pretty well. Did you read that story 'Queens Die Proudly'? The hero was a fellow named Frankie Kurtz. I went through Hollywood High with him. He had just two things he wanted to do: dive and fly. He got to do both. He was on the American Olympic team at Los Angeles in 1932 and Berlin in 1936. He was supposed to go with the team to Helsinki in 1940, but the war got there first. He got his wings at Randolph in 1937; and he was in the Nineteenth Group of Forts in the Philippines. Wound up as a Lieutenant-Colonel and personal aide to General Brett. He was the one who told me that the place to fight this war was in the Air Force. So maybe I'll stay in after the war. Frankie did all right. Maybe I can too. . . ."

That's the story of one Hollywood boy in the Eighth Air Force; and here's another:

William Thomas Kent, Sergeant, wearing the silver wings of a gunner against the blue patch that means "on combat," walked into my office. (See Illus. 53.) He was a good-looking boy, almost sissy. But not his eyes: they looked into mine so hard I had to blink and look down. He started talking:

"I met a friend of yours and he said you could get me a ride in a Flying Fortress. Can you?"

"Well, maybe I can and maybe I can't. Who are you, Sergeant—a gunner in a Marauder? I see you've got wings."

"Nope. I fly in Halifaxes."

"In Halifaxes? Those are British bombers. We don't fly any Halifaxes in the Eighth Air Force."

"Sure, I know you don't. But I do, I fly in Halifaxes."

"But you're wearing an American uniform. What th' hell Air Force do you belong to, anyhow? And where did you get that Air Medal?"

"The Air Medal I got for making twenty-three missions in a Halifax. And the uniform—well, I was in the RAF for two years. But last June I transferred into the Eighth Air Force. I was a tail gunner in the RAF. I knew how to use .30's—never used a .50 like your Fortresses do. So they gave me an American uniform and American pay and told me to go on flying the Halifaxes. What th' hell, it's all the same war, they said. But I'm about through with my ops in the RAF and I'm going to get sent home to be an instructor they tell me, and if I'm going to be an instructor for guys who're gonna fly Fortresses then I oughta get a few rides in a Fortress myself. Doesn't that make sense?"

It made sense. So I got on the phone and called a Colonel I knew and put the problem to him. He listened, and then gave up: "It's a new one on me. What's this boy like? Is he crazy? People get killed in Fortresses. Why doesn't he finish his ops in the Halifaxes and just be smart and not fool with Forts?"

So I passed that verdict on to Sergeant William Thomas Kent. It did not satisfy him. "Listen, I'm willing to go on my own time, Captain. I'm on leave. So why can't I go in a Fortress? Give one of your gunners a rest. Hell, I'll go under his name if you want. But I oughta have a ride in a Fortress before I go home and try to tell other guys what it's like."

I told the Sergeant to come back around dinner time, not because I had a plan to help him, but just because I wanted to hear his whole story.

"I'm a New Yorker. Yes, born there. Old man was an actor. Lot of people over here heard of him. He was the comedian in lots of famous musicals. Great friend of Lee Shubert. *The Student Prince* was the best thing he ever did. Got into one movie, with Paul Whiteman—*The King of Jazz*. Didn't like the movies, so he quit. He's retired now. I was brought up all over America. Went to school in Miami, you know how it is with actors' kids.

"I got a stepfather now. Lived with him for nine years out in Hollywood. He owns a night club there, cost him $150,000 to build it. Like any other business, I guess running a night club makes a difference in the kind of home you run. Not good. I got a sister. Pretty. She married a fellow in Russ Morgan's band. You don't marry into show business. She's got a hot band of her own now.

"You want to know why I went into the Army. Well, I'm not going to tell you it was patriotism, because we weren't in the war when I went into the RAF. And I'm not going to tell you it was any high idealism, because it wasn't. But just the same, I wouldn't have joined up with the Germans or the Japs. Hell no! Maybe I didn't know what the war was all about. But I knew which side I wanted to be on.

"I never worked at anything when I finished high school. What for? I had plenty of spending money.

"Oh, yeah, you wanted to know why I went to war. Well I could tell you it was because I figured we would be in sooner or later and I didn't want to be drafted. Or I could tell you it was because England was losing and I like to fight on the side of a loser. It's more fun.

"Or I could tell you that I wanted to go to war because I would rather get killed than wind up living like what I was headed for. I could give you any of those reasons, but you'd have to decide for yourself which is the right one.

"Anyhow, I went up to Canada and got into the RCAF. I made some good friends up there. Best friend was a big guy from Alaska. An American. He was a mining engineer. Made $100 a day when he was working. Used to carry about $9,000 in his pockets all the time, in $100 bills. Everything was planes up in Alaska—even taxis were planes. So naturally, if this big fellow had to fight, he wanted to fly. He was a lonely kind of a guy, and he wound up doing what he wanted to do. He was a photo reconnaissance pilot—went over and took pictures of what we were going to bomb before we did it, and what we had bombed after we had done it. He found a job where he could work alone and that was what he wanted, so he wound up happy.

"I put in for flying too. Washed out. So I put in for air gunnery. I wanted combat. Had to get combat. They pushed me through. Wasn't very serious back there. Didn't figure then that guys really get killed. Never did much shooting as a kid. Actors' kids play with grease paint more than with guns. Don't know that shooting as a kid would have helped me any—except they say that using a gun when you are a kid will teach you not to flinch when you push the gun buttons in a bomber's turret.

"But hell, you don't flinch from your own guns—you flinch from the other fellow's guns. And boy, they really look like searchlights when they blaze at you at night.

"One reason I'd like to be an instructor back home is so I could tell the kids just starting out how serious it is over here, so they'll learn a lot more before the time when suddenly they have to know what to do, or die.

"Right away after I got over here, I found out that people get killed. When I was in OTU, a bomber came home early one morning and crash-landed where we were. They hauled out the bomb aimer. He was all mashed up from the crash, but he was dead before the landing. He'd been hit right in the head with a 20 mm. cannon shell. That's quite a sight, goddamn, quite a sight, to see a fellow without a head.

"Listen, I'm just like you are. I feel things. I'm no fanatic. No Jap. I don't get any kick out of killing somebody. Maybe it would help. I spent some time with a Polish outfit. Goddamn, they enjoyed killing Germans. They would have rammed the fighters if they could. Every Pole wanted to come home with German blood on his wings. It wasn't enough just to shoot Germans and bomb them. The Poles wanted to see and feel and hear Germans die.

"Oh sure, I have fun on raids. Take the run to Milan the other night. The little villages sure looked pretty. I kept looking at the Alps and saying to the pilot over the intercom, 'Hell, those mountains don't look so big. We've got bigger ones out in California.' And then the pilot said to me, 'Well, just look to your left, right now.' And I did, and there was a big damn peak sticking up in the moonlight with snow all over it. 'Mt. Blanc,' he said.

"A gunner gets moved around a lot in the RAF. I was in Coastal Command for a while, flying Sunderlands. Tail gunner always. That was the only time I was ever higher than the pilot. Dull damn job. Never saw a submarine.

"Then I got sent up to a bomber squadron. English. Been with the same outfit, had the same crew ever since. They've all got commissions now and they started out as sergeants like me, but I still get more pay than they do because I get mine from the Americans. Guess it evens out.

"My first mission was to Dortmund—several hundred planes on that one. And then I went to Dortmund again with a larger number of four-engined jobs. Don't think we'll have to go back there again—finished that place off. I've been to Bochum and Duisburg and Düsseldorf, and three times to Hamburg. All the tough ones. And that once to Milan.

"We don't paint bombs on the nose for an Italian raid the way we do for a German target—we paint on an ice cream cone. Hitting Wop targets was fun, and such pretty scenery.

"Our plane had been holed by flak plenty—twenty-three holes over Bochum. But the night fighters are the worst trouble. Especially to me. The tail gunner has to protect the whole damn crew. He's the quarterback of the team, really, like in football. I keep moving my turret from side to side all the time. And then I call out signals that tell the pilot what to do to get away from whatever is coming up on our tail. I tell him where the danger is and he knows what to do to get away from it.

"Sure we've had trouble. Plenty. On the second Dortmund job we got hit hard. Our port engine blew up. We went into a dive from 20,000 feet and didn't pull out until 2,000. If I could have picked up my parachute that night I would have bailed out and been a prisoner of war right now. But the force of the pullout was too much. I couldn't get out of my seat, so I stuck there.

41. Air gunners of the 8th got a refresher course with water-cooled 50s on the ground in England. But no gunner ever learned on the ground what he needed to know in the air.

42. "See you later" was the stock parting before a takeoff. Haley Aycock often said it to Smitty. (Chapter 4)

43. Smitty's last bombs hit the aluminum plants that worked for the Nazis at Heroya, Norway. The picture shows that the target was smashed. "Our Gang" brought Smitty home from Heroya without a bullet hole in her—but went down with another crew over Schweinfurt. (Chapter 5)

44. "Dinghy dinghy prepare for ditching!" is the crackling command over intercom when a Fort from the 8th can't make it home across the North Sea or the Channel. Instantly, 8 of the 10 men sardine into the radio compartment aft of the bomb-bay. They sit on the floor, pull up their knees, clasp hands behind their heads, get braced for the shock of landing at sea. (Chapter 6)

45. In two dinghies, the crew of "LaMesa Lass" floated for 30 hours before they were picked up by British Air-Sea Rescue. In the picture above, the hand-waver is Bob McCallum, co-pilot. In the picture below, the hand-waver is Skipper Bob Smith from Texas. (Chapter 6)

46. "In distress," with the "drink" below. That telltale plume of smoke from the inboard engine too often attracts long-ranging JU-88's that trail like buzzards behind a homing Fortress formation, waiting to pounce on a cripple.

47. Not a Britisher trawler crew—but the combat crew of an 8th Air Force Fortress, fished out of the Channel by the British Navy, dried off and outfitted on the spot by British issue of greatcoats, slippers, socks, boots and sweaters.

48. Hollywood's war effort has been the target for many jokes—most of them low blows. But one Hollywood name that has had only praise—and deserved it—is that of Capt. Clark Gable. He began as a buck private, went through gunnery school, then came to England and went on 5 missions while he was working on a movie that tells the story of 2 gunners—from Main Street, U.S.A., through the Battle of Germany.

49. Capt. and Mrs. Tommy Wallace (Carole Landis to you) say goodbye to wedding guests. They met on Miss Landis' *Four Jills in a Jeep* tour.

50. *Mrs. Miniver's* director, Maj. William Wyler, came to England to help make a feature picture about the 8th. You saw it—*The Memphis Belle*. Brig. Gen. Hansell, San Antonio, Tex., pins an Air Medal on him for his 5 missions as a cameraman.

51. From the 8th Air Force to Hollywood, after a triumphant tour of the States, went Capt. Bob Morgan and the crew of the *Memphis Belle*, to be filmed in color as they took their Fortress home to her factory birthplace. Here, Capt. Morgan says goodbye to the ground crew, who stayed behind and helped send a new bomber on its missions to Germany.

52. Boss of all U.S. forces in the European theatre of operations: Lt. Gen. Jacob L. Devers, an expert on tank warfare, succeeded veteran airman Lt. Gen. Frank Andrews, who died when his Liberator crashed in Iceland. Eaker said to Devers at an early meeting, "One of our worst problems is gunnery. If we could improve it 10%, German fighters couldn't hurt us." Said Devers to Eaker, "I think I can help you. We used to have the same problem in tanks."

53. A night-club owner was the stepfather of Sgt. William Thomas Kent, from Beverly Hills, Cal. His father was an actor. Tom Kent first went to war with the RAF. As tail gunner of a Halifax, he looked back on blazing targets at Emden and Hamburg and Cologne and Berlin. He made 29 night raids with the RAF. (Chapter 7)

54. Boss of the Fitin'-Bitin' Squadron (Chapter 7) was Major Bob Riordan, from El Paso, Tex. Above, he explains to the King how he set down a crippled Fort for a crash landing. Name of the ship was "Wahoo."

55. Pilots of the Fitin'-Bitin' Squadron—no movie stars, still if you could capture their story and their spirit on the screen, you would have a greater picture than *Mrs. Miniver*—or *The Big Parade*.

56. "I like England . . . England has been good to me," says Sgt. Harris Goldberg from Brook-line, Mass. (Chapter 8) He went to war with the RAF before we got in, made 42 missions in British bombers from England to the Middle East, then transferred to the U.S. 8th Air Force and made 17 more in Forts. "If I live through the war, I'm going to go on living in England."

57. Secretary of War Stimson landed at a Fortress station to award the Congressional Medal of Honor to Sgt. "Snuffy" Smith. As his plane taxied toward the assembled high officers gathered to greet him, Mr. Stimson's sharp eyes spotted a B-17 with a battle-ragged tail. Later, he asked the station CO: "I'd like to meet the tail gunner who rode in that damaged Fort out there." The gunner was Sgt. Goldberg.

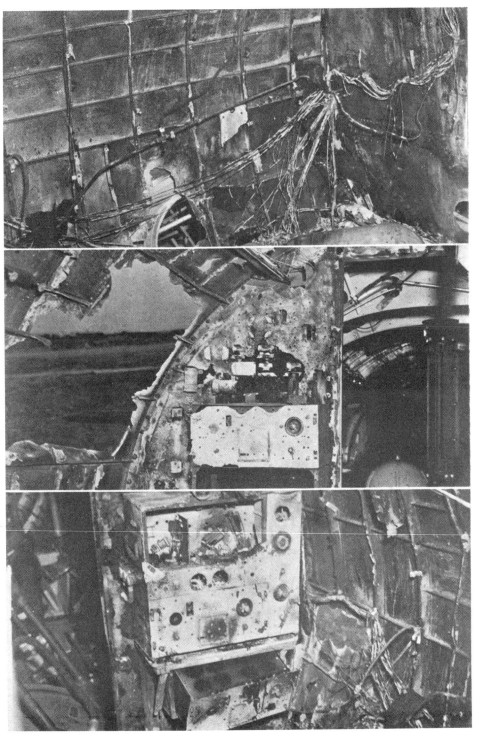

58. Here "Snuffy" Smith fought the fires. (Chapters 6 and 9) The gutted radio room of No. 649, the day Smith brought her back.

59. The Ploesti raid gave the Congressional Medal of Honor to the CO of an 8th Air Force Liberator outfit. Lt. Gen. Jacob Devers, then CG of ETO, fastens the sky-blue, star-studded ribbon of the CMH around the neck of Col. Leon Johnson from Kansas. (Chapters 9 and 28)

60. "Red" Morgan, Congressional Medal of Honor winner, talks to British and American war correspondents. Subject he insisted on talking most about was—"you ought to go get an interview with our navigator. He's the guy who did the great job on that trip." (Chapter 9)

61. Dwarfed by the giant Fortress that towered above him, little Sgt. "Snuffy" Smith, from Caro, Mich., stood at attention while Secretary of War Stimson hung the ribbon of the Congressional Medal of Honor around his neck. Snuffy's Adam's apple raced up and down—he was the first airman of the 8th to win that highest honor.

Had a lot of fun shooting out the searchlights when we got down on the deck. They had all their lights on us when we went into the dive and the guns had us buttoned up down below. They figured our altitude and our course, but they didn't figure our speed.

"I could see the tracer coming up from the ground—goddamn Fourth of July—it would creep up on us closer and closer, and then we would pull away. It was red and green and every color. Down on the deck we were okay. Halifaxes weren't meant to hold together in a dive like that, but ours did. If planes did only what they're supposed to do, the RAF would have lost this war a long time ago.

"And once or twice, a night fighter nearly creased us. One night, I saw one get cocked for the kill. Usually, you can tell when they are going to commit themselves to an attack—they sort of cock their wings like they were sighting on you. Then they crab in, shooting wide open. But this one didn't do any of that, must have been a student. I told the pilot he was out there, but before I could tell what he was going to do, he came in firing. The pilot must have seen the tracers reaching over the nose of our Hally, because he just turned that bomber inside out and went down. He was a professional Rugby player before the war, very strong. Never got rattled.

"And listen, you can tell anybody for me that I think the English are a helluva fine race, or people, or whatever you call them. And I know. Take that navigator of mine. He went up for his commission after 24 raids. And he reported for commissioning in his battle dress—most of them report all spit and polish and trembling. Not my navigator. The Air Marshal asked him the stock question, about well, my lad, and why do you want a commission? He damn near fell off his chair when this navigator said that as a matter of fact he didn't particularly want a commission at all.

"All the men in my crew are English. The pilot got married on a 48-hour pass and we all had a big party. His wife is a WAAF, and so is his sister, and so is his mother. Wonderful family they make.

"You know, you hear Americans talking about the caste system in England. Well, it sure doesn't work in the RAF. We have discipline, damn good discipline. But over there, you never heard a tail gunner call his pilot 'Sir.' There's lots of differences between Americans and the British. For instance, you read about where the British say 'Tallyho' when they see a Jerry. The hell they do! You never heard such language as you get on the intercom when we see a Jerry! A Britisher can outcuss an American any day, and usually does.

"You get to know fellows pretty well after you've been on 24 raids with them. We got to know each other right from the first one. We were all pretty nervous, maybe even a little afraid. But over the target, the bomb aimer laid his eggs, and when he did, he yelled: 'There go my first bombs on those bloody bastards!' and everybody laughed and it was okay after that.

"I've talked to lots of your fellows about the difference between night and day bombing; and for a gunner, I figure it's like this:

"In the daytime, you can see everything that's going to happen to you. The fighters you can see long before they hit you. And the flak, too. Unless the first burst knocks you down, you have time to duck out of the pattern of fire.

"But at night, it's all just waiting and waiting and waiting, maybe six hours on a long job, and never knowing what's going to hit you until you feel it. You can be going along, just quietly minding your own business, when all of a sudden, whoooosh, the lights come up. First one nails you and then the others intersect his beam and move down until you're in a cone, and then the guns get to work on you. Once you're coned you're like a beetle on its back.

"Or maybe it's the predicted flak, that you never know about until *WHAMMM* you're hit and there's cold wind rushing in through the holes and down your spine.

"Or the night fighters that get you. Always you have to keep moving your gun through a half circle of search. Maybe all you'll see at first is just a black blob out there in the night. You've got to hold your fire, because maybe he doesn't see you and there's no use in helping him hunt you. And then, too, you don't really know whether he's an enemy fighter or one of your own bombers. Got to be very careful until he commits himself to an attack.

"And then there's always the danger of a collision. Listen, the way we're dropping stuff now, there's always a helluva traffic jam over a target. And it's getting worse all the time. . . . In May of 1943 we dropped seventeen tons a minute on Cologne, and there were a thousand bombers on that raid. But on Hamburg, July 27, we dropped bombs at the rate of fifty-one tons a minute. That's traffic.

"I got a nice picture if you'd like to publish it—a picture of me on top of our Halifax after it had 39 bombs painted on the nose. The record for our squadron is one that made 40 raids. Ours just fell to pieces after 39, but not before I got my picture on it.

"Say, are you taking all this down? What do you want to write so much about me for? Hell, when I write a letter home, I can't think of enough to fill more than half a page."

That's the other Hollywood boy. There're plenty different ways of fighting it, even in the Air Force—but as he said, it's all the same war.

Chapter 8

ONLY DOPES VOLUNTEER

"...I'm scared of only the things I can't see..."

A LOT of our boys will stay in England after the war—the serious boys who have found here, highly developed, the fine art of living with their fellow men. They have found a depth and breadth of tolerance that does not exist in our own country, where we boast so much about it. Let me tell you the story of one of these boys—it's a story that the Secretary of War accidentally dug up for the experienced newspapermen over here.

Mr. Stimson flew in to a bomber station to confer the Congressional Medal of Honor on a ball-turret gunner named Smith. As his plane rolled down the perimeter, he looked out and saw a Fortress with a chewed-up tail. He said to a General: "I would like to meet the tail gunner of that Fortress." The gunner's name was Sgt. Harris Benjamin Goldberg, veteran of 42 missions in RAF bombers, 17 in Fortresses. (See Illus. 56 and 57.)

I wanted to get Sgt. Goldberg's story—and when a man has had 17 missions, you must hurry. It's a bloody way to look at it, but after 17 missions, the percentage is stretched a little thin; a good story may reach its finish on the next trip. A lot of great stories end long before number 17. Take the case of "Franz Forzmann"—we'll use that name, because there are still relatives in Austria.

Franz was born in Vienna on May 5, 1923—born a Jew, but raised a Catholic. His father ran a chocolate shop on the Esterhazystrasse, one of the early "military objectives" for the Nazis, back in their window-breaking period. Franz left home, and joined a gang of boys who raised hell with the cops; then he drifted to Czechoslovakia. A few Nazi cops got hurt there, too, and so he drifted on to Greece, and on to Palestine. He was only sixteen—

70

he said he was nineteen, and joined the British Army, first with the West Kent Regiment. When that outfit went back to England, he joined the Manchester. The big, brown-kneed Lancashire men liked little Franz. One of them wanted to send Franz home to his parents in Giggleswick, Lancs., to be "raised up proper."

And meanwhile Mama and Papa Forzmann fled to France, and then to Mexico, and finally to America—because a rich man from Chicago saw Mama crying in Mexico City—their permit had expired, they were to be returned to Germany. The big man from Chicago took a plane, saw his lawyers, sent money, and the Forzmanns came to America. And then he cabled money to Franz, told him to come to America, too.

And so little Franz bribed an Austrian consul in Cairo to get a Nazi passport. He got a four-day leave from his Colonel and a long wink that meant: "Go over the hill, my lad, and good luck to you."

Poland and England and France suddenly were at war with Germany. Franz took a neutral American boat and headed West through the Mediterranean. His Nazi passport fetched him "heils" when the boat stopped in Naples, and a searching cross examination at Marseille and Gibraltar, but because everybody on the boat liked Franz and swore they had known him since birth, British officials smiled, and Franz finally wound up in Boston. A Dane on the boat gave Franz a dime to see the city during the stop-over. Franz spent the day on a streetcar, just riding and gawking. And then he went on to New York.

He loved New York. "The so tall houses." He got a job as a machinist, learned baseball from the boys whom he taught how to ski, and started to "look at the girls." On the Monday after Pearl Harbor, Franz was at a recruiting center, demanding admission to the U.S. Army, with preference strongly expressed for "the tanks or bombers, please."

And that's how he got to Britain, as an air gunner in the Eighth. In June, Franz met a "pretty and nice girl," born in Paris of French and English parents. They were to be married. In July, the Group of Forts with which Franz flew made six missions in seven days, all of them tough.

Franz had six colored glass-headed pins stuck in his leather jacket: "Each time I got out to raid Germany, from the briefing map I take a colored pin and stick it here."

He ran the tips of his greasy fingers over the six pins, and talked about what would happen to Germany after the war:

"It will be hard to make straight the boys and girls who have not learned anything but to tell the Gestapo if their parents are not good Nazis. We will have to watch them for a long time before we can leave them to be a nation again."

On Thursday, Franz went to Kiel in the Fortress "Big Jack." Going into the bombing run, where you can't take evasive action because you want all your bombs to hit the target, "Big Jack" stopped a burst of flak and went down. Franz reached Finis on Number 7. So many of them do.

That's why, when you want to talk to a boy who has had 17, you feel, somehow, you'd better hurry. I met Sgt. Goldberg about six one afternoon, and we talked for almost three hours. He really talks Boston. Hadn't heard an accent like that since I was at Exeter.

Harris Benjamin Goldberg was born in Boston—Brookline, really. So were his parents. His father is rather wealthy. Was in the infantry in the last war.

"But somehow he couldn't understand why I wanted to go into this war ahead of everybody else. Parents never can. So I just left him a letter, and one for my mother, and went to Canada to join the RCAF."

If Ben had gone to college, he would have studied psychology; even in high school, he made it a hobby—like some kids collect stamps. He has always been curious, intensely curious about people. And about himself.

"I tried to figure out why I wanted to join the RCAF. I believe there were many reasons: partly for principles; and partly practical, because I was so sure we would be in eventually. I wanted to get a head start. And I picked the air forces because—well, it was adventure. And there was a practical reason there, too: I figured that in the air, if you get it, you get it quick and sudden, and complete."

He put in for flying, washed out—depth perception. Then he took gunnery because it would get him to England most quickly. He landed in Scotland in October, 1941. Saw his first action in a Wimpey—the twin-engined bomber that used to be the backbone of the RAF. Missed the great 1,000-bomber, "scrape-the-barrel" raid on Cologne, but he made the follow-through on Essen. That was his first. Got out of a hospital bed by lying to the Medical Officer in order to go.

His second job was to Bremen: "That was bad. We lost 52 on that raid. Went in at 12,000 feet, got hit, and damn near fell to pieces. We went down to 2,000 feet and sort of stumbled home at about 90 mph. Don't really know how we got home. All my crew were English. We used to have some pretty wild arguments about the States staying out of the war. After that night over Bremen, we argued but we never really got mad any more. Going through something like that brings you pretty close."

I probed to get at the kernel of every story: fear. When and how do you feel it, Sgt. Goldberg?

"It's an old argument, about which is tougher—night or day work. I've had plenty of both. I say it's tougher at night. It is for me—it's the fear of what you can't see that gets you.

"Listen, I'm not ashamed to admit that I was always scared up there. Always. I don't think I will ever get over it. Never. I would be as white as frost when I got on the ground. And shaking, visibly shaking.

"It's all so different in the daytime. You're scared before you take off. And still scared when you go out over the Channel, and everything is quiet. Oh, sure, there's a lot of noise. But when you're waiting, with your back turned to the direction you're traveling, backing into the danger, then there's a sort of silence in the noise of the wind and the engines. And in that silence, there is fear. Trying to fight it with your mind is like trying to fight a toothache.

"But then, when the flak and the fighters come up, something happens to your head or your glands or your heart, and excitement takes the place of fear. You feel all warm, as if your electric suit was out and then suddenly came on again. And then, coming home, I would remember how it was before the shooting started, and I would swear to myself that I would never fly again. But then I would see the coast of England, or, when I was flying in Africa, the Delta of the Nile, and I would forget that I was ever afraid. . . ."

Ben went to Africa in a Wimpey. He had trouble on the way down, got jumped by a couple of JU-88's out in the Bay of Biscay. A lot of planes had started for Gibraltar on this route, and then just disappeared. Ben's plane was almost another of the mysteries. The JU-88's closed in for the kill, and then Ben got his guns on one of them.

Down in Gibraltar, Intelligence officers were very happy to see a battle-scarred, crash-landed Wimpey that had beat the jinx of that trip, and lived to tell what it was. Ben got mention in a dispatch, and official credit for the destruction of one JU-88.

He teamed up with another crew after the crash—five Englishmen and one American: "The American was me."

Ben's log book in Africa is a catalogue of the ebb and flow of the legend of Rommel, from the first fall of Tobruk through El Alamein. Ben's Wimpey worked in close support of the Eighth Army. An entry in his log for August, 1942 reads: "Rhodes Island—forced down in Sinai Desert." The crew wandered without food or water for three days before Arabs found them. Other log entries:

Crete—crash-landed, one dead.
Tobruk—flare-dropping.
Battle area—panzer concentration near El Alamein.
El Daba—supplies en route to Afrika Korps.
Tobruk—shipping.
Fuka landing ground—dispersed aircraft.
Tobruk—combined action.
Tobruk—crash-landed near Cairo.
Tobruk—defenses and searchlights.
El Alamein—15th Panzer Division.
El Alamein—two missions one day, transport and tanks.
El Daba and Landing Ground 104—two missions, Hun aircraft.
Sollum—Motor transport jam at Hellfire Pass.
Fort Capuzzo—chasing Jerry West.
Landing Ground 278—forced landing; fatalities, three.

Harris Benjamin Goldberg, Sergeant Gunner, American, flew 273 combat hours with the RAF, in the desert fighting that punctured the legend of Rommel. Two things he remembers most clearly as acts of bravery and sacrifice that he has not seen equalled:

"There was a pilot of a Wimpey, an American, Tex Holland. One night Holland's whole squadron of Wimpeys were caught in a cone of thirty-five lights over Tobruk. It looked like curtains for the lot. There was one way out. Holland took it. He nosed over toward one rim of the lights and screamed down into a straight dive toward them. The trick worked. The other lights followed his single ship down. All the flak concentrated on him, and the other Wimpeys got away. But for once, a sacrifice had a double-happy ending, because neither the flak nor the lights could keep up with Holland's dive. His plane held together, and he got away, too. But what he did was certain death, ninety-nine times out of a hundred.

"And there was another case like that. There was an RAF pilot on his last mission. The squadron was attacking the Nazi supply dumps at Tobruk. His plane stopped a direct hit from flak, and burst into flames. The pilot climbed it, long enough to let the whole crew bail out; then he banked and plunged into the petrol dump. Did more damage than a whole raid could do with his single blazing plane. His crew lived to walk home through the desert to tell his story."

Ben flew on his last mission in November, 1942—that was the crash. "Three of our crew were killed. They were trapped in the crash and burned to death I swore I would never fly again, and I didn't have to. And so I came back to England—took me until February to get here. I could have had a training job somewhere, got a commission on the ground. But you know how it is. It just doesn't work, staying on the ground. I've heard lots of the Fortress boys say they would never fly any more when they left to go home. I bet you they'll all come back with new groups, on combat."

Ben transferred to the Eighth, became a tail gunner in Forts;—he was doing a good job, a thorough job, until something new and more dangerous came along—the Fortress "pathfinders." They take the bombers of the Eighth to cloud-covered targets, the way the RAF pathfinders lead the way to the target for night raids. Ben shifted to our pathfinders, after 17 raids in the Forts. Volunteered.

"I feel sort of old and experienced among all the new kids coming over— 'sprogs,' we used to call them in the RAF.

"Perhaps you wonder why it is that I have always sought combat jobs. You know there is an old saying among professional soldiers that 'old soldiers never die—because they never volunteer.' I have always stuck my neck out. Why? Because I am a Jew and people expect me to evade danger if I can.

"Of course I have been afraid—but no more than most. I have studied fear. I mean that. I have studied it. There are two kinds:

"There was a bombardier I knew. He was a strong guy, fine, intelligent. I believe he had been a leader in his college. Great athlete. But he did not know how to handle the slow, wearing strain of the fear of death. The fear of being hurt in football—that had been easy. But the fear of death—that was too much.

"Before a mission, I always used to walk up and down before the plane until stations time. They called me 'The Pacer' and laughed about it. It was just a symptom of fear, the pacing. I knew how to recognize it in others, because I knew it so well in myself. And I saw it in this bombardier.

"We got to talking one day after a briefing, and then, day after day, he would look for me and talk more and more. I didn't kid him or call him 'chicken.' He was whipped—he didn't have the guts to go on flying, but neither did he have the courage to go to the Commanding Officer and admit that he was afraid to fly. I had to find an excuse, a way for him to escape, and I did.

"I told him that by flying when he was afraid, he was endangering the lives of his whole crew. Some day, when he would be needed at his guns to stop a frontal attack, he would be frozen by fear, and his whole ship would go down and nine other men would die and it would be his fault. And that was all the reason he needed to prod him into going to his CO and telling him the whole story. And that's what happened. He left the Group and went home. That he had to do. You can't stay around after you've grounded yourself.

"And then there is the other kind of fear, the fear of a coward, of a boy who has always been a coward. There was one gunner who kept getting colds and sinus and toothache and bellyache and earache, anything to keep from going on a trip. But we could tell, all the gunners in the Group knew. And so this Fort got another gunner, a wonderful guy, everybody liked him.

"But the chicken-gunner got worried that he'd lose his rating if he stopped flying, so he came back and the good guy was forced into a new crew. First time the new crew went out, they all went down, over Kiel. And everybody said that the chicken-gunner had killed the boy everybody liked. Of course he hadn't, but everything gets blamed on a coward, and nobody wants to defend him. A real coward, that is.

"Often, I've known that people have expected me to crack, because I am a Jew. But I won't. I don't care how scared I am inside. I won't crack. And honest, it isn't just to show other people. I'm trying to prove something to myself."

Ben has settled down in England—he's engaged to a beautiful Irish girl who is a receptionist in a London hotel; he is a good and close friend of a young English manufacturer who works eight hours every day as the boss and then goes into the factory and works with the men on the night shift. Ben has decided:

"After the war, I don't think I will go back to America to college, or even to live. I want to stay in England. England has gone through so much of what America is just reaching in our history. You know, they say that a Catholic or a Jew cannot be President of the United States. There is no law, but it just cannot happen. Well, a Jew has already been Prime Minister of England."

He feels what so many feel and do not talk about. At least, those with enough intelligence and knowledge to be entitled to an opinion do not talk about it. Many without either knowledge or intelligence talk a great deal about it.

"I know that this war will bring the world no nearer a solution of what they call 'a problem.' But I believe that England has come nearer than any other nation."

Chapter 9

WHAT HAPPENS TO HEROES?

"...and then the Major saw it was me, so he just said,
'Oh, it's you ... okay.' I'm different."

"SNUFFY" SMITH was the first man of the Eighth to win the Congressional Medal of Honor, and live to wear it. His act of heroism "beyond the call of duty" was this:

He was on his first mission. Coming home from St. Nazaire, his ship was attacked, caught on fire. For an hour and a half, Smith fought the flames alone, and finally put them out. The radio gunner and the two waist gunners had bailed out; the tail gunner was shot in the back; Smith crawled out of his ball turret into the inferno, fought the flames, and saved his ship. And Secretary of War Stimson placed the blue, star-studded ribbon that held the Congressional Medal of Honor around his neck, while the group of Forts with which Smith flew roared in tribute overhead. For the newspapers, that was the end of the story. But it was only the beginning for little "Snuffy" Smith, thirty-two years old, grey-haired, red of eye, flat of feet, and big of Adam's apple.

Little Snuffy, though he was the son of a circuit judge from Illinois, and though he read for fun a book called *Glands Regulating Personality*, wasn't quite equipped to cope with the strange forces that work against a man who has been labelled Number One Hero in the European Theatre of Operations.

For instance, he got this cable from his home town in Caro, Michigan:

"NO CARO MAN EVER WAS HONORED AS YOU WERE TODAY
HOME FOLKS THRILLED BY NEWS AND BY YOUR GLORIOUS
EXPLOIT CARO IS PROUD OF YOUR MAGNIFICENT RECORD
CHAMBER OF COMMERCE SEND HEARTIEST CONGRATULA-
TIONS ON BEHALF OF PEOPLE OF CARO   W. H. GILDHART
SECRETARY."

Frankly, being in uniform has slowed me up. I keep forgetting that stories really begin where the newspapers drop them. But Sam Boal, another alumnus of our Galley of Slaves on Forty-fifth Street, over here with OWI now, reminded me: "Listen, I'd like to write a piece about Smith for *The New Yorker*. Sort of a profile. Can you fix it up?"

I did. And Sam came back with a story which included one paragraph like this:

"Late one night, when he was cooking some spam in his barracks, a Major came screaming in to find out who the hell was stinking up the place. But when he saw Snuffy, he just said, 'Oh, it's *you*—okay.'"

Then Jim Dugan wrote a biting piece built on the fact that Snuffy signs his letters "Sgt. Maynard Smith, C.M.H."—as the British put the initials of their decorations after their names.

They took Snuffy off combat up at his station; but they kept him around. It wasn't that he was scared to fly—because he made four missions after the one when he fought the fire. It was just that crews decided that his medal had gone to his head.

It isn't true that Snuffy is conceited. As a matter of fact, he's taken his Congressional Medal of Honor a lot better than a lot of kids take the Air Medal you get for just going on five missions and getting home.

The truth is simply this: When a guy is the Number One Hero, people expect him to get the big head—and things that would have been only funny in Sgt. Smith are fatal in Sgt. Smith, C.M.H.

Or if Snuffy had been a Phi Beta Kappa from Harvard and then done the things he does, he would have been called at worst only "a character." But, of course, the thing is, if he had been a Phi Beta from Harvard—or from Yale—he never would have been C.M.H.; he would have been too smart to stick around and fight that fire.

I mustn't get sore and start a crusade for the appreciation of Sgt. Smith, but I'm trying to arrive at a point:

After this war, hundreds and thousands of heroes are going to come home from distant fighting fronts. They're going to wonder: "What was I fighting for and when do I get it?" Every boy who was under fire was in truth a hero.

I heard the visiting Senator Lodge say to the assembled combat crews in a briefing room: "Listen, when you boys come home, the best will not be good enough for you."

A lot of boys listened and smiled and then did not say, but formed their lips for the sound of, "Nuts."

I often wonder what will happen to all the heroes of this war when they do go home. How many of them will behave like Sgt. York, for instance?

Well, there are two more men wearing Congressional Medals of Honor in the Eighth besides Snuffy Smith. Second Lieutenant "Red" Morgan wears one of them. Red got pretty sore about one hit-and-run correspondent who wrote an article about him for an American magazine, talking about how he was a son of rich parents, a New York playboy brought up in the Stork Club, and a lot of stuff about how he "faced the supreme test with courage because he was an American boy."

If you know Red and talk to him about the trip for which he was awarded the C.M.H., the only story you'll get is the story of his navigator. He doesn't like to talk about himself. Before the war, Red worked with the Texas Company. Red went into the RCAF, transferred to the Eighth as Flying Officer Morgan. The official story on what he did, sent down to Bomber Command by his Commanding Officer, gives far more details than you'll ever pull out of Red.

"On July 28, 1943, F/O John C. Morgan, ASN T-190641, — Bomb. Sqdn., — Bomb. Group, was serving as co-pilot of a B-17 type aircraft on an important bombing mission to Germany. F/O Morgan took control of the aircraft from take-off to the combat area, where the pilot, 1st Lt. Robert L. Campbell, took over the controls. At that time, the formation was 15–20 minutes' flying time from the German coast.

"Just as the pilot took over the controls, the first group of enemy aircraft attacked. The first pass knocked out the oxygen system to the waist, tail, and radio positions. A moment later, a frontal attack from out of the sun at two o'clock put a 20 mm. and a .303-calibre shell through the windshield on the co-pilot's side, totally shattering it. One of them hit the pilot in the head, splitting open his skull. The pilot fell forward over the wheel, wrapping his arms around it, causing the aircraft to nose down sharply. F/O Morgan at once grasped the controls from his side and attempted to pull the plane back in formation. This was accomplished only by sheer brute strength against the struggling of the semi-conscious pilot, who was a six foot, 185 pound, heavily-muscled man. At this time it was determined that the interphone had been shot out as well as the aft oxygen system, and F/O Morgan could not call for help.

"A moment later the top-turret gunner (S/Sgt. Tyre C. Weaver, River View, Ala.) fell to the floor and down through the hatch into the after part of the nose, with one arm shot off at the shoulder by a 20 mm. shell and with a fragment of .303 shell wound in his side. Before toppling through the hatch he cried to F/O Morgan to take the ship down at once. Because of lack of oxygen and inability to stop the flow of blood, it was decided by the navigator (2nd Lt. Keith J. Koske, Milwaukee, Wis.), and top-turret gunner that the only chance for survival lay in quick medical attention. Accordingly, the gunner's wound was bound up as securely as possible and after opening his pilot 'chute, he was dropped through the nose hatch just over the German coast.

"By this time the waist, tail, and radio gunners had all passed out from lack of oxygen and their guns had ceased to fire. For that reason F/O Morgan thought they had all bailed out, they being then only at the beginning of the trip into Germany and return. However, the pilot was still alive, though unable to see or realize what was going on. With his arms wrapped desperately around the wheel, and with head on his chest, he struggled with the wheel, stick, and pedals by virtual instinct. The aircraft was gyrating through the formation before the pilot's struggles could be counteracted by F/O Morgan. F/O Morgan had virtually no visibility ahead, since his windshield was totally shattered by the entry of the shell that hit the pilot. Only straight up, and to each side, could any view be had . . .

"To break out of formation, to go down or fly off alone would have meant quick and sure annihilation at the hands of the swarm of determined enemy aircraft attacks at the time. Thereafter, and unassisted for two full hours, F/O Morgan, doing the impossible, and in the exercise of heroism far above and beyond all call of duty, flew the aircraft in formation with one hand while holding the continually struggling pilot with the other hand, all the way into the target, over the target, making a successful bombing run, out over Germany, and finally out over the sea well on the way back to base. During all this time F/O Morgan was accomplishing evasive action against continuous and concentrated enemy aircraft attacks on the unprotected tail section of his aircraft.

"Two hours of unassisted flying time had elapsed before the navigator decided to go up to the pilot's cabin. There he found F/O Morgan with one arm and hand locked in the co-pilot's wheel and with the other arm holding the still struggling pilot away from the wheel. F/O Morgan told the navigator he could land the ship only if he could transfer to the pilot's seat, where he could see ahead. The navigator and one of the semi-revived gunners, assisted by F/O Morgan, removed the pilot, who fought against their every attempt, and laid him on the floor in the nose, where he was given first aid and the navigator had to hold him down. Then F/O Morgan moved over to the pilot's seat, and for an hour and a half longer he continued to fly alone and unaided.

"Over the English coast, red lights were showing on all the gasoline gauges. It was later discovered that the tanks had been hit and considerable gas lost. A considerable pattern of traffic had developed over the first field observed. Repeated calls to the "control" brought no answer, indicating the radio was out. F/O Morgan, in the exercise of great skill and judgment, moved right into the pattern and effected a safe landing, with the aid of the now revived tail gunner, who lowered the flaps and wheels for the landing. Notwithstanding the efforts made to save his life, the pilot died an hour and a half after the plane landed. The miraculous and heroic performance of F/O Morgan upon this occasion was far and above the call of duty and not only materially contributed to the successful conclusion of the bombing mission, but directly saved the lives of the crew and prevented the destruction of his aircraft.

"The extreme heroism, courage, coolness, and skill displayed by F/O Morgan reflect the highest credit upon himself and the Armed Forces of the United States."

Like every other Fortress crew, the outfit in Morgan's ship that day came from all over America. Read the lineup:

Lt. Bob Campbell, Liberty, Mississippi, pilot.
2nd Lt. Asa Irwin, Portland, Oregon, bombardier.
2nd Lt. Keith Koske, Milwaukee, Wisconsin, navigator.
S/Sgt. Tyre Weaver, River View, Alabama, top-turret gunner.
S/Sgt. James Ford, Chicago, ball-turret gunner.
S/Sgt. John Foley, Portland, Oregon, tail gunner.
Sgt. Reece Walton, Joplin, Missouri, waist gunner.
Sgt. Eugene Ponte, St. Louis, Missouri, waist gunner.
T/Sgt. John McClure, Atlanta, Georgia, radio gunner.

And incidentally, the windup on the story is the point that Red Morgan wants everybody to know about: "Koske made a decision that took guts and brains when he realized that the top-turret gunner would die from loss of blood long before we got home—remember, his whole arm had been shot off at the shoulder. Koske fixed him up the best he could and opened his 'chute and dropped him through the forward escape hatch. Koske figured that the Jerries would find him and save his life, and he was right. The War Department wired Weaver's folks and told them that their son was safe and alive in a German prison camp. There ought to be some medal for what Koske did. The boys who will win this war are the ones who make the tough decision quick, and correct." *

The other Congressional Medal of Honor went to the Commanding Officer of one of the first two groups of Libs over here—Col. Leon Johnson, from Moline, Kansas. A West Point graduate, for two years an infantry officer, father of two tow-headed daughters, Leon Johnson wears his C.M.H. and now a General's star with dignity. When he took over the command of the Lib group he led to Ploesti, it was a "hard luck" outfit. They called themselves the "Flying 8-Balls."

Of the 178 Libs that took off for Ploesti, 37 were led by Johnson. And when they reached their target, it had already been hit with delayed action bombs. Johnson bored in, bombed his already blazing target, and then fought through flak and fighters to bring the battered survivors of his group back to home base. For his courageous leadership that day—remember, 54 bombers did not get home—Leon Johnson was awarded the Congressional Medal of Honor. The day after the order for the award was out, Col. Johnson wrote to the family of every boy who did not come home from Ploesti:

"I am sure that there are many who deserve the award as much, if not more than I do, but, because of the force of circumstances, never received it. I cannot consider this a personal award. I consider this a citation for the leader of the group in acknowledgment of a job well done by the group. I am only the custodian of what belongs to all of them."

* "Red" Morgan was later shot down leading a group over Germany. On March 6, 1944, it was disclosed that he was a prisoner of war in Germany.

Chapter 10

ONE WHO HATED

". . . Great God! There's the
ghost of Jack Mathis . . ."

Two and a half years ago, when I tried so hard to get somebody interested in an air training program for high school kids, I was convinced that if you started training a boy at about fifteen, you'd be bound to wind up with a good airman—pilot, bombardier, navigator, radio operator, or air gunner. I was wrong. It takes more than that. You've got to start much younger to wind up with the kind of a boy you need to stand the strain of air combat, the kind of air combat they would get in the Eighth. Let me explain what I mean in terms of a story about two boys from San Angelo, Texas. You can't produce such boys as the Brothers Mathis by waiting until they are fifteen to start the job. It begins at birth.

The name Mathis (See Illus. 62 and 63) is one of the legends of the Eighth Air Force, for good reason. This terse and yet eloquent citation by Lt. Gen. Jacob L. Devers, Commanding General, European Theatre of Operations, sums up the first chapter of that legend: it is a recommendation for the Congressional Medal of Honor, "beyond the call of duty."

"For conspicuous gallantry and intrepidity above and beyond the call of duty, in action with the enemy over Germany in March, 1943: Lt. Jack Mathis, as leading bombardier of his squadron, flying through intense anti-aircraft fire, was just starting his bomb run when he was hit by enemy anti-aircraft fire. His right arm was shattered above the elbow, a large wound was torn in his side and abdomen, and he was knocked from his bomb sight to the rear of the bombardier's compartment. Realizing that the success of the mission depended on him, Lt. Mathis, through sheer determination and will power, though mortally wounded, dragged himself back to his sights, released his bombs, then died at his post of duty. As a result of this action, the bombs were placed directly upon the assigned target, under most hazardous conditions, for a perfect attack against the enemy. Lt. Mathis's undaunted bravery has been a great inspiration to the officers and men of his unit. It reflects the highest credit upon himself and upholds the finest traditions of the Armed Forces of the United States of America."

There is a stilted style about a citation that waxes the image of heroism—but the simple facts of what Jack Mathis did before he died shatter the restraint of official language and thunder the story through the pages of history that are reserved for heroes.

Even on the fields of the Eighth Air Force, where danger is a daily diet, the story of Jack Mathis grew quickly into a symbol, a legend, almost a subconscious battle cry. Every bombardier lived in his own imagination the bloody agony of effort with which Jack Mathis pulled his broken body back to his bomb sight—the torture of will that kept him at the complex gadgets that guide bombs down onto a target, kept him at his sight until one word rose up through the blood that rattled in his throat, one word that was half the exclamation that means a bomber's job is done—"Bombs." That was all he could say of "Bombs away!"

Every boy who had ever seen or known Jack Mathis nursed the memory of his face, the inspiration of his courage as a stimulant to conquer fear. Jack Mathis was more than just another dead bombardier.

One night at a station near the one from which Jack flew, a tall boy walked into the officer's mess and looked around. A bombardier grabbed the arm of a pilot and whispered: "Great God! There's the ghost of Jack Mathis."

It wasn't. It was Mark Mathis, and this was Mark's half of the Mathis story:

The Brothers Mathis went into the Air Corps together and to bombardier training together—and there they got split up because Mark got into a little trouble with the authorities, a kind of trouble in which the Brothers Mathis specialized: practical jokes. Jack got through school first, went into heavies; Mark trailed and got put into mediums.

On March 17, Jack Mathis had 13 missions behind him. And on that day, Mark arrived as a visitor at Jack's field; he had landed in England with his outfit of mediums. There was quite a reunion that night—cut a little short by a warning that a "deal was on" for the morrow. The deal was Vegesack.

Before Jack took off, he told brother Mark: "Listen, why don't you get a transfer into our outfit? Hell, you'll never have any fun in the mediums. I'm going home soon as I finish my ops, and put in for pilot training. You could take my place in 'The Duchess.' Helluva fine crew. Think it over."

That mission ended half the Mathis story—Jack came back, dead. And Mark began pushing the papers that shifted him from mediums to Forts. He went into "The Duchess," flew in the nose where Jack had flown, used Jack's old bomb sight. You could still see the scars on it where flak had gashed through the black paint to shining white metal.

I got to know Mark Mathis pretty well; got him over to a station one morning to meet Sir Stafford Cripps. And after the meeting, we got him to stand in front of a bomber and talk a little bit about the meaning of Memorial Day for a newsreel we wanted to send back home. He explained that "Memorial Day for us over here is a day of saying 'thanks' to those who have died to make the job we gotta do a little easier. As for me, I got a pretty personal debt of gratitude. The Germans killed my brother Jack over Vegesack. But Jack got his bombs away and they messed up some shipyards that were making submarines. And so what Jack did maybe saved a lot of lives at sea. Reckon you can say he did his job."

It was a bitter cold morning, raining. We came back to Number One mess afterwards and sat in a corner and talked. Mark drawled as Texans are supposed to; his words were as deliberate as the falling of a redwood tree.

"I've had 3 missions. Don't reckon I'm a-gonna quit at the end of my tour. I want to git all of my missions and then I wanna git the 12 that Jack never had a chance to make. That way, I figger I can sorta even up things for him."

Mark, you've heard a lot of guys say that "this is a gentleman's war" over here; they'd rather fight the Japs because they can't learn to hate the Germans. How do you feel about that? Obvious question. Eloquent answer:

"Well, I figger it this a-way: You don't start hating till you been hurt. Me, well, I been hurt. So I hate the Germans. I wish we bombed their cities instead of just their factories."

After the crew of "The Duchess" finished their ops, Mark was transferred to a new Fortress, one that had arrived on the birthday of President Roosevelt, and so it carried a bold "FDR" painted on its nose. Inside that nose, Mark Mathis rode into battle.

Vegesack had been a momentous mission—we did great bombing, knocked down some 50 Jerries, and lost only 2 Forts. That is the mission that clearly proved the case for daylight bombing, proved that Forts could fight through to their targets.

Mark's first mission was to Bremen—that was the one on which Oscar O'Neill was lost. His next was to Meaulte—that was the one on which Red Cliburn finished his ops. And more important, it was the first time that the groups from the new Wing had worked in strength.

Then Mark went to Antwerp. And then to Kiel, and he didn't come home from Kiel. Bill Calhoun, the boy who led the great raid on Huls, was leading the Group that day. The "FDR" was hit hard, and began to straggle out of the formation.

Breaking all rules, Bill dropped his squadron back to cover the straggler, but not in time. Out of a cloud screamed a flock of FW's. They pounced on the wounded Fort, hammered it down and down. Some gunner in the nose was still blazing away at the attacking planes as the crew of the "FDR" dropped free and pulled rip cords that popped their 'chutes into billowing umbrellas against the sky—one, two, three, and on through seven. And then the Fort plunged into the sea. Smoke rose in a great cloud, and that was a good sign. Meant that the Fort had stayed afloat long enough to burn a bit and make that smoke —long enough for those still inside to get the dinghies loose and scramble in.

The boys who knew Mark and Jack Mathis simply will not believe that both of them are dead, and neither do I.

Chapter 11

HE STILL WANTED WINGS

"... listen, I don't have to get hit in the
belly with a chunk of flak to know how it feels to die ...
I've got plenty of imagination ..."

THIS story is only incidentally about the Eighth Air Force. But it ought to interest anybody back home who's got a husband or a sweetheart fighting anywhere in this war. It's about a guy whose name has had a lot of publicity—but always tucked away deep down in the screen credits on movies. Beirne Lay is the name. (See Illus. 86.) He wrote the book called *I Wanted Wings*. It was his own story, sort of an autobiography in a way. Any resemblance between his book and Hollywood's picture of the same name was purely coincidental. There wasn't any Veronica Lake in the book—there wasn't much but Veronica Lake in the movie. Anyhow it was a great book. He used to get letters from kids over here, letters that would start like this:

"Dear Col. Lay: I just found out that you are over here, and I have a copy of your book, which is about the first thing that I ever read about flying that talks like I feel about flying. And I wonder if I sent it to you, if you would mind writing your name in it for me. And if you ever come up to our station, will you please let me know because a lot of the guys here want to talk to you—etc."

I don't suppose any kid ever wanted to be a preacher or a doctor or a piano player or anything half so much as Beirne Lay wanted to be a pilot, when he got out of Yale. He went into the Marine Air Force and washed out; and then through some finagling he got into the Army Air Forces. He was in and out of the Air Forces, between jobs in Hollywood, working on *I Wanted Wings,* which was supposed to be propaganda for the Air Forces, but turned out to be a starring vehicle for Miss Lake.

And for five years, there was one other thing that Beirne wanted to do even more than he wanted to fly—he wanted to marry "Luddy." Guys these days don't stick to a courtship for five years. Our grandfathers did, but not us. Excep. Beirne. He finally won, both his wings and Luddy. I don't know Luddy, but I saw her picture. It was on the second night I was in England. I had gone down to Bomber Command, to begin learning about our Eighth Air Force. And I was spending the night with Beirne. It was December, cold. We were lying under about a dozen blankets, talking about Topic A, but respectfully, because we were talking about girls we love. He was talking about Luddy. He flipped a picture across the room, a picture of her and their two children, and I turned on the bed lamp to look at it. Even in a snapshot, she was beautiful.

"I brought a picture of Luddy with me, but I didn't bring any pictures of the kids, and for ten months we agreed that she wouldn't send me any pictures of them, because that would only make me want to go home all the more. Then she sent me those pictures."

Beirne was one of the seven officers who came over here with General Eaker in the late Winter of 1941 to plant the seeds of the Eighth Air Force. It had been a tough ten months. One thing sustained Beirne—he loved Luddy; he felt strongly about flying, and he worshipped the Old Man—Eaker.

The newspaper I worked on, the New York *Mirror*, always specialized in printing news about divorces and disloyalties and failures. "Rape, riot, and ruin" was the formula. I once had an idea that maybe we ought to print a page once a week, or maybe twice, and just call it "Good News"; and on that page, we would print only stories about people who had not jumped out of a window; people who had been happily married for fifty years; people who maybe weren't making a million dollars, but whom everybody in the block loved and respected; stories about politicians who wouldn't tell a lie for another vote, or even for ten thousand. You know, just good news about good people. It was a pretty silly idea, and the veterans of the newspaper business said nobody would be interested. And after eight years on the *Mirror*, I got to where I agreed with them. Until that night I was lying there in the dark at Bomber Command, listening to Beirne Lay talk about his wife.

"When I said good-bye to Luddy there at LaGuardia Field, I died. I've been dead for ten months."

And while we were talking, a guy came into the room and switched on the lights and yelled: "Hey, Lay, you're gonna get to go home. I swear it. I just heard the Old Man say so."

Beirne pushed himself on his elbows. He grinned, and said "Thanks—thanks—Christ—thanks."

Then the lights were out again. No talking for maybe five minutes.

"Did you hear what he said? Jeesus! Going home! Home, did you hear him? I said that I died ten months ago, didn't I? That's what I said. Well, Tex, now I know how it feels to come back to life."

But Beirne didn't get to go home just then; that's how things always happen. He took a tough job to help somebody else out. It damn near broke him, because it was another chair-borne job. And then finally he went to the Old Man and told him. "Sir, I'd like to get back on combat. The Government spent $30,000 teaching me to fly. I want to fly. May I, sir?"

Because the General knows as much about human nature as he does about flying he said okay. And Beirne went up and spent two weeks with Col. Chick Harding's outfit, brushing up on the combat side of flying. He checked out on a B-17—"God, what a helluva lot of airplane a Fortress is."

He flew as co-pilot to Regensburg, the toughest job the Eighth has had since the Libs went to Ploesti. He saw planes explode in his face—11 planes out of his own Group were shot down. He saw human bodies come hurtling back through his Group because his was the last over the target. He saw all the serious side of this war, the bloody side of it, and some of the fun, too, when they got to Africa. (See Illus. 64, 65, 66.)

"It was dark by the time we got our planes staked out on the base down there. I started walking across the field toward the Hq. tents. I was walking along with another guy and suddenly I just wasn't with him any more. It was pitch dark and we didn't have any flashlights. About fifteen minutes later, they found me. I had just dropped out of sight into a seven foot trench, the end of it—one of the trenches that had been built to stop Rommel. I got through the whole raid, and then damn near got killed by falling into an old trench."

Next morning, he got a brief Cook's Tour through Africa by trying to barter with the natives.

"Little kids, dirty from the dirt of ten years without washing, come up and mob us, wailing, 'No father, no mother, me just poor little bastard. Chewing gum, please?' "

He came back to England, and we sat and talked all about it. He was going home, to train with a Group and come back here to fight. Had he told Luddy about all this yet?

"No, I didn't have the heart to write her. But somebody must have tipped her off. Because the other day, I got a letter from her, and she wound up by telling me that all the ribbons she ever wanted to get from me had nothing to do with medals. All she wanted was the kind you buy across a counter, to put into children's hair. I guess she knows. I don't know how I'm going to convince her, but I've got to."

Nobody ever knew better than Beirne what he was getting into; he's seen the Eighth grow up; he knows what's ahead for it, and as he said before the Regensburg job, "Listen, I don't have to get hit in the belly with a 200 mm. shell to know how it feels to die. I've got plenty of imagination, and I've seen it happen to others, so I know."

He could have had such a good chair-borne job. But the trouble is, with Beirne, like so many others in the Eighth, "he still wanted wings." *

* In May, 1944, Colonel Lay led his group on a raid from Britain. Coming home his plane was shot down. Eleven parachutes were seen to open.

Chapter 12

FABULOUS FABIAN

*"... sometimes, a crew chief gets to know his
pilot* too *damn well ... it's hell when
they take off and don't come home at night ..."*

PILOTS and bombardiers and gunners and navigators get pretty fat and soft.
Doubt if any of them could do two laps around a football field. And as for the
ground officers, the Paddlefeet, well, you know what happens to guys who
never got much exercise except on a golf course, and they don't equip our
Fortress fields with golf courses.

But the planes, listen, they're in better shape than Tunney was ever in. And
the guys who keep them that way are the crew chiefs. This is the story of one
of them—he isn't "typical"; he's the tops. But he is typical of what all of them
try to be. Every crew chief has a fierce, possessive pride in "his" plane.

The pride of a Lib's crew chief is belligerent; he knows there is nothing
beautiful about his "pregnant cow," but he'll fight you over her other fine
points. There is cockiness in the pride of a Thunderbolt's groom. But there is
a brazen conceit in the pride of a Fort's crew chief. To him, his Fort is the one
and only glamor girl.

Fabian Folmer, from Mansfield, Ohio, twenty-five years old, married,
father of a six-months-old baby girl born after he left the States, is the crew
chief of a very big baby, the famous Fortress "Hell's Angels." (See Illus. 77.)

The "Memphis Belle" was the first and most famous Fort to go home from
the Eighth. The Belle went home after 25 missions. But "Hell's Angels" put in
50 before she went home. Fabe went with her.

At the time I talked to Folmer, he had nursed "Hell's Angels" through 31
missions without an abortion—a turn-back—and he had graduated two pilots
who finished their combat tours of duty in "his" ship.

Back home, he started out on combat status as a gunner; when he went into the Army, he had been headed for college and training as a Certified Public Accountant. But he was taken off combat and grounded, not to a clerk's job, but to a mechanic's; that was after his outfit left Boise. There were a bunch of old Army sergeants in the Group. They taught Fabe "to love a bomber like it was flesh and blood."

Over here now, "Hell's Angels" is his only love, almost his only emotion. Fabe comes from German stock, or rather, Austrian. He was born on the east side of the industrial city of Mansfield, Ohio. The whole east side is· full of Austrian people. "I speak German pretty well, well enough to talk my way out of the country if I ever got shot down over there."

There is a strange and strong relationship between a pilot and his crew chief —stronger than between any other two men in the air force, stronger often than the tie between pilots and co-pilots.

"When I tell a pilot that my plane is 'ready for combat' he's got to take my word for it. Sometimes, you sort of flinch when you say it, especially in the beginning, because you know so much depends on your being right. I haven't been wrong yet."

First skipper of "Hell's Angels" was Capt. Irl Baldwin, from Washington. (See Illus. 67.) "One night, 'The Angels' came home with an engine blown out. Capt. Baldwin climbed out and looked at me and pointed at the engine and asked one question: 'Okay for tomorrow?'

"We worked all night, and lucky for us, there wasn't any mission for the next day. So we worked all that day to change the engine. It had to have two hours of slow time on it before it was okay for combat. Capt. Baldwin came over with his co-pilot, Capt. Joy, about eight o'clock in the evening and took 'Hell's Angels' up for two hours of slow time. She went out next morning on a mission."

And just as a ground crew chief develops loyalty and pride in his bomber, so does its combat crew. Take the case of "Hell's Angels' " crew. The ball-turret gunner and one waist gunner took two more missions after they finished their ops, in order to stick with Capt. Baldwin until he finished at Kiel.

After you've passed 20 missions, you're living on borrowed time; to take two extras out of loyalty to a skipper and his ship is one hell of a test of devotion.

Fabian Folmer's "My Day" would run about like this: "We're alerted for a mission tomorrow at about 6 P. M. We get a hint as to whether it's going to be early or late next morning—can't tell definitely, but whatever the system of guessing is, it usually works. The Engineering Officer checks each Crew Chief —'Is your ship okay?' And then we give it a last minute check. Oxygen. Get ready for the armament man to put the bombs in. We wait until all the civilian workers finish their day and leave the field. Security. And then the bombs are loaded on. We don't have anything to do with the loading. Sgt. Tooey is our armament man. Each ship has two of them usually. All of the armament men team up to load the ships. They have a tough job, especially in the winter. There is a specialist for the gun turrets. Another for oxygen equipment. We check the troubles, report, then see that the specialists do the work on our ship. And then bed. Up about three to four hours before take-off. Ready the ship. Crew chief pre-flights the engines, warms them up after the ground crew 'pulls the props through.' The crew chief walks his bomber out of the hard-standing, waves so-long. Then the real work starts—the sweat of waiting for their ship to come home.

"We can tell our ship in several ways. In the first place, all her camouflage is faded from weather. She's a lot lighter than the new Forts. We can tell her long before she's close enough to read her identification number and letter."

Sometimes the crew chief will fly a couple of missions with his bomber "just to show the combat crew they can trust me to keep my ship in shape."

The crew chief of the "Memphis Belle" made one mission with her; Folmer has never gone out with "Hell's Angels." He's not scared, but neither is he foolish; his skipper has never had cause to question his judgment.

"Sometimes, a crew chief gets to know his pilot too well. You know what I mean? One thing I hate is telling somebody good-bye."

For three weeks during October, three Forts in the Group with which "Hell's Angels" flew were in a nose-and-nose race to see which would reach 50 missions first. Once the "Angels" was well out in front, and then slowly another Fort named "Knockout-Dropper" edged into the lead. Trailing by only 2 missions as the "Angels" and the "Dropper" crossed 45, was an unnamed Fort. The crew of No-Name was composed of ten rugged individuals; each had a name he wanted to paint on the Fort; nobody would give in, so the Fort got no name at all.

Folmer was contemptuous of his rivals: "They're heaps of junk. The 'Angels' is as strong as the day she left the factory. She's got exactly four holes in her now. Two of the holes came from the same bullet, going in and coming out. You call that lucky? Maybe so, but I got a theory about luck. Luck is only condition, and condition is brains and sweat. If you're quick enough to take the breaks, you'll get plenty of 'em."

Chapter 13

THEN, BACK TO THE JAPS

*"... air power will get warmed up on Germany, and
then just plain burn the hell outa Japan. ..."*

A STOCKY, red-headed, freckle-faced young man of about thirty-three, named
Paul Smith, used to be editor of the San Francisco *Chronicle*. He went into the
Navy on the day after Pearl Harbor, into Public Relations. Had a good job.
But of course he didn't last. Editors don't make good public relations men.
He resigned his commission as a Lieutenant Commander, and enlisted in the
Marines as a buck private. Last I heard of him was in a letter on *Chronicle*
stationery, from California, in December. He had worked for and won his
commission as a Second Lieutenant in the Marines. At the time he resigned
his Navy commission, he told reporters:

"A Lieutenant Commander is supposed to know how to run a destroyer. I
couldn't boss a lifeboat. I want to get into a job where I'll learn how to use
a bayonet, and then I want to use it."

He's got that job now, somewhere out across the Pacific.

Paul and I "reported" together in England back in 1941. We both convinced ourselves then that Germany was the first enemy; Japan didn't count,
except in the vague sort of way that has always given bad dreams to all Cali-
fornians.

Then the Japs slugged us behind the ear at Pearl Harbor, and they pushed
on through the Philippines, and Burma, and Singapore—and slowly, Paul
began to feel, as a lot of Americans did, that for us at least, Japan had become the first enemy.

There was another young newspaperman that Paul and I got to know over
here in England who had a slightly different slant on things. Frank Owen was
his name, editor of the *Evening Standard*, toughest and ablest of Lord Beaver-

brook's young men. Frank has had a rough and exciting career. He was once the youngest Member of Parliament, from Wales. He was the spearhead of the non-Communist agitation for a Second Front in Europe. And finally, he went in as a buck private, too, into the Armored Corps.

Frank felt this way about the Japs—they are not the first or the worst of our enemies, but they are definitely the last enemy of all free men.

He's out in the East now, on the opposite side of the battle area from Paul Smith. He's attached to the staff of Lord Louis Mountbatten, editing a newspaper for the Allies. From what I hear, he's a damn fine editor and circulation manager and reporter—the works.

He's just as good at wangling native mules to deliver his papers as he is at writing editorials. But the point about Frank is this:

He is typically British in that he fought in his own way to hasten a Second Front against Germany. And now he has gone on to fight in person on the Second Front against Japan.

Americans must understand this: Nobody in Britain will quit fighting when the Huns are whipped. Nobody will quit until the Japs are beaten, too.

I hope Paul Smith realizes that the British are in this with us to the end. And he will, if he remembers the things we saw over here in the blitz: that Sunday we sat in a roofless church in Bristol as the sirens wailed the warning of another raid, and nobody left the church or even stopped singing; the people he talked to in the caves at Dover; the people Jeannie Norton told him about, the people who slept in subways and ate in canteens and shipped their children to the country and went on working in front line factories.

These people will want the armies of Britain to march on to Tokyo after the Yanks and the Tommies meet the Russians in Berlin.

And the RAF—the men who have learned how to destroy Germany "city by city," they are aching to have a crack at area-bombing Japan. Even if they didn't have a grudge against the Japs that dates back to Hong Kong and Singapore, sheer professional enthusiasm would urge the RAF to steal a thousand Lancasters and go wage a privateers' war on Tokyo, if their Government so much as seemed to hesitate about sending them out to operate from Chinese bases when the Hun collapses.

And the Royal Navy—Britain is an island that takes a fierce and fighting pride in her Navy. Every admiral and tar is itching for the day when he can set course for the Pacific and even up a debt that dates back to the ambush off Malaya.

But the avalanche of vengeance must come in the proper order of things. I met a young Lieutenant Colonel the other day who has seen the full cycle of this total global war. He started the war at the other end, in the Pacific, and now he's the boss of a Fortress Group in the Battle of Germany.

The name: Eliott Vandevanter, from Baltimore, graduate of West Point, and of Kelly and Randolph Fields. But most important, he's an alumnus of Del Monte Field, Philippine Islands. He was out there two months before Pearl Harbor. He saw the war the way Colin Kelly and Shorty Wheless saw it, for six months. It was a different show out there.

"The most Forts I had ever seen in the air at once was nine. The first time we went on a mission to Germany, we had about 300 Forts on the job—prettiest damn sight I ever saw.

"Out in the Pacific, it was like what you read about in the last war. The combat crews would gas and load the plane. We wouldn't be briefed for a mission, any more than just be told that the enemy is somewhere 'out there.' No weather information. Nothing. Just take off, and find the enemy and bomb him. And most of our missions were single ship jobs.

"Once, we landed on a strange field. Had one flat tire. Took us two days to fix it up. I finally got a message through for instructions. And the reply finally came back—very brief. 'Take off into the wind'—that was all. So we did.

"This is real air war over here. The way it ought to be. We don't fight just with squadrons or groups. We fight with whole damn air-madas. Just think of the bombers we'll have by the time we finish up Germany and then move on to Japan."

That's how this alumnus of the Pacific Front looks at it, now that he's over here. And that's how everybody in the RAF and the Eighth AAF looks at it, too.

The only thing that worries most of the bombardiers in the Eighth is that the RAF will lay down the first heavy raid on Tokyo, and then, by God, they would be sore. The way the boys in the Eighth feel is this:

"Listen, the RAF got to Berlin first. Tokyo is OUR target!"

62. Hatred for Hitler, burning hot, deep, is in the face of this 8th Air Force bombardier, a boy from San Angelo, Tex., named Mark Mathis. (Chapter 10) Most airmen are impersonal about the war. Not Mark Mathis. The Nazis killed his brother. Mark had a reason for riding his bombsight into Germany.

63. The Congressional Medal of Honor was awarded posthumously to Jack Mathis, bombardier of the B-17 "Duchess." Mortally wounded, he got his bombs away over Vegesack—the raid that proved the case for daylight bombing—then fell dead across the bombsight. Brother Mark Mathis used that same flak-scarred bombsight, until he, too, was reported missing in action. (See also Chapter 34)

64. Regensburg . . . Before . . .

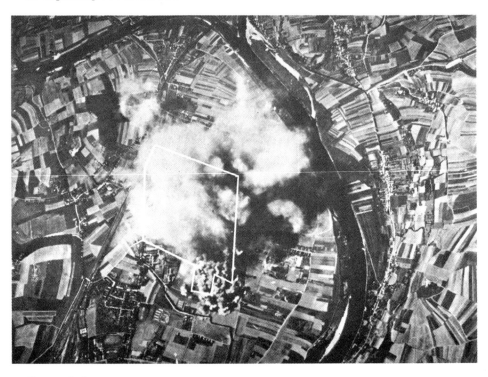

65. . . . during . . .

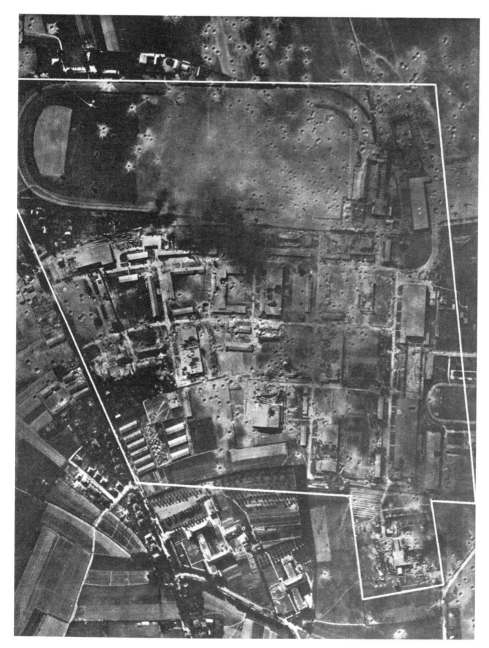

66. . . . and after. (Chapter 11)

67. "Hell, it's mostly luck," (Chapter 12) said Captain Irl Baldwin from Yakima, Wash., first skipper of the four who have had "Hell's Angels" at one time or another. Baldwin was the first to finish his "ops" in the "Angels" and win a rest.

68. "Hell, it's mostly luck," said tail gunner Michael Arooth, Springfield, Mass., in the hospital convalescing after his 6th mission, on which he knocked down 4 Jerries to raise his bag to 7. Tail gunners don't get much shooting unless their ship is in trouble and falls out of formation. Then the Jerries line up on the tail and blaze away for the kill. Flying again, by the end of 11 raids, Arooth's score had risen to 9. For that record he was awarded the DSC, the Purple Heart, the Air Medal with 3 Clusters, and recommendations are in for Clusters to his Purple Heart and DSC.

69. "Hell, it's *all* luck," said a new bombardier of "Hell's Angels," as he rolls the snake-eyed double aces in a crap game beneath the nose of the lucky bomber.

70. "Luck . . . and a little hard work" brings a bomber home. Fabe Folmer's ground crew once changed an engine on "Hell's Angels" overnight; she was slow-timed at dawn; flew on a mission that afternoon. At Mission 45, the Angels were still flying. Favorite song of Fabe Folmer is one he learned from a "Limey." Name of it is "Old Soldiers Never Die." (Chapter 12)

71. First enemy and foulest foe of every mission: the weather. Pilots of the famous Fitin'-Bitin' Squadron sweat out another "heavy English dew." (Chapter 7) Airmen of the 8th may grumble a bit about a tough mission, but they growl and cuss when weather weights their wings and "scrubs" a mission—cancels an attack order.

72. Ground fog haunted the twin mission to Regensburg and Schweinfurt on August 17, anniversary of the first Fortress raid on a Nazi target. (Chapter 14)

73. Brows were furrowed in grim attention . . .

74. God's guidance was asked . . .   75. Bombs were "cocked" for destruction. . . .

76. Combat crews rode to their action stations . . . faces mirrored the strain that chewed at nerves.

77. The weather held one formation grounded, while the other roared on to Regensburg, bombed it and shuttled to Africa.

78. Depression, gloom and foreboding go when the sun comes out. Every branch of the services has its toughest job. In the grins of these 2 gunners, Ed Lawler from Camden, Ark., and Bill Dickson, of Selma, same state, you get the answer to the question "How the hell do they stand it?" The answer is, "Guts!"

79. Famous were the names of some of the veteran Forts that made the birthday raid on August 17th. "Delta Rebel I" fought the first rounds in 1942; "Rebel II" kept fighting in 1943, until her skipper, Mississippi George Birdsong, went home. Old crews would not take over the "Rebel." They said, "George used up all the luck in that ship." A new crew, brash, confident, took the "Rebel" on their first mission and did not come back. (Chapter 5)

80. Like eagles the Forts looked as they screamed down the runway, blue flame from the super-chargers blazing through the prop wash, until finally their wheels seemed to push them free from the earth and their wings lifted—intoxicating instant—airborne!

81. The day the blow fell on Schweinfurt. The birthday punch was aimed at the center of the Nazi ball-bearing industry. By destroying machines that made ball, roller, and taper bearings, the Forts knocked off production in a hundred plants that made German war machines and moving parts of machines. This was strategic, precision, daylight bombing.

82. Like fathers, "sweating out" the birth of the first baby, say, "My wife thinks *she's* having a tough time," so do the watching, waiting ground crews at a bomber base claim they suffer as much as a combat crew during a mission.

83. Spam and java make the menu for Interrogation chow. To stomachs shriveled by altitudes of 25,000 feet and temperatures of 40 below, spam is filling and coffee warming.

84. "Make with the hands." A pilot explains how a Jerry flew over him and dropped aerial bombs on the Forts below . . . and missed. Interrogation is the time when Intelligence officers ask combat crews, "What happened to you?", and combat crews ask each other, "What happened to Bill, and Joe, and Johnny, and Spike. Did you see any 'chutes open?" Finally the missing are added up and each group knows its share of the percentage of another mission's "MIA"—missing in action.

85. Last picture of the last crew to fly in Smitty's "Our Gang" was the one above (Chapter 14). Standing l. to r.: Lt. Denver Woodward, bombardier, Portsmouth, Ohio; Lt. Joe Newberry, navigator, Crookston, Minn.; Lt. Clive Woodbury, co-pilot, Fresno, Cal. (who didn't go to Schweinfurt); Lt. Bill Wheeler, pilot, Scarsdale, N.Y. Seated, l. to r.: T/Sgt. Jim Cobb, radioman, Freemont, N.C.; S/Sgt. Jim McBride, tail gunner, Akron, Ohio; S/Sgt. Jim McGovern, waist gunner, New Haven, Conn.; S/Sgt. Lloyd Thomas, ball-turret gunner, Larussell, Mo.; T/Sgt. Bayne Scurlock, top-turret gunner, Gladewater, Tex.; S/Sgt. Ray Gillet, waist gunner, Stockton, Cal. Subbing for lucky co-pilot Woodbury in "Our Gang's" last trip to Schweinfurt was unlucky Lt. Louis Bianchi, Bakersfield, Cal. At the first dawn's station-time Woodward laughed and said to Newberry, "Let the fighters come in close today before you knock them down. We got a photographer riding with us in the nose and we gotta let him get some pictures for our albums. We gotta have something to show our kids when they ask us, 'Daddy, what did you do to win the war.'"

Chapter 14

LUCK IS NO LADY

". . . luck is funny . . . you look at a fellow who's
got a lot of it . . . and you wonder why . . ."

JOHN GOLDEN once told me the safest formula for turning out a stage hit:

"Put some real people into the middle of a situation where they've got to make decisions, fundamental decisions, and then just leave your characters alone and they'll work out a play for you."

Well, if that's the formula, then every damn mission of the Eighth Air Force into the Battle of Germany holds a hundred plays, all hits. I sat through one of them the other day. I was in the audience, but sometimes I wandered onto the stage and got mixed up with the props and the action. I'll try to tell you what happened.

The scene is a Fortress field. Even in the early fog light of English dawn, you could tell that this Fort had a new wing. And on her nose there was a familiar name: "Our Gang." Remember what happened to the old wing? That was the one that got chewed up at Huls weeks ago. This was the dawning of August 17, first birthday of the brazen, bloody daylight storming of Hitler's Fortress Europe by the Flying Forts of the U.S. Eighth Air Force.

Forts of the First Wing this morning were cocked for a raid on the ball-bearing factory at Schweinfurt, deep inside Germany. (See Illus. 72–85.) Forts carrying "Tokyo tanks" of extra gas were cocked for a deeper thrust, at the fighter factories at Regensburg; from there they were to fly on to "a secret destination"—that's how it read in the combat order that came down to First Wing. They were shuttling to Africa.

Before this day's air battles were done, the Luftwaffe would lose some 300 fighter planes; we would lose some 60 bombers—more than 600 boys.

This was to be a rugged day. I felt it. Didn't know whether or not anybody else could tell that early, but I was scared as hell when I pulled up inside the nose of "Our Gang," to tell Bill Wheeler that he was carrying a hitch-hiker. Fear had been piling up in the coils of my guts for days.

Every station had clamped tight every possible leak after a first take-off had miscarried; all passes were stopped. Weeks before, the lead crews had been briefed for the job, but they kept their secret. Now the whole station knew. More important, they all knew that, sooner or later, the deal would be on again. It was like Huls, only worse. They had time to think. And to sweat. And they were to get more time today.

This job would rank with the first raid on Berlin in drama and importance. It would be far tougher, too. The 8th was not to hit Berlin until long-range fighters were operating to give cover over the target. Over Schweinfurt today, the only fighters would be German fighters.

I knew from the beginning that I would have to try to sneak in on this job. Curiosity. Two kinds. This job would rank with the first raid on Berlin and the first night raid in drama, excitement, importance. I wanted to be at the ringside. And I wanted to find out if I could "cure" fear. I found out. I couldn't.

The last few days had been full of contrasts. Saturday night, I went to a movie, Bing Crosby and Dorothy Lamour in *Dixie*. Went with Bill Hearst, the widow of a famous RAF pilot, and a red-headed girl whose fiancé was with the British Army in Sicily. *Dixie* was a perfect British wartime movie. Took in another movie Sunday afternoon, *Bataan*—Robert Taylor. The critics warned that this was "grim film fare—realistic closeup of war." It was a damn fine movie—but nobody enjoyed it. People shuddered and said: "Well, I'm glad I saw it"—but they weren't.

Back to the office, met young Congressman Will Rogers, Jr. Talked politics. He said he had made a speech to combat crews at a Fortress Station and warned them that after the war was over, they would get only what they continued to fight for, no "forty acres and a jeep" stuff for the returning warriors. He looked so much like his father. Needed a haircut. Suit needed pressing. Tie was half under his collar. You expected him to start chewing gum, twirling a rope, and drawling the old opening line—"All I know is what I read in the papers." His trouble is my trouble—nearly all we do know is what we read in the papers. He's trying to cure his trouble.

At Claridge's, for dinner, young Will Rogers and I talked about Bill Hearst and watched Ambassador Winant at another table and thought a lot about "second and third generations." Walked back across Grosvenor Square after dinner and ran into Mike Santorra, the General's aide. He said the Boss had left for Africa. That meant he would not fly with the Forts as he had ached and schemed to do. I found afterwards that General Devers had said flatly "No." Reckon everybody is a "little boy" to somebody who has the authority to say "No." Wonder if the Boss was as peeved as I would be. Twice as peeved, I bet.

Up early the next morning, beautiful day. Drove Paul Holt, *Daily Express* Moscow correspondent, out to have a look at American fighter and bomber pilots and crews. At lunch with Christiansen, editor of the *Express*, I had proposed this idea: Assign one of your best men to write a series of articles on not more than five or six of the kids in the Eighth Air Force; tell not only their story and the story of what the Eighth Air Force is trying to do, but also the story of just what kind of Americans are fighting this war. Couldn't have picked a better man than Paul Holt for the job. Keen, sensitive, searching.

I wondered if Holt would believe as I do that the Eighth Air Force has made the greatest single contribution to the support of Russia's war effort by drawing most of Hitler's fighters to the Western Front. I wanted him to find out for himself what the kids in the Eighth are doing to lift the pressure off the Red Army. He talked discerningly of relations among the United Nations; especially keen was his crack about the psychology of Russia's distrust of the democracies:

"A mistress suspects that her man cheats on her and hates it; a wife expects it and is resigned to it."

If there were no suspicion between Russia and us, then our bombers and the RAF could shuttle to Russian bases across German targets, instead of down to Africa. We talked of that—Paul Holt said it would never happen.

I thought of these things as I scribbled reminding notes, leaning in the nose of the Fortress "Our Gang," waiting for a take-off that I prayed would be scrubbed. Especially since Hub Zemke (See Illus. 118)—he's the CO of a group of Thunderbolts—had told Paul when we picked him up at Fighter Command:

"A third of all the guys who try to be pilots are washed out in training. Another third drop out further along the line, because they don't like to fight. It's in the heart more than the guts. Those that do like to fight aren't necessarily killers, and those that don't like to fight aren't necessarily yellow. But if you don't like to fight, you don't belong in the Air Forces."

So damn true. It's like football—some guys *like* to tackle; they enjoy the challenge of impact. And that joy of impact makes the difference between a great football player and a fair one. Same with pilots and gunners.

We took Zemke out to the field where he had left his Thunderbolt when he flew down to Fighter Command, watched him take off—no stunting show-off for Holt, just a quiet and steady climb, and a turn north toward his home base. And then we drove on to another fighter field and talked to another Thunderbolt pilot—Capt. London, from Long Beach, California, nesting place for a large share of the aviation industry. (See Illus. 131.)

"I call my plane 'El Jeepo.' My own nickname is Jeepo, after the Jeep in Popeye. When I went to flying school, I didn't have any other nickname, so they called me Jeepo. Dunno why, they just did."

Handsome, calm, strong face, London's, completely typical of the best American type. He didn't talk much; Holt had to pull it out. I'll never forget one thing he said:

"We like to go out with the Fortresses, because the Jerries will come up and fight to stop the Forts. They have to, and that gives us a chance to get a crack at them."

Capt. "Jeepo" London, first ace of the Eighth Fighter Command, measures up to Col. Zemke's definition—he likes to fight.

Talked to Major Roberts at that station, too. He was struggling to write a letter to the mother of one of the pilots in his squadron, who was missing in action:

"We have to do this. It's tough to word it. We feel pretty bad when one of the boys doesn't come home, and we try to make his folks hope like we do that he bailed out and is okay. It's extra hard sometimes. One of the boys was married to an English girl. She was about to have a baby. I had to go in to town and tell her he was lost. She took it pretty hard—lost her baby, too. I think the wives have the toughest time in this war."

The wives and the mothers. And like Mr. Winant and his son, it doesn't help to be close to where the boys are flying and fighting and sometimes not coming home. Major Roberts knocked down three Jerries in one day, scored our first triple; he likes to go out with the Forts, too.

"Too bad the Fortress boys and the fighter pilots can't get to know each other better. I know a couple of them. We're going to start asking them to our dances."

Out on the squadron bulletin board was a letter from the crew of the Fortress

"Tough Stuff," addressed to the Thunderbolt pilots who had covered its crippled withdrawal to a point where they could safely crash-land in the south of England. The "TS" had collided with an FW. For fifty awkward, labored lines on both sides of a piece of paper, the crew of "Tough Stuff" expressed its deep gratitude to all Thunderbolt pilots. "Boy, you sure looked good to us that day."

The Thunderbolts were covering both thrusts of the Fortresses' deep penetrations today. They would "sure look good" again and again.

I don't know why I suggested to Paul Holt that we drive by a Fortress station after we left the fighters that Monday evening. It was the station where I had done most of my hitch-hiking. I hadn't been back there since the Huls job. They had a new CO now, a young Lieutenant Colonel who had trained in mediums. The boys all liked him, said he was a "raunchy guy." We drove over after dinner, dropped in to see Major Alford, Operations Officer. The Colonel came down, and the four of us sat around and talked. Alford asked me if I was staying over to take a ride. "Got a good one cooking tomorrow."

I knew this was the Big Deal, thought of every good excuse why I shouldn't stick around, finally stopped dodging, and told Holt he better drive on in alone. That was after an hour of mental nickel-flipping in the operations room, watching the guys playing checkers, waiting for the combat order to come in, smelling the special pre-mission steak sandwiches cooking next door—all the old atmosphere that digs under your ribs and spars with fear, then slugs it out toe-to-toe inside.

I told the driver to go by Claridge's and pick up Bill Hearst, tell him nothing, just to get on some warm clothes and come on back up and ask no questions. She was a wonderful girl, the driver, MacDonald. Veteran of lots of those midnight drives. I went back to the operations room. The sweat was on.

For ten days, the Luck that writes out the orders on each of us had been winding up this deal like a vast slot machine.

Around the station, about three hundred boys were sleeping, or trying to sleep. They knew with their dinner that they were alerted. None of them knew for sure who would fly—perhaps four hundred altogether thought their number might be on the hook for the deal that was cooking.

There was a deep difference between their sweating and mine. They had to go if their name was put down for the mission; I could make my own choice, pick my own crew.

This Group was full of new faces, now. There was only one boy, Lockhard, who had been flying a year ago when the meager Eighth Air Force made the first raid. He had been badly wounded on his 5th mission, spent a lot of time in the hospital, and now he was up for his 19th. There were a few other familiar names. I stuck around, watching the checker game, chiseling a steak sandwich, waiting for the attack order to come in. It arrived about midnight. Alford drew it out of its sealed envelope.

Yes, it was the Big Deal. Alford grinned, looked at me, pointed out the course that we already both knew: "Don't stick your neck out. You better watch this one from the control tower."

Capt. Sheeler looked up from his absorbing game of checkers. "Hell, this one will be easy. The Wing will take the rap and we'll have a breeze."

If we're lucky, brother, if we're lucky. More than 60 bombers wouldn't be lucky before this was over.

I walked out into the night. Clear as crystal. Stars out. RAF bombers were rumbling out overhead. Good football weather. First really cold night. Or maybe the cold was inside me and not the weather. The evil omens started to work as I stepped out into the darkness.

A black kitten—not a cat, but a kitten—walked across the road. Then it wasn't satisfied just to walk across; after I growled at it, frightened, it doubled back and circled me. Remember, it was a kitten—hadn't had much time to scatter its bad luck around. I stalked the kitten—not to kill it, just to catch it. I took it inside and examined it in the light. It wasn't grey, or black and white. It was all black. All bad luck. 100%.

Does this sound silly? Maybe so. But it's all part of "sweating a mission." Different people do it in different ways. But as the pressure mounts, the pressure of percentages, the sweating increases. I walked on through the dark. Stumbled into a low barbed wire fence. Tore my britches at the knee.

The barbed wire seemed to be holding me back—that's the kind of trick your imagination plays when you're scared. You seize upon every omen, and cling to it, nurse it, magnify it. Sure, I was scared.

Briefing was to be at three, take-off at dawn. I went up into the Combat Wing headquarters. Alford was there talking to Col. Gross. He was flying in the lead ship next day, leading the whole show over the target. I've always thought that any man who said he wasn't afraid before a mission like this one wasn't just a damn fool or a damn liar—he was just a damn liar, period.

But Col. Gross wasn't afraid. I really don't think he was. He was to fly co-pilot to Lt. Col. Wurzbach, the new CO. And General Williams was to fly in the lead ship of the second element—he was the CO of the First Wing. Col. Gross laughed and said:

"Looks like there are going to be a lot of promotions to fill a lot of high rank-ing vacancies around here in a couple of days."

There was a lot of joking about a special mission of high ranking gunnery experts who had come over here to study their problem under combat con-ditions; three of the experts had been lost on one raid into the Ruhr the other day. After the raid, one of the others phoned the expert who was "observing" at this group:

"Listen, I've got a lot of papers and letters and other things over here that I'm leaving in my bag, with a letter of instructions as to what to do in case I don't come back from this next raid. Wish you'd take care of it for me. I'll do the same for you."

The veterans were still laughing at the way his color changed from deep tan to light grey as he listened. But there was no scorn in their laughter—each of them had felt the same way at least once, many of them often, some of them still.

I laughed with the rest of them when the story was told; and then I told Major Alford what I knew I would tell him: "Guess I'll go along tomorrow."

He grinned. He knew that my guts were in a vertical dive. "Okay. Who do you want to ride with?"

"Let's wait until after the briefing. Think I'll try to grab a little sleep."

Sleep, hell! I knew I couldn't sleep. I walked back across the road to the officers' club; found my quarters, flopped on the bed, stared out the window at the stars and thought about all the good resolutions, the "sensible and real-istic" resolutions I had made as the fire died out of the inboard engine of "Our Gang," and the hazy shape of England showed up ahead after we fought our way back to the Channel from the Huls raid—"never again, never, never, never."

After an hour of squirming and tossing, I got up, went over to the briefing, looked at the flight plan, asked Alford whom he wanted me to fly with.

"You better go with Harry Lay. He's a good boy, leading the high flight. Know what he looks like? Here, I'll show you who he is. Look for the boy with the sloppiest cap farthest back on his head. That'll be Lay."

I looked and found the face, a long jaw, a square jaw, a good smile, a veteran. And he had slept well, had not squirmed and tossed since dinner. He was a good man, this boy. Comes from Denver. Other boys were asking him questions. His answers were short and accepted without further questions. He was respected. Alford called him "raunchy." I would call him rugged.

The briefing held no new horror for me, but it was a jab into raw nerves. These boys knew what this job was to be; they had been briefed for it once before. But again they whistled when Intelligence told them how many Jerry fighters would be up and hammering at them. Again they grunted when Intelligence showed them where fighter cover would leave them and they would be on their own, four hours inside German territory, five hours on oxygen. A slug through the oxygen system and brains would blur.

Major McNaboe had told me before the briefing that Col. Ordway, my boss, was bringing General Crockett, Theatre G-2, down to the briefing. Col. Ordway had never ordered me not to fly again—but he had told me that he would issue orders grounding me unless I promised not to fly.

I knew that he would not get too sore if I sneaked in on this one. But I also knew that if he saw me there, he would have to order me not to go. And because, before the briefing was half over, standing there among the kids who had to go and go and go again until they were shot down or until they fought through to the end of their missions—standing there among those boys, because my nerve would not measure up to the job they would do beginning at dawn, I deliberately bumped into Col. Ordway at the end of the briefing. He said hello, then suspiciously:

"You're not going to try to go today, are you? Remember what you promised. You are not to go. Get that. You are not to go."

And only because some of the other kids heard what he said—only because it took more nerve to admit in front of them that I was scared than it took to go on the mission, I laughed and said:

"I'll flip a shilling. If it's heads, I won't go."

Col. Ordway looked straight at me. Tight-lipped, he said: "You are not to go." And walked off to the club, to sleep until breakfast.

I walked over to see if Bill Hearst had come up. He was waiting for me, wondering why I had hauled him out of bed. I told him: "Stick around and you'll see the most exciting thing you've ever seen in your life or ever will."

We ate breakfast together. Ralph Housman, the Group Navigator, ate with us. The deep scars of the 20 mm. shell fragments that had hit him on his last mission were still quite visible through the hair over his forehead, still thin from the time they had shaved his whole head to dig metal out of his skull. I told him I was going on the trip. McPartlin, the Operations Officer of O'Neill's old squadron, had suggested that I go with Bill Wheeler in the Composite Group, low flight, instead of Lay. "Better place for pictures." So I shifted plans.

Ralph said: "Listen, that Wheeler is the best pilot in the outfit." (See Illus. 85.)

That was the first warming news I had had. For a few minutes, I had to swallow only once to get my pancakes to go down and stay down quietly. Bill tried to talk me out of going, tried hard, and sincerely. Shrewdly, he planned his tactics, based his whole attack on the simple question: "Just why do you want to go?"

That wasn't one I could answer easily. What I said was: "Because I want to." What I wanted to say was:

Listen, Bill, these kids who are going to take their Fortresses into Germany today and hammer the hell out of a factory that makes most of the ball bearings going into damn near every war machine Hitler needs to keep fighting—these kids who are going to do this job are the best that ever came out of America; they are the richest harvest of all American history. I never knew they existed, or maybe I just forgot they existed, or maybe they really never did exist until the challenge of total war revealed the same high qualities that have always been beneath the skin of the American people when the time of great testing has stripped them lean. I want to measure myself against their standards and try to grow a little by stretching to reach up to where they live and fight and, some of them, die. This to me is education essential for usefulness beyond the war. I shall never be able to understand the ideas and the desires and the hopes and the demands that our generation will bring out of this war if I avoid or evade what they can neither avoid nor evade.

But you can't talk stuff like that at 5 A. M. over pancakes and thick bacon to Bill Hearst and a guy with flak scars on his head. So I just said "I'm going because I want to go," and went and collected my duds and cameras and crawled into the car, and Bill and I drove out to the plane.

Remember, the plane was "Our Gang," with one new wing and a whole new crew. I was wearing the boots of a pilot who had finished his missions—and Smitty's helmet. . . .

Bill Wheeler—he comes from Scarsdale, New York—was already up in his seat when I got there, running up the engines. I pulled up inside, stood up in between the pilot and the co-pilot. The regular co-pilot, Clive Woodbury, from Fresno, was off that day. Sad-faced, dark Louis Bianchi, from Bakersfield, California, was riding his saddle. I told Wheeler I was hitch-hiking—he looked worried, cold, unfriendly: "Okay, if Operations say okay. Take-off is at dawn." (See Illus. 85.)

That was that. The crew was squatting around on the scattered flying gear. Guns were installed. The gunners were checking their parachute gear, strapping their knives in their boots, adjusting their escape packets in their knee pockets. I hadn't been able to get anything for my escape kit: pleasant thought.

The crew's roots were stretched across the whole of America. Look:

From Stockton, California—Waist Gunner Ray Gillet.
From New Haven, Connecticut—Waist Gunner Jim McGovern.
From Gladewater, Texas—Top-Turret Gunner Bayne Scurlock.
From Akron, Ohio—Tail Gunner Jim McBridge.
From Larussell, Missouri—Ball-Turret Gunner Lloyd Thomas.
From Freemont, North Carolina—Radio Operator-Gunner Jim Cobb.
From Crookston, Minnesota—Navigator Joe Newberry.
From Portsmouth, Ohio—Bombardier Denver Woodward.
From Bakersfield, California—Co-pilot Louis Bianchi.
From Scarsdale, New York—Pilot Bill Wheeler.

At stations time, the crew was kidding around—a little too much laughter. Joe Newberry, the navigator, said, very loud, to bombardier Denver Woodward:

"Gotta let the Jerries get in close today so Tex can get some good pictures. Don't shoot until he says we can."

Loud laughter again. Too loud again. I swear to you that every man in that crew knew "Our Gang" would not come home from this raid. I knew they knew it. It hit me suddenly, sharply, like a kick in the groin. They knew it. And I knew it.

I don't know whether or not it was the crew or the ship or me that had run out of luck. But I knew "Our Gang" would not get home. As taxi time ticked on, we crawled into the ship. Bill Hearst tried once more to get me to stay on the ground. I never searched so desperately and so fast in my life for a reason, for an excuse as I did then. But now the difference between me and combat crews was too sharply drawn—they had to go, I had a choice—and so, I had to go, too.

We sat there in the nose. The engines rose and fell in their rumble. The ship quivered. There was a chill sitting beside me and around me and in the bottom of my pockets when I stuck my hands there in search of warmth. Still there was the joking that could not hide the strain. And now the brakes were off and we were creeping out of the hard-standing, out on to the taxi strip, nosing toward the runway that was our "point of no return."

And then suddenly the engines died. The flash came over the intercom that there was a delay of thirty minutes. Instantly, speculation was hot. Will they scrub it? Nobody said he hoped there would be a scrub—instead, Joe Newberry said:

"Goddamn it, I hope they don't scrub this one today. We're flying in a good position. I'd like to get this mission behind me."

We were flying lead of the low flight, the Purple Heart Corner. And Joe Newberry did not hope this mission would not be scrubbed. I know that everybody in that plane hoped it would be scrubbed.

When Death creeps into a Fortress, you feel it. I'm not kidding. You feel it as surely as you feel the chill of dead air in a refrigerator.

We didn't get out of the ship. Not worth it for thirty minutes. We settled down and tried to wriggle up a little warmth against the grey fog that still clung to the field. The sun was trying to burn a hole in it. No luck.

There can be no tension contrived by Man alone to equal the strain of waiting to see whether or not a "delay" will turn into a complete "scrub" on a tough mission. All the special weaknesses that have been inherited from generations protected against Man's original struggle for survival, each crack in the armor of insulation against panic, widens as the pressure grows.

At the end of thirty minutes, engines whined and peevishly coughed and angrily roared all over the field again. There was no scrub. There was no laughter now. We taxied a little further out from our hard-standing, only about twenty yards. And then, once more, the engines choked and died. Once more there was the flash: "Delay thirty minutes."

At first, there was relief. Now, surely, the mission would be scrubbed. But then the relief was routed by fresh nerve-strain.

Each delay only snafus all the carefully worked out plans for attacks— further loosens the timing of the diversions and the fighter escort—bet the Jerries know what we are cooking up by now—bet they'll be waiting—

Yep, fears were fulfilled. At the end of thirty minutes, the same routine: Engines, whine, cough, roar. And the taxiing begins again. Once more the engines die. This is too much. Nerves snap. Rich cussing crackles over the intercom, through the ship. This time, the zero hour is delayed two hours. By now, the navigator has made so many changes on his forms that he can't figure out exactly when the take-off will be.

This much is certain: this time, we do not sit inside "Our Gang" for two whole hours. This time, we tumble out to fight the chill that has damped our spines.

And quickly, I prayed that Col. Ordway was awake by now, that he would find out that I was in the plane and order me out, the way he did that time when I was heading for Vegesack. Bill Hearst had heard back at Control Tower that Zero Hour was shoved back; he drove down, and together we went back to the officers' mess, and sat out in the rising warmth of the sun, as it wrestled with the morning fog. Bill and Major McNaboe both argued with me now.

I wanted to help them shape their arguments so that I could not find rebuttal; I wanted them to help find an excuse for me to duck out of this raid. God, how I wanted to help them. And then Col. Ordway joined the argument. He did not "order"—he argued. Let's shrink my part of the story. I gave in; sure. I went out to the plane, invented a lame story about being "sure that they're going to scrub it," collected my cameras and flying clothes out of the nose, and drove on back to the officers' club.

And let's shrink the middle part of the story, too. Col. Ordway and Bill and I drove over to a fighter station where the old Eagle Squadron is now flying Thunderbolts. The place was full of generals; we watched the take-off after the briefing. On this mission the fighter pilots were not told where the bombers were going. I wondered why, and asked Col. Ordway—he used to be A2 for Fighter Command. It seemed wrong not to tell the fighter pilots the whole story of what the Fortresses were trying to do this day—certainly the fighters would try harder to make their half of the deal work if they knew how tough a job the Forts had laid on for them.

We stayed with the fighters through lunch, heard their interrogation, heard them tell how the Germans had ducked tangling with them, how Jerries had flown on to stalk over our Forts beyond the range of our Thunderbolts. And then Bill and I drove back to the bomber station to join the rest of the "sweaters-in."

There hadn't been a sweat like this one in a long time on this station. We saw other whole groups fly past to other fields. Ours had been the first over the target. They should have been the first home.

Long minutes after other groups had gone by, straggling ships, first one, then only two more, circled our field and dropped their wheels and flaps to land. The lead ship with the two Colonels came in. I watched them climb out as the ground gang pushed close around their Fort to look at battle damage.

Without asking a question, I knew that today had been "rugged." In seven hours, the CO had aged at least one year. There was a great exhaustion in his walk, in his face, in the way his arms hung at his sides.

We stayed on the field a while longer. Two more ships came in, then the one with the General in it. It was a moving sight to see him get out and walk around and shake each man warmly by the hand, each man in the crew. The pilot of his ship used to be the jockey of a Spitfire in the RAF—he finished his ops in Spits, then shifted to our own Air Force, and now he's finishing up in Forts. The things he learned in Spitfires helped him fight Focke-Wulfs with a Fort today.

And then we went over to the interrogation of the three or four crews who sat in the still emptiness of the interrogation room. The customary wild chatter was not there this day. Nobody wanted to make too much noise. Everybody had one ear cocked for the sound of Fortresses coming home.

Dixie Tighe, hardest working reporter in England, was there. She had watched the raid going out today from the waist of the old Fortress "Yankee Doodle"—the one that General Eaker flew in on the first raid just a year ago. Dixie knows the kids in this group better than their mothers. She was a barometer of their losses today, sad, solemn, silent.

Capt. "Doc" Ross came in and reported on the first ship that had landed. She had fired two red flares. One boy had been taken out. He was dead.

The ship was Capt. Harry Lay's—the one Major Alford had wanted me to go in. And the dead boy was the radio operator—just like the first raid I ever went on.

We went back to the Control tower, and checked the list that had phoned in from other fields, where they had been forced down without gas. I studied the list—11 ships were still missing, no word from them.

One of the missing ships was "Our Gang."

I walked back over to Operations Room. A bunch of the guys were standing around, talking, quietly, the way you talk at a funeral or in an elevator—going down. Bill Martin looked up from behind the operations board and said:

"Hello, luck."

Chapter 15

HARTFORD IS HEAVEN

"...you can see the man in the moon tonight...
I never could see why it looked like a man in
the moon...until Doris Anne showed me..."

THE future development of postwar commercial aviation will not be decided by conferences of elderly and powerful gentlemen as much as by the
direction of somewhat older young men who were on combat in the first of
the war, and in combat, earned the right to be grounded. Able and aggressive
young men like Whitney Straight, for Britain—for us, with boys like Lt.
David A. Tyler, Jr., son of a worker in the City Department of Hartford,
Connecticut.

Just so that you will know quickly what kind of a boy Dave is, he was a
great swimmer in college; he travelled a lot in America in swimming meets;
he could have gone to Yale on an athletic scholarship, but he preferred to
go to Trinity College, because it's in Hartford; he trained for the Air Force
all over America; he came to England by way of South America, Africa, and
North Ireland; he has flown on bombing missions over Germany, Denmark,
Norway, Holland, Belgium, and France.

"And you know, the more places I see, the more I want to go home to
Hartford. Hartford is Heaven, believe me it is."

You know Hartford. It isn't Heaven at all. It's just another New England
town built along several Main Streets. But not to David A. Tyler, Jr.

Every home town in America is going to be "Heaven" to thousands of homesick, overseas-sick American boys after this war. You watch. Far places have
never had any real enchantment for American boys; not after the last war
wound up in a charred France; not in the peace between the wars. It may be
different this time. We'll see. Only if it is different will America challenge

Britain on the international airlines, after another Peace Conference decides how much there will be and who will get what.

Dave Tyler's crew in the Fortress "Ex-Virgin" makes a pretty good cross section of America. Meet them:

Wayne Hendricks, from Salt Lake City, Utah, co-pilot, twenty-two years old. He was born on a farm between Idaho and Utah; his father was the State Veterinarian. He's married to a Salt Lake City girl. He saw the sights in Brazil and French Morocco on the way over here. He didn't like the smell. Salt Lake City is the cleanest city in America.

Louis Nelson, from Minneapolis, Minnesota, bombardier, twenty-one years old. His sister is in the WAC. His father is in the lumber business. He was a student in the University of Minnesota, majoring in history; he wanted to be a teacher of ancient history. When we got into the war, he tried to be a pilot—"I already had a white silk scarf and I wanted Uncle Sam to give me a P-38."

Malvern Sweet, from Livermore, California, navigator, twenty-three years old. His father used to be a rancher—"but the ranch died when the spring dried up." Now he drives a school bus. Mal's kid brother is in pre-flight training; Mal wanted to be a pilot, but his eyes washed him out. He was in college, San Jose State, studying to be a teacher of manual arts. The one thing he talks most about, according to his pals, is "Blondie. No, she's not a girl, she's a pony. I raised Blondie from a colt."

The other members of the crew were Fred Boyle from Reno, Nevada, top-turret gunner; radio operator and gunner, Colin Lee, from Sun River, Montana—his geography is the tip on his background; ball-turret gunner, Hugh Johnson, from somewhere in Illinois; right waist gunner, a boy named Daugherty—really a man, not a boy. He used to be a second pilot for TWA. Transferred from the RAF. Don't know where he came from. And left waist gunner, Wayne Frye, killed on the Schweinfurt deal; tail gunner, Stan Soloman, from Scranton, Pennsylvania.

They were all damn fine boys. Let me tell you about their last trip, to Schweinfurt.

As I told you, the name of their Fort was "Ex-Virgin." The Fort in which they flew over here—and they damn near landed in South Ireland after wandering around in an overcast until all the red lights were showing on their tanks—was called "Deadly Nightshade." And then they got one called "The Vanishing Virginian."

"We didn't like that idea of 'vanishing' and nobody was from Virginia in the crew, so we just painted out everything of the old name except "The Virgin." And then one day we came home with a flak hole just about dotting the V, and after that we called our Fort the "Ex-Virgin."

The bombardier and the navigator had been briefed for six weeks on the Schweinfurt show. "We didn't know where the target was, but we could draw pictures of what it looked like. And when they told us that we could recognize a certain five-story building, we knew we were going to hit at less than our usual altitude. None of us knew until we got back from Schweinfurt that the new Air Division had gone on to Africa."

Dave's ship was in about the fifth group over the target, but by the time they got to the target, there wasn't enough left of the two preceding groups to make up a good squadron. The Eighth Air Force lost more Forts on that Birthday Raid than we could put into the air on some missions last winter.

The "Ex-Virgin" got hit hard at 14:05 hours—2:05 to you—just after the fighter escort left them. Dave was packed into the center of Purple Heart Corner down in the low squadron that always takes a beating.

A couple of 20 mms. socked the ship, blew out all the oxygen system on the left side, and "just tore the hell out of the waist gunner. He never knew what hit him. I didn't start to hate the Germans until I lifted the waist gunner out of our ship when we got back home," said Dave, later.

This was the last mission for Dave, and Nelson and Sweet, and Lee; next to last for Hendricks and Boyle. A rough one to pick for the Goal Post trip.

The same shells that knocked the oxygen out, blitzed the intercom too: "It's hell when you can't talk to each other. You can look at each other, but you can't talk. It's hell."

That's when the boys in the back of the ship started bailing out. The whole tail end was swirling with a strange white smoke. Plenty of reason to jump.

"I couldn't tell them to stick to the ship, and I don't know what I would have told them if it had been put up to me. There wasn't enough oxygen for all of us to live and get to the target and then get home at altitude. And if we broke formation and tried to get home down on the deck by ourselves, well, that would have been curtains for all of us."

With only the pilot, the co-pilot, the navigator, the bombardier, and the top-turret gunner left in the front of the ship, the "Ex-Virgin" plowed on. They added up the oxygen in the emergency bottles, set the indicator to 10,000 feet to make it last twice as long, and moved around as little as possible to conserve their strength for the trouble ahead.

The tail gunner had been the first to bail out in the back. "I guess he remembered the time we saw a Fortress go screaming by us after everybody had bailed out except the tail gunner, still blazing away at the fighters on his tail. A few minutes later the Fort went into a spin. The first thing that happens when a Fort spins is the tail snaps off. I guess our tail gunner figured he didn't want that to happen to him. Don't blame him."

When Dave's limping Fort got over the target, the bomb racks wouldn't release their load. Flak had jammed all the controls:

"Boy, we were really mad. Louis told the top-turret gunner—he's the engineer, too—to go back there and get to work with a screw driver, see if he couldn't pry the bombs loose. And that's what he did. He got them all set until we were coming over another German target and then he kicked the bombs away. That sort of made up for what they did to us that day."

By that time, most of the tail surfaces were shredded and flopping in the prop wash; the power was failing; the red lights were showing.

"When we left the target, we started hoping we'd reach the coast. When we reached the coast, we started hoping we'd reach mid-channel so the British Air-Sea Rescue would get us instead of the Jerries. When we got to mid-channel, we started hoping we'd reach the beach, and when we crossed the beach, then we started hoping we'd reach home. But we didn't."

They crash-landed on a fighter field, skidded in on the "Ex-Virgin's" belly, smoking down the runway.

I talked to the survivors of that crew a few nights later. We were driving in to London. The moon was bright; the RAF was going out to do its job. Dave was whistling and Mal was humming and Louis was furnishing the words to a song I had never heard before. Somehow or other the subject came up, in the dark, about the ethics of shooting Germans as they bail out of their planes.

Dave was vehement: "I wouldn't have a guy in my crew who shot at a German in a parachute. He couldn't ride with me."

Hendricks was practical: "Besides, we'd be fools to start shooting at guys in 'chutes. There's more of us go down over there than Germans over here, and besides, in the Forts we got to keep going, we can't hang around banging at boys in 'chutes. The Germans can."

Nelson split hairs: "I think it's okay to shoot a guy just as he is climbing out, but as soon as he leaves his plane, I guess we oughta leave him alone."

And then we got onto the old subject: Why don't we hate the Germans as much as we hate the Japs? Dave had half a good answer:

"I feel this way about hating the guys we're fighting. They aren't the ones that made me leave my wife and my home and come all the way over here to fight. Those guys, we never get a chance to shoot at. Just let me get my guns on Hitler or Goering and then I'd have fun killing, because I hate those guys. They're the ones made me leave Hartford."

Chapter 16

A WEEK OF SIGHT-SEEING

". . . where the pressure is greatest,
there you will find the most heroes . . ."

ONE job I sometimes had to do was to help conduct VIPS (Very Important People) on tours of the Eighth Air Force. For instance, when the five Senators paid us a visit, I was detailed to go along.

That week of sight-seeing was one of the best I've had over here. I saw a lot of things I wanted to see myself while I had to be on hand to point out things to the Senators.

Our gang of greeters and photographers went up a day early to International Airport to cover their arrival. At lunch, the first day there, I stumbled on the first bit of the "It's-A-Small-World" Department. Across the dining room was Stan Washburn, in the uniform of an Air Transport pilot, a guy I hadn't seen for more than a year. Went to school with him. Quite close friends. But the meeting was strangely casual, as though we'd seen each other only the day before. "Hello, McCrary, how are you?" Just like that.

Being an ATC pilot does that to you. He was to take off in a Skymaster for Africa that night; two days before, he had seen his wife in New York City. Flying all over the world like he does, I guess you get used to bumping into people you haven't seen for months or years.

Sitting in the sun that afternoon, a bunch of other ATC pilots, and some combat pilots who had been in the Middle East, and one who had fought in Burma, swapped atrocity yarns.

"Gotta be careful not to crash in the desert. The natives don't like white men. They cut off your toes and sew them up in your mouth."

"Yeah? But you oughta see what they do to you in the jungles. Yeah, they

117

sew up worse than your toes in your mouth. All the pilots used to carry a bottle of henna dye in their first aid kit. When they got shot down, they'd dye their hair red. The natives think that white people with red hair are gods, or something."

Sammy Schulman gave Washburn a telephone number in the city at the African end of his southern run. "And say, if you'll go by the hotel and pick up my laundry, I'll give you one of the silk shirts I left down there."

In the lobby of the Administration Building of the Field, some talented RAF pilot stationed there had painted a striking series of murals, pictures in vivid colors of all the places to which airplanes fly today. Landscapes in vivid jungle green, with crocodiles in the foreground, and a Skymaster splitting the horizon; the skyline of New York City from LaGuardia Airport; kangaroos in another foreground; a native wearing nothing but a basket of bananas on her head; camels in another panel of the mural, with beautiful Arab women in the foreground. Heavy emphasis on the women in all the panels.

The people in the lobby reflected the panels on the walls. There was a most handsome Polish officer in tropical uniform, with many medals on his chest; not just ribbons, but medals. There were six young French officers, dark, sunburned, in shorts—airmen. They sat there all day and watched the other people and waited for their plane and smoked stubby black cigars. There was a bronzed Norwegian seaman with many medals, and only one eye.

Then our Secretary of War, Mr. Stimson, walked in, with his upturned grey hat, just back from Africa, on his way home. Elmer Davis, worried, head down, hair whiter than ever, with the funny black bow tie he always wears, came through the lobby. On his way to Cairo. A lone British paratrooper with a limp came in. His rifle was dusty but not rusty; his hair was dusty, his skin was a little grey with dust, and the lids of his blue eyes were raw and red with dust and the glare of the sun. He was an officer. He wore expensive brown suède shoes. Home for leave.

There was dust on everybody who came in from the South. Those who came from the West looked crisp and clean and fresh.

A flotilla of British admirals entered—naval delegation from Washington, with gold braid so high on their sleeves they could scarcely bend their elbows. An Indian RAF Squadron Leader and a Commander in the Indian Navy stood in a corner, in earnest argument about a cable. A very ugly and very strong looking pilot in the uniform of the Royal Australian Air Force walked past.

He had USA on his shoulder patch, and his teeth were much whiter and better than any you find in England.

A bunch of American officers came in from the States; all with their Colt pistols strapped awkwardly around sloppy, new—very new—uniforms. The British all looked like professionals, we like amateurs.

It was really Grand Hotel, wartime.

At dinner, ran into an old friend, Major Bob Campbell from "Wray's Ragged Irregulars," the outfit where I got in most of my missions. Bob was through with combat, had finished his trips, was going home now. Comes from Marshall, Texas. Married, but no children. "Reckon I'll work on that when I get home."

At dinner, too, was a kid who had been in the first Eighth Air Force outfit that went down to Africa. He was a little tight, complaining about how they had a lot more missions in the Twelfth than in the Eighth to finish their tour of combat duty. Claimed that it was just as tough down there. Bob shot him a couple of sharp facts about relative losses. The boy subsided.

Went to bed that night. Was about to go to sleep when three crews from new Fortresses piled in, laughing, talking, cussing, kidding. "Goddamn, bet it don't get as cold in England as it did in Maine. Better not, or I'm gonna fly right down to Africa the first time we get sent over to do a job on the Germans. Gonna fly right on to where it's warm in the winter."

That boy didn't know it then, and neither did I, but he was about to do just that.

Next morning, Bob and I had breakfast, then we went over and played croquet. Bob teamed up with a boy named Calvin Swoffer, from Memphis. (See Illus. 95.) Swoffer and his Fort, "The Memphis Blues," went down into the Channel on his Mission X, last one before he wound up his combat tour. Air-Sea Rescue fished him out. Funny to see these two veterans playing peaceful croquet now. And later, we sprawled in the sun and talked. Bob is a wise young man; went into the Army as a buck private.

"You know, I don't expect any special treatment because I've got a few medal ribbons. Swear I don't. But people treat us like they think we do want something special because we've had a rough war. Why do you suppose that is?"

I didn't have an answer to that one. Do you? We watched a bunch of enlisted men, gunners, sorting out their baggage by a truck—they were going home, too. One of them wore a leather jacket with a skull and crossbones on the back, and the name of the Fort he flew in. Very famous name: "Southern Comfort." The original one crashed; there's a "Southern Comfort, Jr." flying now.

It's pretty good, sending enlisted men home by air the same as officers. That's what I like to see.

A shining new Fortress without any paint on it came rumbling in for a landing and braked to a stop down the long runway, turned, and taxied back. The new crew piled out, stretched, and looked around as if to say: "So this is England. Well, where's the war?"

"I'll never forget the time we landed here last fall. All our gunners were on the alert, ready for trouble. And when we took off from here and flew on further south, we were nervous as hell. We thought sure we'd be attacked before we got to base. We didn't realize that the RAF had already won the Battle of Britain two years before."

First one, and then another Marauder thundered over the field, circled, and landed.

"Look at those damn things—twin engines. Well, by the time I get back here with a new Group, they'll be flying from bases in France or Norway or somewhere they won't need any range to reach the Jerries. I hope I don't ever have to fly anything but a Fort. They're the queens!"

Bob was in the "two-man Air Force" with Haley Aycock when they had two bombers for patrolling the Gulf of Mexico and lived in style in Houston.

"There are certain points in getting through to the end of your missions where you get more scared than at others. 10 and 15 and 20—those were the missions that scared me stiff. But when I got through 25, I figured I could go on flying forever. And I still believe it. If I come back here with a new Group, I'll fly again—on combat."

That afternoon, the Senators came in, and Campbell and Swoffer and the rest flew West. The Senators spent the night in their special train. Next morning, there was Washburn back from his African run, to split a fresh melon with me for breakfast. Then we went on down to London.

I've got a debt to Senator "Happy" Chandler—he made me get up that Sunday morning and go to St. Paul's with him and General "Doc" Rankin. Last time I had gone to church anywhere was two years before in Bristol in the middle of a blitz. It seemed strange, rising and sitting and kneeling between a Senator and a General in St. Paul's that Sunday. The congregation was pitifully small. The scars of the Battle of Britain were still plain on some of the walls of the great cathedral. There were only very old people, and women in black, and children, in the congregation that morning, as the preacher said over and over again to punctuate his long prayers, "Lord, have mercy on us, miserable sinners."

We went out to Eighth Air Force Headquarters for lunch with General Eaker, and after lunch we went into the War Room and the Boss told the Senators all our secrets. He pulled no punches, hid nothing. Col. Ordway told them everything the Jerries were doing to us and the General told them everything we were building up to do to the Jerries. I remember especially one thing he said:

"We'll keep building bombers and fighters, until one day we won't mind if Goering knows when we're coming. We might even tell him in advance, so he'll get his fighters up and try to stop us. But he won't be able to. We'll be too strong."

The Senators went out and looked at our Air Force. They gave us a pretty short time to show it to them, though. It took the Old Man fifteen months to get it up to where they saw it—for two days.

If they had given me more time and the Boss had given me permission, I would have run a very different show.

First, we would have gone up to Col. Chick Harding's outfit, one of the best over here. We would have tried to pick a day when the weather looked like a hot mission coming up. We might have pulled in about dinner time and sat around and pitched the bull about the team that Chick quarterbacked for West Point, one of the greatest teams in Army history. Chris Cagle was on it. The great names of that team are great names in the war now: Bud Sprague, Blondy Saunders, "Light Horse" Harry Wilson, Moe Daly, Tom Trapnell, Art Meehan, Chuck Born, Gar Davison, Bill Wood, Tiny Hewitt. Some have been killed in action, some are prisoners, some have more medals than others, and some are generals. And the quarterback is the boss of a Fortress Group here in the Big League of this war—Chick Harding. (See Illus. 97.)

If we were lucky, we would have landed there on the morning before they went to Regensburg, and on to Africa. The Senators would have shared a room with Col. Bill Kennedy, a gunnery specialist who came here to study the way we use the .50's on the Forts. They might have talked to Bill after the lights went out, and that would have given them a special "stake" in the mission. Getting to know Bill would have made the Senators feel the way a lot of us so often do when a good friend goes out and does not come back. The last anybody saw of him was when he went around one side of a big mountain in the Alps and a German fighter started around the other side. Nobody knows what happened when they met. It was over Switzerland.

Chick Harding's outfit was to lose 11 of its 24 bombers over the target on Regensburg. The Senators would have had a good dose of the special tension of a Fortress raid. They would have had to wait and wonder not just for that day, but for several—because the Forts were to land in Africa.

Chick would have pulled us out of the hay in the dark of the night because the take-off was to be at dawn. We would have sat through the briefing, then tried to kill time, while everywhere in the dark boys were dressing and lacing-up and zipping-up and going out to their frosted Forts.

We would have stood on the control tower roof in the half-light of dawn and and heard the engineering officer curse in a deep Kentucky growl about the loads we ask the Forts to carry on these long raids. We would have seen them rise through the haze and climb into the sky even before the sun melted the mist of the morning. We would have gone back to mess for another cup of coffee and some more combat breakfast eggs. And probably, if the Senators had done what I would have done, they would have piled back in bed for some sleep.

But the sleep would have been short, because the Forts would have come back and the roar of them would have made us jump out of bed, wondering if they had been to Africa and if we had slept for a week. But not only had they not been to Africa, they had been recalled from this first take-off—weather or something else. The men would pile out of their Forts and cuss and growl and grumble—because once you take off, the worst of the strain is over. Might as well finish the job. It is so often like that—as Marc Blitzstein puts in the words of his symphony:

"Oh, the Air Force is always hurry-up, hurry-up, hurry-up, hurry-up—and then wait."

We would have had to wait for a week before they took off for Regensburg again. And for another ten days before they came home. Only six of Chick's Forts were in shape to come home.

Then I would have taken the Senators back up to Chick's station, and put them in front of an open fire to talk to one of the guys who went on the show. He would have told them a story of Forts going down in flames, sixty parachutes in the air at one time, human bodies hurtling back through the air from groups that had gone ahead, debris like the wake of a hurricane, the debris of shattered fighters and Forts.

And because I would have picked the right officer to tell this story, he would have told them what he put into a terse report on the mission. A report in which he made this recommendation for a medal, for a boy named Major Gale Cleven, from Odessa, Texas (See Illus. 87):

"Throughout approximately two hours of constant fighter attack, Major Cleven's squadron, flying the low flight, was the focal point of the enemy's fire. Early in the encounter, south of Antwerp, he lost his entire second element of three B-17's, yet he maintained his vulnerable position as leader, exposed to the brunt of attacks, in order to keep his guns uncovered to protect the bottom of the rest of his Group.

"About thirty minutes before reaching the target, his airplane received the following battle damage:

"A 20 mm. cannon shell penetrated the right side of his plane, exploded under the pilot, damaging the electrical system and radio compartment, killing the radio operator, who bled to death after both legs were cut off just above the knees.

"Another 20 mm. shell entered the left side of the nose, tearing out a section of the plexiglass about two feet square; it also tore away the left gun installation and injured the bombardier in the head and shoulder.

"A third 20 mm. shell penetrated the right wing, went on into the fuselage and shattered the hydraulic system, releasing the fluid in a flood into the cockpit. A fourth 20 mm. shell crashed through the cabin roof, and cut the cables to one side of the rudder.

"A fifth 20 mm. shell hit the Number 3 engine, destroying all engine controls. The engine caught fire and lost its power—luckily, the fire later died out.

"Confronted with this structural damage, partial loss of controls, fire in one engine, and serious injuries to personnel, and faced with fresh waves of fighters still rising to the attack, Major Cleven had every justification for ordering his crew to abandon ship. And his crew, many of them inexperienced youngsters, were already preparing to bail out; no other alternative seemed possible. The co-pilot, with good reason, pleaded repeatedly with Major Cleven to leave the ship. Major Cleven's reply, deliberately intended to shock the crew out of its panic was this: 'I'm sticking, see, and you're gonna sit there, you sonofabitch, and take it too.'

"Those words, heard over the intercom, had a magic effect on the crew.

They stuck to their guns. The airplane continued to the target, bombed it, and reached base in North Africa.

"Sgt. Ferrorgiarro from San Francisco (married, with a nine-year old daughter), left waist gunner and a veteran of the war in China in 1942 and of seven months at the front in Spain in 1939, voiced the opinion of the whole crew to me when he stated that the completion of the mission was solely due to the extraordinary heroism and inspired determination of Major Cleven. And hence I believe that Major Cleven's actions were far above and beyond the call of duty, and that the skill, courage, and strength of will and wisdom of leadership displayed by him as airplane and squadron commander in the face of hopeless odds have seldom, if ever, been surpassed in the annals of the Army Air Forces."

This officer was recommending Major Cleven for the Congressional Medal of Honor.

That wouldn't have been the end of the story. We would have had to wait until Sunday evening, October 10. The Regensburg raid was an old story by then—it happened during the last week in August. People still talked about the raid—it was part of the twin thrust, one Force hitting Schweinfurt, one Regensburg. It was strategic bombing at its best. The target at Schweinfurt had been a ball-bearing factory—a nerve center of Hitler's whole Factory Front; the target at Regensburg was a factory that made fighter planes.

On that day, the Eighth destroyed fighters in the air as well as in the factories—307 Jerries knocked down was the total bag, 20 of them by the Thunderbolts.

But as I say, by Sunday, October 10, Regensburg was an old story. The Sunday papers were full of the news of the longest daylight raid ever pulled from British bases.

The Forts and Libs had hit Anklam, east of Berlin; Gdynia and Danzig in Poland; and Marienburg in East Prussia—a very short flight from the Russian front. All those targets had been hit on Saturday. On Friday, they had hit Bremen; and on Sunday, Münster in Westphalia. It was a big three days.

General Eaker made a broadcast back to America on Sunday night. For the first time, he gave some idea of the size of the operations of the Eighth, in the speech he shortwaved to America:

"On Friday, we sent more than 4,000 Eighth Air Force fighting men against German industrial targets. And again yesterday, more than 4,000 fought their way through the German defenses to destroy vital Nazi aircraft factories. And here is a message direct from my combat crews, a message which they want me to give tonight directly to their greatest supporters, the working men and women in the factories at home who build our fine planes and the weapons they carry. This is the message: We have not yet won this battle. The battle has not yet even reached its climax. The fight is now on at white heat. We have just passed the fifth inning, but we have not yet reached the seventh inning stretch. We are not going to relax over here. And you must not relax at home."

The Boss was trying to puncture the wave of too early optimism that he knew would blossom out of headlines like the ones in the London *Daily Sketch* on Monday morning:

"U.S. Forts Shatter Münster—
814 Nazi Fighters Down in 40 Days."

But if the Senators had been here, they would not have needed the broadcast by The Boss to make them know this war is still bloody, still far from won.

I would have made them stick to the story that started back in August, the story of Major Gale Cleven. I would have ruined their appetites Sunday night by telling them that of the 14 planes from Chick's outfit that got to the target at Münster, 13 did not get home Sunday morning.

And then we would have gone to the office and called the station. Chances are, we would have got through to an intelligence officer.

"Hello—hello—this is McCrary, calling from London. I want to get a little information. You know Major Cleven? Well, could you tell me—er, that is— he's okay, isn't he? What's that? You can't give out that kind of information over the phone? Oh, sure, I know. Well, I just wanted to know. There's a friend of his here who would like to come up to see him tomorrow. Wouldn't come up, eh? I see. Thanks."

But you never get stories like that when you spend only a week in a country that has been fighting a war for four years. In such a country, such a story fades into all the other stories that are hidden in the calm of England. At home, if you told the story of Gale Cleven in New York they'd be talking about it in Los Angeles within the week. That line of his—"I'm sticking, see, and you're gonna sit there, you sonofabitch, and take it too"—that line would be grabbed up by politicians and advertising agencies, and by historians, too. It would rank with "Damn the torpedoes! Full speed ahead!"

But over here, the story of Gale Cleven is "just another story" in the Eighth

Air Force, "just another story" in England—for there are so many of them.

Where the pressure is greatest, there among the people fighting on our side, you will find the most heroes.

I wish the Senators had met more of them. They should have spent a month here like young Will Rogers did, just moving around, meeting those guys who fight the Battle of Germany, carrying the war directly into the vitals of the first and worst of our enemies.

Then they could have gone home and fought in their own way to see to it that whatever is made, whatever is shipped, whatever is planned, whatever is decided back there, will be worthy of guys like Gale Cleven.

Chapter 17

"THE WOMEN"

"...he called me Princess, not Duchess..."

CLARE BOOTHE LUCE aimed *The Women* at a lot of ladies she knew. Scored a direct hit. There are women in London like that, too. The war has only given them an excuse to be what they are.

But you'll find women like that in every city and town and village, vicious and useless in direct proportion to the length and brilliance of the Main Street of the place in which they live. There are plenty of women like that in England. Most of them like Americans. We are "fresh." But there is the other kind, too, over here—the kind that healthy American kids fall in love with, the kind that some of the kids are lucky enough to marry.

I know that a couple of newspaper guys, cooking up good stories, have worried a lot of wives and mothers and sweethearts back home about the "Piccadilly Commandos" who prey upon our innocent American boys. Sure, there are those, too—the kind that work the streets and also the kind who struck it rich and don't have to work any more. But they are in the negligible minority in London, just as they are in New York and Chicago and Los Angeles and Dallas and Atlanta and every railroad junction at home.

Let me tell you the story of one of the good ones. This is really a lot of stories, bundled into one—and needless to say, all names are fictitious. Stories of a number of girls, good girls inside, who have given a lot of airmen of the Eighth what they needed to keep them from going off their nuts—what no doctor could give them. And the girls often got little in return.

Jackie Beauvais used to be a telephone operator at the Air Ministry, until she met Capt. Donald Schyler, pilot of a Fortress in the Eighth. Let's start the story with a little dope about Donald. New Yorker, St. Bernard's, then Groton, then Yale. At Yale, he was not Deke and Bones—he was the Fence and Scroll and Keys. His clubs were the Links and the Racquet and the River in town, Meadowbrook in the country. He piddled at polo in New Haven—but he never was very good at Meadowbrook, because he was always looking up to watch the planes coming in or taking off from Mitchel Field, when he should have had his eye on the ball. He had to fly.

He came to England too late for the Battle of Britain; he joined the Third Eagle Squadron just in time to transfer to the Eighth. By that time he was getting a little old for fighters, so he shifted to the Forts, flew first as a replacement co-pilot, finally went out as a skipper of his own ship. He had about three raids under his belt when he met Jackie Beauvais.

There is a famous fellow around New York called Georgie Hale, who used to bring American show girls to England and France before the war. Donald knew Georgie pretty well. Donald is the kind of a boy who knows citizens like Georgie. When Donald came to England to fight the war, he did not close his mind to fun. He called up Georgie. "Listen, you've probably got the names and numbers of a lot of the dames you took to London and left there. Give, brother, I'm off to London."

And that's how Capt. Schyler happened to call up Miss Dixie Mahoney, Bayswater 6974.

"This is Don Schyler from New York. Georgie Hale told me to call you up when I got over here. You remember Georgie. You're not Dixie Mahoney? Well, then, who?"

"I room with Dixie. My name is Beauvais. Dixie is in the show now, down at the Windmill Theatre. She won't be home until about 6:30. So sorry."

"Hey, wait a minute, Duchess! No, not Duchess—I mean please don't hang up, Princess! Please! Gosh, where did you get that voice? Are you English or just an actress? What I mean is I never could tell whether all actresses talked like they were English or all English dames talked like they were actresses."

"That is not amusing. Miss Mahoney will be in at 6:30. Good-bye."

He did not call Miss Mahoney. But next morning at eight, he started calling the Air Ministry and heckling the operators for somebody who sounded like "she's a princess." He got no satisfaction, but he kept calling Abbey 3411, like playing roulette, until finally her voice came up.

"Princess! It's me! The guy who wasn't funny yesterday. Please, I know you are busy. Yes, I know I was rude. Yes, I know a supervisor is standing right over your shoulder, but please, please, please meet me tonight. Where? I'm staying at the Dorchester. Meet me there when you finish work. Oh, I'm sorry, what I mean is, I'll pick you up. How'll I know you? It'll be dark when you get through work. Listen, I'll be standing right outside the Air Ministry, right where everybody comes out, and I'll have a flashlight inside my pocket, turned on. You look for a guy with a glow—that'll be me. Please. Remember, the guy with the glow."

And that's how it turned out. She didn't want to do it, but curiosity won, and she looked for the "guy with the glow," and they had dinner at Claridge's, "because that's the only place stuffy enough to take a Princess," and each thought the other was attractive, and both were right.

Things rocked along very nicely after that—except that Miss Beauvais, her first name was Jacqueline, lost her job at Air Ministry because Donald called her up once too often. She didn't have the heart to hang up on him, because he was calling from his bomber station and he had just come back from a long raid. She had heard the Forts going out over London that morning. Toward the middle of the day the supervisor finally exploded: *"Miss Beauvais, never in the field of telephony have so many people been indebted for so many wrong numbers to one person! What is the matter with you today?"*

Jackie tried to explain that she had heard the Forts go out and hadn't heard them come back—but that's hard to explain to a supervisor. It was hell around the flat, too. Dixie was in love with the mid-upper gunner of a Lancaster. She worried every time the RAF went out over London at night. And Jackie worried when the Forts went out by day. No peace at Bayswater 6974.

But Donald sent some cables back home, and somebody sent some cables back to London, and Jackie got a job on the switchboard at the American Embassy. Before long, everybody was calling her Princess and some of her words began to show a trace of an American accent. She went to all the dances up at Donald's bomber station. Once she brought Dixie and a bunch of her show girl friends and after that the whole station called her Princess, and she got silk stockings and American cigarettes and lighter fluid and hairpins and lipsticks, out of gratitude from all the kids at the Fortress field.

One Saturday night, she went up for a dance. The boys were out on a long raid, deep into Germany. She had heard them go out that morning while she was at the station, catching her train. But she wasn't nervous today. This was his next-to-last mission. One more to go, and then they would get married. He had already asked his Commanding Officer, and his parents, and because they liked her picture, and trusted their son, everybody had said: "Yes." There were several other girls on the train, all going up for the dance.

They got to the station about noon, rode to the field in a bus. She knew where to go, and so did some of the other girls. At officers' mess, they sat around with the Red Cross girls and watched out the windows. There was a little tension now. The boys were due back in a half hour. That was a long half hour. She smoked seven cigarettes until they burned her fingers. She chewed one nail until she remembered how scarce nail polish was. She poked Donald's fountain pen into the curls of her hair—Don had left the pen with her—she was keeping "our" diary. She twisted a ring on her finger, a man's ring, with a crest on it. It was Donald's ring, on her left hand, the correct finger. Donald always said about the crest, "Every American family tries to dig one up after it's had money for three generations."

The half hour was up and the first of the Forts came home. She tried to count them, but they circled and it was hopeless—the sounds were all mixed up. She just waited. And then a grimy bombardier burst through the doors of the officers' mess and ran to grab the hands, and then to hug all, of his girl. Jackie didn't know him, or she would have asked about Donald. A navigator came in, one of Donald's best friends. He saw her at the same instant she saw him. He didn't have to tell her.

I called the station about dinner time to talk to a pilot I knew. There was a lot of noise. The party was on. I asked about the raid, who was missing. He called the roll. Eleven planes were lost.

"And listen. You knew Don Schyler's girl, didn't you? Well, she was up here for the party. We put her on a train. She wanted to go on back home. You might just call her up and take her out to dinner or something. Be a good guy and do it, will you? Yeah, she took it pretty tough."

She was dry-eyed, not even a quiver in her chin to tell me that her guts were tied in a knot with an agony of grief. I tried to make conversation, tried to crack first feeble, and then, in desperation, dirty jokes. She laughed. And finally I took her home. "Good night, and thank you very much. But don't worry, because, you see, I know Don is all right. I know it."

I didn't see her for a couple of months after that—but she was right. Don was okay—prisoner of war. Then, one night, I ran into her at the Ambas-sadors' Club. She was doing a good rumba with a tight, but attractive pilot. I cut in. We danced a little, and then I took her back to my table. We talked.

86. *I Wanted Wings* was the name of a story by a red-headed guy named Beirne Lay. (Chapter 11) It will be remembered as the movie that made Veronica Lake famous. It was written originally to tell what happens inside a boy who "just *has* to fly." Beirne Lay had a responsible chair-borne job in the 8th Air Force, but he, too, had to fly. He went back on combat, and his last ride before he went home was the 8th's "roughest deal," to Regensburg and on to Africa. He got home once—but in May, 1944, his Liberator was shot down as he was leading his group back from a German target. Eleven parachutes were seen to open.

87. This heavy-jawed young pilot gave the 8th Air Force its best battle-cry in the shuttle-raid to Regensburg and on to Africa. With his ship shot to shreds, and every man in the crew ready —with good reason—to bail out, he yelled at his co-pilot: "You sit there, you sonofabitch, and take it!" The co-pilot sat. The pilot's name: Maj. Gale Cleven, from Odessa, Tex. (Chapter 16)

88. The oldtimers began the Battle of Germany by hitting targets on the North Sea edge of Hitler's Fortress. This was Wilhelmshaven, Forts going into the target, June, 1943.

89. The new groups, with longer range in their Forts, reached out for targets like the U-boat pens way down at La Pallice, once out of reach for all but the Libs. The locks of the U-boat pens are beneath the smoke at A and B. The circled bursts show how another group plastered a fighter field.

90. Boldest thrust by the Forts was made by "the new boys," all the way to the Messerschmitt fighter factories at Regensburg on the banks of the Danube, then on to Africa, then home again, bombing U-boat installations on the Bay of Biscay on the way.

91. Fighters (that's one going down in pieces, smashed by Fortress guns) had learned new tricks by the time the 8th reached out to Regensburg: they were dropping bombs and using rocket-projectiles on the Forts by then. But still, on the birthday raids to Regensburg and Schweinfurt on August 17, Forts and Thunderbolts scored their biggest bag of Jerries: 307. (Chapter 16)

92. The Germans had learned a lot about defense by the time the "new boys" got into the battle—flak, for instance, was heavier and more accurate. The new boys got into the fight late, but they did not have it easy by any means.

93. Fighters weren't the only peril on the Regensburg job. Beyond the Danube were the Alps, and beyond the Alps were more Alps, and beyond that the Mediterranean—and only beyond the Mediterranean lay their journey's end—Africa.

94. Once down on Africa's hot sands, the airmen of the 8th turned the blue Mediterranean into an "ole swimmin' hole." Natives stood on the beach and around their airdrome, bartered shoeshines for "chew-gum."

95. Two of the "first of the many": RAF transferee Lt. Calvin Swoffer from Memphis, Tenn. Now he's home, and so is Maj. Bob Campbell, from Marshall, Tex. (Chapter 4) Bob was in the same outfit with Oscar O'Neill and Haley Aycock and Red Cliburn and the rest. As they were going home, others were coming over—the first of the "new."

96. Moe, the donkey mascot of a bomber crew flown back from Africa, mans a 50-caliber machine gun. Holding Moe is Tail Gunner S/Sgt. Marshall R. Lord, Providence, R.I., and looking on is Ball-Turret Gunner S/Sgt. Louis Klimchak, Josephine, Pa.

97. New to combat, but old to Fortresses, is Col. "Chick" Harding, from West Virginia. He piloted the fifth Flying Fortress that left the factory. Once quarterback of a great Army football team, he's the CO of Gale Cleven's group now "and up to my damn ears in paper-work!"

98. Heroes are as plentiful in the new Air Division as they were in the old Wing. Among the earliest was Ball-Turret Gunner Floyd Thompson, a Cherokee Indian from Durant, Okla. Nicknamed the "Chief," Floyd once had the electric heating go out on his flying boots over Germany, stuck to his guns with frozen feet until the fighters were driven off.

99. The CO of the job was then Col. and now Maj. Gen. Curtis Lemay from Ohio. He is deeply respected in his new Air Division. Quiet, studious, he is a careful planner—and hence a successful performer.

100. Ambassador Winant's son, Capt. John, Jr., was the skipper of one of the new Forts. In his crew were Lt. Dick Walker, bombardier, Albany, Ga.; Lt. Bob Tredinnick, navigator, North Caldwell, N.J.; S/Sgt. Weidemann; Sgt. Alonzo Swope, waist gunner, Harlington, Tex.; Capt. Winant; Lt. Don Arns, co-pilot, Algona, Iowa; S/Sgt. Elmer Fjosne, ball-turret, Cornell, Wisc.; S/Sgt. Paul Hurles, radio-gunner, Columbus, Ohio; S/Sgt. Wirtz; S/Sgt. Frank Malone, tail-gunner, Hones Bath, S.C.

101. "Spook" Bender, million-dollar pilot. Colorful, too, were these "first of the new." Perhaps a little more than typical is the story of Capt. Bob ("Spook") Bender, from Pollockville, N.C. He used up a million dollars worth of Fortresses on 15 missions to German targets. Uncle Sam doesn't mind the expense, however, because Capt. Bender has always bombed his targets, always brought his crew home alive, and 3 times brought back enough of a B-17 to call it salvage. The name of each of his 4 Forts was "Spook." First 2 crash-landed, shot to shreds. Third had to be ditched in the Channel—that one sank in about 3 minutes. Number 4 had to ditch too—but that one floated a half-hour. "We're getting better with practice," said "Spook." That time they took to their rubber-dinghies and paddled around in the North Sea for 22 hours before Air-Sea Rescue fished them out.

102. Bombs away! Another load of high explosives goes down on German installations—this time a Nazi fighter base—from Flying Fortresses of U.S. 8th Air Force Bomber Command. Flak bursts above and below the nearest Fortress bomber, sending shrapnel flying through the air.

103. FW-190 production goes up—in flames! Flying Fortresses of 8th Bomber Command hit 2 of their favorite targets: the huge FW-190 factory at Marienburg in East Prussia and the Arado Fleugzeugwerke at Anklam, approximately 90 miles north of Berlin. Picture, made from one of the Forts during the attack at Anklam, shows the entire factory burning fiercely.

104. Marienburg during and after a successful attack.

105. If this were a movie, this picture of a tailless Fort going to its death would be neatly centered on the page, dramatically lighted. In action, pictures like that don't happen. The cameraman's attention is too much on the Focke-Wulfs and the bucking evasive action of his Fort—and on the fate of the men who were—and maybe still are—in that plane.

She wanted to talk, and I must admit that I wanted her to talk. I had heard she had quit her job at the Embassy and that she was dancing in a show with Dixie. Somebody had told me that she was drinking a little. Didn't show it now.

"I couldn't stand that job at the Embassy any longer. I don't like people to be sorry for me, especially when they are sorry only so they'll have an excuse to put their arms around me and then kiss me on the forehead.

"And I know what a lot of Don's friends are saying about me."

For the first time I saw her chin pucker, then quiver, and her eyes were not dry now. I wondered.

"The other day a fellow from United Press who was a good friend of Donald's, called me up and asked me if I had had any letters from him since he was a prisoner of war. I told him sure, one a week, regularly. He wanted to read them. I didn't mind. They are beautiful letters. You can't put much into a letter from a prisoner of war camp, but somehow Donald managed to write a dozen lines of feeling between every two lines of writing. There was nothing there that a German censor would have understood. But I did, and so did this newspaperman. He wanted to publish the letters, to write a story about Donald. He said it would mean so much to so many people back home whose sons or sweethearts or husbands were prisoners, but hadn't had time to get a letter through yet. It sounded all right to me, so I let him have Donald's letters.

"About a week later, he brought them back—said he had decided not to publish them after all. I was just curious, so I asked him why not. He could have lied, but I'm glad he told me the truth. He was mad. He said that he had talked it over with Donald's Commanding Officer, and the Colonel had advised against it, for this reason: 'Suppose when Don comes back after the war he finds out Jackie has been a show girl. Suppose he doesn't want to marry this girl when the war is over. If you publish these letters, he'll pretty much have to, won't he?'

"And so the letters were not published. Listen, Donald knows I'm a show girl. He knows that; he knows everything else about me. He knows I've gone out with other men since he was shot down, and he knows why."

And now her chin was quivering like a child's; and there was such a flood of tears banked up in her eyes that she poked at them with her fist, and smudged mascara on her cheeks.

"All right, maybe Donald won't want to marry a girl like me after the war is over. Maybe he'll want to marry some woman with the label of 'lady' even if that's all she's got. He'll find plenty like that in Paris or in New York or wherever he goes when he's free again."

But suddenly, her chin went up, no quiver now, and almost fiercely, she said—as much to herself as to me:

"But if Donald wants me, Jackie the show girl, well, he'll only find one like me and he'll find me right here in London. I'll wait."

Donald's CO is a full Colonel, so I couldn't call him a damn fool; but next time I saw him, I told him the story and gave him 100-to-1 odds that Donald Schyler would come back to London at the end of the war, and maybe before, to marry his Princess. He wouldn't take the bet. He knew I had a sure thing.

Chapter 18

RAINBOW CORNER

"... if you want a good wife, you better
marry an airlines hostess ..."

THERE'S a place in the heart of London called Rainbow Corner, run by the Red Cross. You know some of the people who work there—Mrs. Harvey Gibson and Lady Cavendish—Adele Astaire to you, Delly to the GI's. Delly told me about one of the girls down there, named Jo Sippy. No kidding. Sounds like a song. And so does she. (See Illus. 108.)

I'd always heard that if you want to get a good wife, go find an airlines hostess who isn't already engaged. Jo Sippy used to be an airlines hostess. And so, not that I'm hunting a wife, but because I've got some friends who might be, I dug up the story of Jo Sippy.

Typical American girl, typical of the best. Comes from St. Louis, went to a girl's school in Pennsylvania, then to Iowa State University, then to Washington University in St. Louis. When she was a senior in college, she took flying lessons. Has 25 hours solo time—and 1,200 hours time as a hostess on an airliner. She likes planes, and the men who fly them. Over here, airmen of the Eighth worship her. They all say, "Geez, what a relief to find a girl who knows something about planes!"

One of her best friends was Johnny Perkins, pilot of the "Windy City Challenger." Sure, he came from Chicago. When he came over here, he was co-pilot on the "Chuck Wagon." His two best friends were the pilot and the bombardier. They finished their tour of duty and went home. Jo says:

"Johnny was very lonely after that. The four of us used to go around together in the city here, saw all the sights, took all the tours. On a furlough he had once after a rough ride, he took me down to Cornwall to spend a week-end with his great-aunt. His father is English. Johnny was a wonderful guy, so light-hearted, always laughing."

He was a wonderful guy. The "Windy City Challenger" went down, with Johnny at the controls, on his 19th mission. (See Illus. 109.)

"Nearly everybody on the station called me up and told me. They all knew we were good friends. One boy who was a part of the 'Windy's' crew called up and said he missed the ride because he'd gone that day in another ship. He said he was sorry he wasn't with Johnny, because now all his gang are gone. The boys all saw a number of parachutes open out of the 'Windy' as she went down—some said seven and some said eight and some said nine, but nobody said he saw ten. It's bad when it's like that, because you always figure that the very one you wanted to come home was Number 10. I think everybody on his station loved Johnny. They all come in and talk about him."

Jo has a picture taken of herself with Johnny; it was up at the station— Jo is loaded down with the bundles she always takes to the kids up there, and Johnny was walking along behind her, not carrying any of the bundles, laughing. Jo does a million little jobs for the bomber boys—gets their pants darned, and their socks; buys presents for their girls—after first learning all about each girl; gets dogs to be mascots, and then gets collars and brushes and medicine for the dogs. She makes and cancels dates, theatre tickets, and hotel reservations. Quite aside from the fact that she is very pretty, she is popular as hell at a bomber station:

"I go to all their dances. It's just like a fraternity dance back home, only lots more riotous."

Jo has one burning ambition, one ambition that keeps her loyal to the Fortresses—even though the food seems to be better at the Thunderbolt stations, and the orchestras are always better, too, at the fighter dances:

"More than anything I want to go along on a Fortress raid. And then I would like to go home in a Fortress, as hostess. We had a plan to try to persuade General Eaker or somebody to let the 'Windy City Challenger' go home to Chicago, like the 'Memphis Belle' did. But now I guess that won't ever happen."

Don't give up, Jo. There's a Fortress flying now with most of the name of Johnny's ship—"The Windy City Avenger."

Chapter 19

HER HEART BELONGS

"... it's nice to have a PRU pilot in love
with you—he appreciates company ..."

It's a long time since I sat down in Billy Rose's office and looked at all his elaborate plans for Jeep Shows to entertain the troops. Some of Billy's guesses about what would make soldiers laugh were pretty good. But you know and I know what they all want. They all want a girl—and you know the kind of girl they want. Any pilot I ever saw would pass up a pushover for a dinner and dance with a nice girl. But then you probably know that.

Sometimes the lucky ones find what they want and need. About the best match I've seen come out of this war is that of Tris Henderson (See Illus. 113) and "Pappy" Crandall, Photo Reconnaissance pilot. You know what the PR pilots do. They go out in stripped-down Lightnings loaded not with guns but with cameras. It's a lonely job, a challenging job, and a vitally important job.

Major "Pappy" Crandall comes from Detroit. But this isn't really his story. It belongs to Tris. Let me tell you about her. She was born into show business. You've certainly heard of her father, maybe seen him work. Dick Henderson is his name. There are three kids in the family.

Tris has a twin sister, now married to an Air Transport pilot, living in New York; and a brother Richard, 1st "leff-tennant" in the Army. Tris's full name is Theresa Claire Madelaine; her sister's bountiful name is Winifred May Mary Henderson. They were sent to a convent at four and a half, and the folks went to America, to Hollywood.

"They came back to get us after four years. Mary and I didn't know them."

They lived back in Hollywood until Papa Dick lost all his dough in a real estate deal; then they came home to England. The sisters went to dramatic school and to another convent in Belgium. They finally got a job with Jack Hylton's orchestra, and toured Germany and southern France in 1937–39. In 1941, the brother and two sisters did a trio act in London. Then marriage got Mary, the Army got Richard, and Tris got a job in a show—*Strike a New Note*. Tops the list of all the shows the Eighth Air Force wants to see on leave.

Tris met Pappy when she was doing a show down at her brother's training camp. Pappy was in the RCAF then, Pilot Officer James Crandall. There she met two more Americans—Tex Roberts and "Dago" Stephen Frell. That's where a typical story begins:

Tex got off to a fast start; he went into a Spitfire squadron near London, and spent many a leave leaning on the stage door, waiting for Tris to finish her show. When Tex was stuck at his station, Dago would find it out and sneak in for a date. Pappy was slow to move in; not until about a month before the other two shoved off for Africa did he muster the nerve to ask Tris for a date. He got it.

And then, two weeks later, all three called on Tris at once, same evening, same time. There was a heavy strain on friendship for a moment. Laughter was the cure—they all went out on the town together. So night after night, it became the same. Then Tex and Dago transferred to the Eighth Air Force, and were part of the slice of the Eighth that got sent to Africa. Tex wrote and cabled Tris at least once a week.

"And I heard from Dago, too, until he was shot down on a patrol flight, near Gibraltar. That was in November, 1942. Just after that, I got the last letter from Tex. Don't know what happened to him. Suppose he went down, too, or he would have gone on writing."

There was only Pappy. You see them together now and you know that's how it ought to be. But you know how seldom things like that work out the way they should.

This war grinds out an inexorable elimination that has no apparent rhyme or reason. Sudden death scrambles lives and shatters dreams and faith and often even hope. An awful lot of boys get so tired that they cannot believe in God or country or in any of the lofty things for which men are supposed to fight. A few lucky ones find a girl they can believe in, and on that girl, more than on the speeches of Presidents and Prime Ministers, they build all their war aims.

Do these ideas sound phony? It's tough to put them into words. Billy Rose was only one who tried to write a song that would be *the* song of this war. He couldn't do it. The whole damn song-writing industry couldn't do it. And you'll find the music long before you'll find the words.

But you might find the words for a great war song already written. Just listen in some night when a Photo Recon pilot comes home from a long and lonely mission deep into Germany, when the first thing he does is to get to a telephone and ask Trunks to get him through to London, like Pappy calling Tris, for instance. There's a saying that "girls have brought more airplanes home than gasoline or prayers."

Chapter 20

THUNDERBOLT LOVE STORY

"...I wasn't like other wives...I didn't mind
his flying...I really wanted him to fly..."

I ONCE thought that the only movie that could "explain" aviation would be documentary, or perhaps a job like Disney did on *Victory Through Air Power.* My mistake. The job can be done, as most other jobs can be, with a love story. As a matter of fact, this particular love story. The names are false, to protect the boy, but the rest of this story is fact:

Henri "Hank" Derain was a child of the last war: father, American; mother, titled French. Jenny Cathrop was a child of the last war: father, Canadian; mother, English. (See Illus. 111 and 112.)

Henri's mother died when he was three—Granny raised Henri and his sister. His father went back to America, became a famous architect, and sometimes visited his children in Paris. Jenny's mother was a nurse in the last war—that's how she met the man she married, a Canadian, badly wounded and still lame. They have lived in the country near London ever since.

After Henri became twenty-one, he had the right to choose his citizenship. French, like his mother, or American, like his father, which would he be? France had fallen; Vichy was turning the stomach of millions of Frenchmen— including Henri. He chose to be an American.

On the day France knuckled under to the Nazis, Henri was in the air, fighting Germans. He shot down a Hun, and was himself shot down. He bailed out, and walked home toward his station. Half way there, he learned that France was out of the war. He went to a field where Poles were stationed; borrowed a Polish uniform, and escaped to England with them. In England, he joined the Free French Air Force.

Jenny was telling me his story:

"It was very difficult in those days. We did not know whom to believe, if they were French. But finally, at Dakar, the good and the bad were sorted out. Those who went with De Gaulle to Dakar were told that, when they came back, they could have planes and fly with the RAF in Free French Squadrons. Henri went to Dakar. For a time he flew from the 'Ark Royal.' But when he came back, he still could not fly because they did not give the French any planes. That was when I met him. I was working at the Canadian Legion Club."

They were married soon after that. Their marriage was two years old when I met Jenny. It was then so deep and strong that they must have begun to love each other from the instant they met. In two years, they had built up a whole lifetime of understanding.

"Henri transferred to the RAF, and right after that we got married. It was such fun, moving from station to station with him. They move you around a lot in the RAF. And then, because he was an American by choice, he transferred into the Eagle Squadrons.

"Again the change was wonderful. It is so good, I think, for people when they are first married to have to make new friends together all the time. The Americans were wonderful to us. They called him Hank and they called me Jenny. My name is Jeannette. And then Henri transferred to your Eighth Air Force with all the other Eagles, and we moved into a little farm house on the edge of the field from which he flew.

"Henri lived at home. There was a phone by his bed, and actually he slept nearer to his plane than if he had been in the barracks. He would have breakfast with me and lunch at the mess—because the food was better there—and then dinner at home at night. We didn't ask the boys over often, because when you do, you like to have food and something to drink for them, and we had neither.

"Henri always talked to me about flying. He explained everything, when he was mad and when he was afraid and when he was excited, and how he felt when he was making a kill. He told me everything.

"I've always been keen about flying. When the war is over I shall learn to fly myself. I've got one brother back from training in Canada. He's a navigator, flunked his pilot's training. Henri and I told him that we are ashamed of him. And now my younger brother is going into the RAF. He will be a pilot or I shall give him no peace."

Jenny doesn't have many friends in London, and of course Henri had none; Jenny has always lived in the country and Henri had always lived in France:

"The first time I ever saw St. Paul's was when Henri and I were driving from the hotel to the Liverpool Street Station. Always before it had been hidden by buildings, but the blitz opened up the whole place so you could see it from the street we took to the station. I was disappointed. It looked much smaller than I had expected. Like Niagara Falls did when I saw it for the first time.

"I went to New York and Canada once. New York is a wonderful and exciting place. Henri and I had talked a great deal about what he would do when the war is over. Like all titled young Frenchmen who are without great wealth, Henri is not equipped to earn a living. America would startle Henri. With them, if they do not have money, they just go into the Army or the Air Forces. What we hope he can do is to get into the diplomatic service for America somewhere, perhaps as an assistant military attaché or something, very little at first."

I suppose these two talked together and planned together and dreamed together more than any pair I ever knew of. They both loved one thing as much as they loved each other: airplanes. Henri's friends were nuts about Jenny, because they could talk shop around her, and either she kept her mouth shut or, when she did speak, it was to ask an intelligent question.

"You see, I really had a feeling about planes. I loved the sound and smell and feel and look of them. And the boys knew that, and so I sort of belonged."

Henri talked more than just generalities of flying to Jenny; they talked about what he would do if he had to bail out:

"He always said he would never crash-land—he would always bail out. It was so easy. He had it all figured out: if he had to come down over water, he would bring his plane down as far as he could under control, and then he would stand right on the edge of the cockpit and just before his plane hit, he would dive out—he always said that was how they did it in the French Air Force.

"And we often talked about what he would do if he came down in France. He knew every inch of France so well, we always figured it would not take him long to get out. He said he would be out in a month for sure. And he gave me three jobs that I was to do while he was away:

"I was to finish reading a book on psychology that he had studied in school in France. I was to learn to speak French so I could go and live in France at least some of each year when the war is over. And I was to keep up my physical training exercises so that I would not get fat and lose my figure while he was away.

"That was quite a lot to keep me busy, and now I shall have to do all these things, because, you see, Henri was shot down in France.

"I've talked to boys who saw it happen, but it was so far down it was hard for them to see everything. He went down after one Jerry, and then another got on his tail. A Thunderbolt can outdive anything, and Henri seemed to be pulling away as they went down over the Seine, when the flak opened up and seemed to hit both Henri and the Jerry. They both seemed to dive into the Seine. I don't know what to believe.

"Somehow, though we always talked about his being shot down, we never really thought he might be killed. Of course, we did decide not to have any children until after the war, so I suppose you can say that we did worry a little about the thought that he might not live through the war. But we never talked about it.

"I always knew his plane by the identification letter on the side—T for Tommy was his. I would watch it take off, and then I would wait for it to come back.

"He never telephoned, because he knew that I knew his plane, and that I would know whether or not he was back safe. But on the day that he did not come back, I was not there. I had gone into town to do the marketing that day —the buses run only twice a week. I saw them go out, but they came back while I was in town. I didn't know until the wife of one of the other pilots came over and told me. This was not the first time it had happened to one of the pilots' wives—just two weeks ago, there was another."

She was fingering a strange, silver identification bracelet with a saw tooth-edged plaque. I asked her what it was.

"This? It's Henri's identification, his dog tag, you call it, from the French Air Force. Naturally he does not wear it now—the Nazis do not take kindly to Frenchmen who have left France to join the RAF and the Eighth Air Force.

"You see how this is in half? One half of the Frenchman's identification marker stays with him when he is dead; the other half is broken off here along this saw tooth edge, and nailed to his coffin. I don't know what became of the coffin-half of Henri's tag.

"This war is certainly all scrambled up. Henri's uncle was a famous fighter pilot in the French Air Force, a professional soldier. He was killed in Syria, fighting against the British."

I asked Jenny what she will do now. Her lips trembled a little for the first time.

"I am going back to the station and work there with the Red Cross. Why not? It is the place he loved, the last place that we loved and lived together. His friends, I know, will for a long time remind me of Henri by the silence that they will keep about even the mention of his name, and then slowly they will talk about their old friend Hank as if he had gone away for a week's furlough, and then everything will be all right again.

"I will be very happy there. I can hear the thunder of the planes going out in the morning, the going out and the coming back—that is a beautiful thing. And besides, Henri's ground crew is starting a pool on when he will get back to England. So far, nobody will buy a chance that says it will take him more than a month to get across the Channel. The ground crew of his plane are willing to bet he'll steal a German plane and come flying home in it. Until he does come back, my life is there—where he left it."

Chapter 21

FIRST OF OUR FIRST

"...even Noel Coward could not
find the words..."

YOU'VE heard of the Eagles, the American kids who formed three squadrons in the RAF and then transferred back to the Eighth U.S. Air Force. They flew Spitfires in the RAF and kept them for a while when they shifted from blue to khaki. They loved those Spits, as one of them put it, "with the kind of love that makes babies." It's possible to feel that way about a Spitfire.

Those were the kids who were given the big-bellied Thunderbolts to take into battle. There was damn near mutiny. Orders had to be issued instructing the Eagle pilots to keep their opinions about the plane to themselves. "Don't talk to newspapermen!" It was like that for almost a month. And perhaps the most violent critic was a kid named Avey Clark—nephew of Tommy Hitchcock. He used cuss words that seamen reserve for U-boats, to describe the Thunderbolt. That was in the beginning.

Then one evening, I ran into Avey. He was with a girl, at a London night club, obviously celebrating something, with a big, almost drunken grin on his face, but he wasn't drinking. I sat down beside him. What goes, Avey? The story tumbled out:

"It happened today—first crack at the Jerries—short, but we found out— hell, I could outdive him and turn inside him. Couldn't climb with him, but it's okay because I can do all I need to do. Did I get one? Those fifties just ate him up. I saw it in the film."

And that's what happened to all the Eagles. You know how it is: a man will be faithful to a plane, until he finds another that can kill for him, and then his love learns another song.

Now the Eagles have still another plane—you know the one, even better than the Thunderbolt. It had to pass the Eagles' test, too. There is no better test than "Do the Eagles like it?"

A lot of people have tried to tell the story of the Eaglés since Quentin Reynolds first struck gold with them. Their story can never be "told out," because it's still going on. Let's bring it up to date:

I crossed the Eagles' trail first in 1940, when Bob Scheftel got me to write some stuff in the *Mirror* about his good friends, the Sweeneys, and about an idea of theirs. The idea was the Eagles. Next time I got tangled up with their story was in January, 1941. I went up beyond the Eastern Hump of England to the Eagles' nest. They weren't on combat yet; almost, but not quite. Bill Taylor was their acting CO then; their actual CO was Walter Churchill, an Englishman. I spent that first night in his rooms. I prowled around and looked at the things I could see without breaking locks, to find out what I could about this Englishman who was worshipped so by these typical American boys.

I talked to many of the Eagles, sopped up their stories, and then began to ask the question to which I have not yet found a universal answer:

"Why did you go to war before your country did?"

There were perhaps four times as many answers as there were Eagles. I like this one best: it is the story of Don Willis, from Fort Leavenworth, Kansas, now a Captain in the Eighth Air Force, married to an English girl.

One evening, out in Chicago, he heard a guy playing a violin in a night club, and the music the guy made with his fiddle was beautiful. Don talked and drank with this man late into the evening, and early into the morning. The man came from Finland, and Finland was at war with Russia then. Don decided—he wasn't drunk—that any country that could produce men who could make music like his new friend, such a country must be a helluva fine country. So he went to Finland and joined her air force and fought wing to wing with the Finns. Just like that. It wasn't idealism. He'll call you an idiot or a liar if you say it was. It was just that "this guy with the fiddle made such goddamn beautiful music and he was a Finn."

He fought with the Finns until Germany muscled in on the war with Russia. Then Don decided that something was wrong, so he joined the Norwegian Air Force. He doesn't know why he did, but he did. Norway fell, and he came to England and joined the RAF. And then, along with all the others, he swapped the blue for the khaki of the Eighth.

I went up to the ceremony at their station, when RAF Air Marshal Leigh

Mallory of Fighter Command gave each of the transfers a special silver emblem to be worn on the right—it meant they had fought with the RAF before America got into the ring. Run through the list of the names of the boys who got those medallions that day—you'll see how the story of "the first of our first" was rooted in every corner of America:

Lt. Col. Peterson, Santaquin, Utah. (See Illus. 115.)
Maj. Oscar Cohen, Carbondale, Illinois. (See Illus. 115.)
Maj. Gus Daymond, Burbank, California.
Capt. Hollander, from Hawaii.
Capt. Halsey, Chickasha, Oklahoma.
Capt. Stepp, Ketchikan, Alaska.

Just in the first six of the names on the list that day, you get a pretty wide coverage of America. But go on with the list.

Capt. McMinn, Salt Lake City, Utah.
Capt. Andrews, Costa Mesa, California.
Capt. Fetrow, Upton, California.
Capt. Dufour, Ford, Essex, England.

Dufour had a good story, too. He began fighting with the British on the ground, wound up in the RAF. But there are many more.

Capt. Don Gentile, Piqua, Ohio.
1st Lt. Smith, Molokoff, Texas.

By now you know all about Gentile. And how in the hell did a town in Texas ever get named Molokoff? I'm going to look that up when I get home.

Lt. C. V. Padgett, Bethesda, Maryland.
Lt. R. L. Priser, Troy, New York.
Lt. J. A. Clark, Long Island, New York.

This is Avey Clark; he's got a kid brother coming through the RAF kindergarten now. I've forgotten why Avey couldn't get into our own Air Forces at first—maybe it was because he hadn't been to college, maybe because he was just too damn tall.

Lt. E. L. Miller, Oakland, California.
Lt. D. A. Young, Buffalo, Kansas.
Lt. F. R. Boyles, Mt. Vernon, New York.
Lt. A. H. Hopson, Dallas, Texas.

Do you remember that line in the Canadian Air Force picture, the one Warners made with Jimmy Cagney, where Billy Bishop is talking to a boy who has just won his wings. "So you are from Texas—fine, that's one of Canada's biggest provinces"? A lot of Texans got in early.

Lt. J. A. Wilkinson, Swarthmore, Pennsylvania.

Lt. W. T. O'Regan, Los Angeles, California.

Lt. J. E. Lutz, Fulton, Missouri.

Lt. H. D. Hively, Athens, Ohio.

Lt. D. E. Booth, New York City.

You don't get many boys from New York City doing things like joining the Eagles. Don't tell me there's something about living in New York City that shakes all the adventure out of a boy.

Lt. L. R. Cover, San Carlos, California.

Lt. G. J. Smart, Sedan, Kansas.

Lt. W. C. Slade, Draham, Oklahoma.

Lt. D. K. Willis, Fort Leavenworth, Kansas.

This is the boy who went to war because he heard a fellow make beautiful music on a violin.

Lt. George Carpenter, Oil City, Pennsvlvania.

2nd Lt. S. H. Pissanos, New York City.

Steve Pissanos talks American with a Greek accent straight out of a musical comedy. He is always good for at least one laugh at a briefing.

2nd Lt. R. G. Care, Angola, Indiana.

2nd Lt. H. L. Mills, Leonia, New York.

2nd Lt. E. D. Beattie, Albany, Georgia.

2nd Lt. D. D. Nee, Long Beach, California.

2nd Lt. H. L. Ayres, Indianapolis, Indiana.

2nd Lt. A. W. Chatterley—can't remember where
    he came from.

2nd Lt. R. A. Boock—same with him.

2nd Lt. R. C. Braley, Lemoore, California.

2nd Lt. K. D. Peterson, Mesa, Arizona.

2nd Lt. P. M. Ellington, Tulsa, Oklahoma.

2nd Lt. A. J. Stephenson, Los Angeles, California.

2nd Lt. K. G. Smith, Boise, Idaho.

2nd Lt. F. J. Smolinsky, New York City.

There's a boy whose roots are on the continent of Europe, somewhere; but I'll bet you couldn't pick him out of a crowd of Eagles.

2nd Lt. V. A. Boehle, Indianapolis, Indiana.

There was another boy on the list from Indianapolis—Ayres. It frequently happened like that. Two friends, neither could decide to go separately; but together, it was easy.

2nd Lt. F. M. Fink, Philadelphia, Pennsylvania.
2nd Lt. F. J. France, Oklahoma City, Oklahoma.
2nd Lt. J. L. Bennett, Tucumcari, New Mexico.
2nd Lt. D. H. Ross, Huntington Park, California.
2nd Lt. V. R. Castle, Bluffs, Illinois.

My kid brother knew one of the first of the Eagles to get killed—Phil Lechrone. He came from Salem, Illinois—Douglas was working in the oil fields out there.

2nd Lt. R. K. Merritt, Rockland, Maine.

Now these boys were not all in the Eagles, nor were they all the boys who did make up the Eagles. They were just the ones who had been in the RAF, and were now in the Eighth Air Force Group that did hold most of the Eagle transfers.

The present commanding officer of that Group is perhaps the most famous of the Eagles—Lt. Col. Chesley G. Peterson, 23 years old, from an alfalfa farm in Utah. (See Illus. 114.)

Quent Reynolds made some of the Eagles who died more famous than Pete —boys like Anderson and Fenlaw and Flynn and Kolendorski and Mays and McGerty and Olson and Tobin—"Red" Tobin. They had more of what you call "color" than Pete.

Don't know when Pete started being serious; must have been early. He's a student of air combat, just as some people are students of history and mathematics and physics and chemistry and astronomy. Pete is a student of killing at 400 miles per hour. More than a student, he's a Ph.D. But he still studies.

Pete saw his first Jerry killed at his first training field after he came to England. Squadron Leader and later Group Captain Walter Churchill was the "professor." The Americans had just arrived at the field. It was near Liverpool. A Heinkel roared over and dropped its bombs one day. Churchill went up and knocked it down, almost on the field.

"That's a damn fine way to teach," says Pete. He's done a lot of the same kind of teaching. But first, he learned a lot from others. For instance, from Churchill, he learned many of the things a leader must know:

"Study tactics. Never stop studying, because they always change. You hear a lot about the Germans making frontal attacks on our Flying Fortresses today, but that is not new with the Germans. Churchill knocked down the first bomber with a frontal attack, a Jerry, in 1940. It is important for a leader to do first what he recommends that others do."

I suppose the first time this stringy blond boy ever studied flying was about fifteen years ago, when a barnstorming outfit with a ramshackle plane tried to rent his father's alfalfa field—for selling short hops to the local yokels in Utah at $2.50 a ride. Young Peterson prodded his Pop into this barter: "You fellers can use my alfalfer field for your flying machine, but you are gonna have to pay me rent the way I say. You're gonna have to take this boy of mine for a ride until he says we been paid off."

That was the first of many hours in the air for Pete. You probably know the middle part of his story: Two years in Brigham Young University, quit to go into the Air Forces, lied about his age by two years and was nailed for it. To spare him more serious charges, a kind officer bounced him out with this verdict—"lack of inherent flying ability." Twice he tried to get around our neutrality laws to join the Canadians; and then, the way a busted jockey would drift to a job on a stud farm, Pete took a job in the Douglas plants out in California.

And finally—because his story had to end this way—along with a bunch of other American boys who could get into the air no other way, he sailed for England on August 13, 1940. Their passage was paid by a man named Col. Charles Sweeney. These were the first of the Eagles.

Actually, they weren't the first Americans in the RAF. There is a plaque in St. Paul's Cathedral in London, and a small headstone beside an English fighter field, that commemorate the very first of our first to die in the RAF. He was Billy Fiske. (See Illus. 190.) But Fiske was not like these Eagles— though he came from Chicago, he had spent much of his time in Europe; he married a famous English beauty, the former Countess of Warwick; and most of his best friends were English boys already in the famous 601 Squadron of the RAF.

These Eagles were far more American than Fiske. They were Main Street. Take a boy like Gus Daymond—he was a make-up man in Hollywood; he made the first kill for the Eagles, when he was only nineteen. Before he finished, he destroyed 8. Pete's score was 6.

Pete and Gus were two of the Eagles' seven COs; they were the last two before all the Eagles put on the khaki of the Eighth, on September 29, 1942. There were three Eagle Squadrons; and before they transferred, in eighteen months of combat they destroyed 73½ Jerries—the half they shared with the RAF.

Of that 73½, the original Squadron killed 45 Huns. Of the boys in that Squadron, 8 were killed in action and 17 on active service, 3 are missing, and 6 are Prisoners of War.

As I told you, Pete is the CO now. He had been CO before, but in the Dieppe show, while they were still flying in the RAF, Pete got the first of his two dunkings in the Channel. He was shot down on August 19. It wasn't bad. Pete had time to take off his new boots and reluctantly throw them away, and he tossed away a pistol he always carried, but not before he emptied it on the way down, in the general direction of the Jerries. He was quickly picked up by a launch of the Air-Sea Rescue.

I'm convinced that Destiny puts the finger on some boys and marks them for survival—Pete is one of them. He was drying in the wind on the deck of that launch, sitting and talking to a Canadian who had been fished out just before him, when an FW came dusting over the waves and sprayed the deck of the launch with cannon shells. The Canadian was killed instantly. Pete was not touched.

Once more Pete was shot down, in one of the first brushes between the Thunderbolts and the Jerries. This time, he came out with two black eyes—slapping his face against the water in the fall did it. After that, he was grounded.

Pete is married. To a Hedy Lamarr type of girl with a wonderful sense of humor—Audrey Boyes, she was, from South Africa. A movie star over here. After he was grounded he was sent to U.S. Fighter Command and given a staff job that permitted him to commute to work from a London flat. But you know enough about guys who fly to know that you could never keep Pete out of a plane.

Last time I saw him he was coming through town, on the way to make a speech to some British factory workers who were making the "drop-tanks" that give our Thunderbolts the extra range. It was to be one of those pep talks the British use to boost production. Pete dreaded it. As he got into the elevator, I kidded him about the brief case he carried. "That's really the mark of a settled old man, Pete—you'll wind up a brief case brigadier if you aren't careful." Pete just laughed, and patted the worn brief case.

"You know, I've carried that ever since I came to England. Makes me look older, but I've never carried anything in it except a toothbrush. That's all that's in it now."

I suppose Pete knows the British and gets along with them better than any other American I know. They like him, and respect him. I've tried to get out of Pete an answer to my question—"Why did you come to war before our country did?" No luck. Nor is he sure why he fought for the British instead of for the Chinese, for instance, and Pete is generally pretty sure of why he does whatever he does.

The Eagles can't tell you why they came ahead of the rest of us; but none of them have ever been guilty of the crime that some of us committed when we came to England and our manner shouted: "Okay, Britain, relax—we'll win the war for you."

There has been a lot of that talk; too damn much. Noel Coward, who sometimes sticks that knife of his to the heart of a sore, wrote a piece that most of the Eagles would endorse. Perhaps you haven't read it:

LINES TO AN AMERICAN OFFICER

These lines are dedicated to a man
I met in Glasgow, an American.
He was an Army officer, not old,
In the late twenties. If the truth were told
A great deal younger than he thought he was.
I mention this ironically because,
After we'd had a drink or two, he said
Something so naïve, so foolish, that I fled.
This was December, Nineteen Forty-two.
He said: "We're here to win the war for you."

Now listen . . . I'm a Britisher.
I love America and know it well.
I know its fine tradition, much of its land
From California to Maine. I know the grand
Sweep of Colorado mountains; the sweet smell
Of lilac in Connecticut; I close my eyes
And see the glittering pageant of New York

Blazing along the evening sky; I walk
In memory, along Park Avenue, over the rise
Before Grand Central Station; then Broadway
Seared by the hard, uncompromising glare
Of Noon, the crowded sidewalks of Times Square,
So disenchanted by the light of day
With all the sky-signs dark, before the night
Brings back the magic. Or I can wait
High on a hill above the Golden Gate
To see a ship pass through. I could recite
All the States of the Union, or at least
I think I could. I've seen the Autumn flame
Along the upper Hudson. I could reclaim
So many memories. I know the East,
The West, the Middle West, the North, the wide
Flat plains of Iowa; the South in Spring,
The painted streets of Charleston echoing
Past elegance. I know with pride
The friendship of Americans, that clear, kind
Motiveless hospitality; the warm,
Always surprising, always beguiling charm
Of being made to feel at home. I find
And have found, all the times that I've returned,
This heartening friendliness. Now comes the war,
Not such a simple issue as before.

More than our patriotism is concerned
In this grim chaos. Everything we believe,
Everything we inherit, all our past,
Yesterdays, todays, tomorrows, cast
Into the holocaust. Do not deceive
Yourself. This is no opportunity
For showing off; no moment to behave
Arrogantly. Remember, all are brave
Who fight for Truth. Our hope is in Unity.
Do not destroy this hope with shallow words.
The future of the world is in our hands—

If we remain together. All the lands
That long for Freedom; all the starving herds
Of tortured Europe look to us to raise
Them from their slavery. Don't undermine
The values of our conflict with a line,
An irritating, silly, boastful phrase.

Remember, I'm a Britisher.
I know my country's faults. Its rather slow,
Superior assumptions; its aloof
Convictions in its destiny. The proof
Of its true qualities I also know—
This lies much deeper. When we stood alone,
Besieged for one lone agonizing year,
The only bulwark in our hemisphere
Defying tyranny, in this was shown
The temper of our people. Don't forget
That lonely year. It isn't lease or lend,
Or armaments, or speeches that defend
The principles of living. There's no debt
Between your land and mine except that year.

All our past errors, all our omissive sins,
Must be wiped out. This war no nation wins.
Remember that when you are over here.

Also remember that the future peace
For which we're fighting cannot be maintained
By wasting time contesting who has gained
Which victory. When all the battles cease,
Then, if we've learned by mutual endurance,
By dangers shared, by fighting side by side,
To understand each other, then we'll forge a pride,
Not in ourselves, but in our joint assurance
To the whole world, when all the carnage ends,
That men can still be free and still be friends.

All these ideas that Noel Coward with his special skill has put into words —some impatient, some almost angry, but all wise—the kids in the Eagles could never phrase.

But writing was not their way of saying what they felt. These "first of our first" just came to England in "that lonely year" and swapped themselves for a Spitfire and a chance to fight.

Even Noel Coward cannot find words tall enough to reach their story.

Chapter 22

"MOY TOVARICH"

"...That's Russian for 'My Comrade'..."

THE Boss asked me to get together all the best film we had on Eighth Air Force bombing—especially the color film on the shuttle mission to Regensburg and the briefing film for the Ploesti job. He wanted Averell Harriman to take it to Moscow with him. That was about the time when all the war commentators on the papers over here were predicting that soon RAF and Eighth Air Force bombers would start shuttling to Russia.

I collected the film, showed it to the officers who were going along with Harriman, and wondered if they were going to take with them the one man best qualified to tell the story of the Eighth to the Russians—Hub Zemke. (See Illus. 118, 119, and 124.)

Col. Hubert Zemke, commanding officer of the first Group of Thunderbolts to see action in the Eighth, is the ablest young man I have ever met. Far and away. Got to know him well in the fall when we were making an indoctrination film on the Thunderbolts for him to take back on a trip around the training units back home. I pulled his story out of him in scattered talks while we were working on the film.

"I was one of the two Americans who went out to Russia in 1941 to make delivery on about 200 P-40's that we shipped first to Britain. They weren't hot enough for the RAF, but the Russians made damn good use of them.

"We had four English kids as mechanics, and there wasn't anybody else but Allison and me to supervise the assembly of every damn one of those kits. They'd been lying around for months in England, in crates, stuck away in barns. The Russians put them together and I test-hopped each one of them. Brother, that was when I was really scared to fly. You never knew what would happen. Helluva lot of deterioration in stuff that's stored like those planes were. But we got all but one of them into the air.

"That's when I started to have real respect for the Ruskies. We always knew that the P-40 had damn bad ground loop tendencies—but they flew every one of those kites and never ground-looped one. And the mechanics—well, I always thought I knew everything about a P-40, but those grease monkeys were asking me about the carbon content in the steel of the engines. What th' hell."

Hub studied Russian on the boat going over to the North ports. His teacher was a Russian-Polish girl, whom he called a "long-haired dictionary."

"The first Russian words I saw when we got into port were painted in big red letters on the side of a long warehouse. I studied them and tried to say them to myself, and finally I figured out what they meant—'NO SMOKING.' I felt as smart as a college professor."

For the first few months they worked in the North. "We used to shiver by a fire and watch the Ruskies out in the snow, backing out runways for the planes as fast as we put them together. They had a brass band that used to play damn near all day long while the men worked. Played on old beat-up instruments—kept one hand in their pockets and played with the other one. I damn nearly fell off my stool one day when I heard the band strike up the 'Peanut Vendor.'"

After that job, Hub went on down to Moscow; he worked in the Embassy there for a while, studying all the latest military reports on the German Air Force, translating them into English for the Military Attaché at the American Embassy.

"I always spoke and read German—learned it from my parents. They weren't German—they came from Switzerland. The Swiss learn to speak every language in the hotel register."

Hub's father is a sheep rancher in Montana. Hub was raised out there, and went to the University of Montana, where he boxed and played football. He still looks like a halfback, hard and lean and young at thirty. He used to slip down to London from his station and enter the Rainbow Corner boxing matches as "Corporal Zemke."

He's certainly had a wider experience than any other young pilot of this war. After he left Moscow, he went on and served in the Military Attachés' offices in Irak, Iran, Cairo, Khartoum, and Nigeria; and of course, for a while, he was in England, working with the P-40's, trying to persuade the RAF to use them. The RAF never did. Home from his travels, he trained forty-eight

Chinese pilots in fighter tactics, teaching them with a sign language he had invented. He is quick to admire skill and courage wherever he finds it; he has a realistic admiration of the Russians, for instance: "In the factories, I have been told, the Russians shoot those who don't work, or let them starve. In the air, if a Russian runs out of ammunition, he will fly his fighter into the tail of a bomber until the fighter's prop just chews the bomber's tail off. I've been told that, and I believe it. The Russians are a damn fine people."

And his feelings about fighting are sharp and clear: "You've got to want to fight or you are no good. You don't have to want to kill—but you do have to want to fight."

He brought the first group of Thunderbolts to the Eighth, usually led them in combat, and certainly had as many combat hours as any man in his group. At thirty, he has destroyed 7 Huns, holds the British and American DFCs, the Silver Star, and the Air Medals with however many Clusters you get for about 80 missions.

In short, Zemke is a damn able man, for any job. The training you need to survive 80 missions in a Thunderbolt teaches you a lot more than just how to fly.

Before they came over here Hub's outfit trained for a while up in Connecticut; there, they got to know Walter Rompel, advertising manager of the *Mirror*. Through him, the whole damn group started reading the *Mirror*, and in it they found the comic strip that has given America a new national hero: "L'il Abner."

In "L'il Abner's" comic strip community, there is a day set aside once a year upon which any woman who catches a man can keep him as her husband. It's called "Sadie Hawkins Day." I've been away from home so long I've forgotten just what day it comes on, except that it's early in November.

Typical of the spirit of Hub's outfit was their victory goal: to shoot down 100 Germans by Sadie Hawkins Day. On the eve of the day, the score stood at 98. They went out that day, knocked down 7. Hub got Number 100.

Quite aside from the box score, I think Hub's outfit was the hottest in the Eighth while he was leading it. General Eaker was sort of partial to him, too. He told me about the first time he ever saw Hub:

"I was at Wright Field then. Mr. Henry Ford had decided that his production methods could turn out a lot of airplanes and he wanted to get one of our fighters down so his people could have a look at it. I arranged to send him a P-40. A second lieutenant reported in my office to make the delivery. He was a group engineering officer at Langley. He walked in. Typical fighter pilot, chip on his shoulder, looked you right in the eye. Not insolent. Just confident. It was Zemke."

And Zemke remembers that too: "Hell, I'll never forget it—the biggest kick in my life. Mr. Ford let me go over to Indianapolis and look at some racing cars his people were testing, and they let me drive one. You sit there with your hip pockets dragging. That's the first time I ever really felt speed. That's the first time I ever fully appreciated that speed is relative to what's near you. The next time I appreciated that was when I got a Focke-Wulf on my tail."

Like every fighter pilot, Hub tinkers with his plane to find new ways to make it faster, more maneuverable, ways to make it "special." Hub takes out all the excess weight. He even took the thick shatter-proof glass out of his windscreen. Next mission, he got a .303 bullet neatly through the thin screen; it barely missed his head. Unlike most pilots, Hub did not put back the thick glass.

You wonder what will happen to a boy like Hub after the war. He says he wants to stay in the Air Forces, because he always wants to be able to fly fast planes, and the only way he can do that is to be rich or in the Air Forces, so he figures he better keep his wings.

But at night, with his boots propped on an oil-drum stove and battered pipe in his teeth, he'll talk about his wife and show you the silver mug he bought for his baby son and tell you that after the war he's going to buy a ranch and settle down and never leave it.

U.S. industry should comb the Air Forces after this war and grab guys like Hub Zemke—he's learned far more than just the best ways to fly and kill.

He has learned the value of learning thoroughly.

He's the kind of American who will be able to explain America to China and to Russia after this war. His language is universal because it belongs to Tomorrow. He is an airman, and tomorrow is the Air Age.

Chapter 23

BOMBER'S BEST FRIEND

*"... I'd sure hate to be the pilot
of a bomber ... when somebody shoots at me,
I want to be able to shoot back ..."*

WHEN the Assistant Secretary of War for Air, Mr. Lovett, came over here, the Boss assigned me to him as an aide. His inspection trip was pretty well laid out for him by Fighter and Bomber Command, but he had a knack of seeing a lot more than most people. For instance, take the time he went to a hot fighter outfit. What he wanted to do was to talk to the pilots; talk, and listen. This Group's flying time covered a broad experience.

They trained on P-40's back home; they brought P-38's to England; and they went into combat in P-47's. Didn't give them much time to develop any prejudices against anything but the Germans—their first CO, Col. Arman Peterson (see Illus. 127 and 128), who was later shot down and killed, never called them Germans or Jerries or Huns. They were always just "those bastards."

Mr. Lovett was good with the boys. General Hunter collected every pilot who had made a kill into the projection room, where their best combat film was projected. And then Mr. Lovett got up, hands in pockets, very shy—talked so quietly that the kids had to sit up and sort of turn their heads to hear what he said.

"I know how some of you probably feel about people who come over here from Washington to talk to you. But I would honestly like to help where I can. Now suppose you knew that your brother, your kid brother, was a pilot back home, and coming over here. What things would you want us to do to the Thunderbolt back home before your brother had to fight in it against the Focke-Wulfs?"

158

That was a good approach, and it thawed out the boys. But when they aired their gripes, at first they talked as if Mr. Lovett were only a politician, as if he had flown as a mere passenger on the airlines between New York and Washington. These boys didn't know, of course, that the shy man in the brown suit was a helluva pilot in the last war, that he had bombed some of the targets the Forts were hitting now when he flew with the first Naval Unit from fields in France, where Nazi fighters were based today—that as one of the best educated men in America, he had fought and won a long crusade to knock down the bars that made a boy have two years in college before he could get into the Air Corps.

But the kids over here are keen as foxes, and so, as Mr. Lovett skillfully juggled technical terms like "zoom climb" and "flash boost," as he discussed with broad knowledge subjects like the vision from a Thunderbolt's canopy as compared with that of the FW, slowly, the boys caught on: this guy knows his business. And they spilled the works, because they knew that here was a man who understood, and wanted to help, and had the authority to move the immovable.

Don't get the idea that all their talk was complaint. Col. Peterson's conclusion was typical:

"Sir, we don't ask that they give us a 500 m.p.h. fighter that can carry anti-aircraft guns and outmaneuver a Spit at any altitude. Maybe our sons will get such a plane for the next war. All we want is a few little changes in the planes we've got now, and then, *plenty* of those planes."

I suppose you can say of any fighter or bomber group, "They are remarkable boys." But this outfit was more than that. Like any outfit, it had its "stars," and they got the kills. But you felt somehow that, more than any other group, this one fought as a team. Maybe it was because they had had three different kinds of fighting planes since they won their wings. Facing a new problem together once knits co-operation; facing a new plane three times forges and tempers a sharp-edged weapon.

Take a boy like Major Gene Roberts, twenty-five, squadron commander. The time the Eighth Air Force made its deepest penetration into Polish and East Prussian targets, Roberts was the leading ace, with eight Jerries to his credit.

He looks exactly like what he would have been if the war hadn't swept him out of his competent but colorless niche—an electrical engineer. His background and education was the routine kind that produces such a multitude of very different Americans. Born in Spokane, he graduated from Gonzaga University. (See Illus. 130.)

He married a girl from Caspar, Wyoming—"she was the secretary to the Major who was CO of the base where we trained in California."

He flies a Thunderbolt over here, and though it looks exactly like every other P-47, it's different: first, because of the way Maj. Roberts flies it; second, because of the crew chief, T/Sgt. Negely Sapper, from Noblesville, Indiana; third, because of the assistant crew chief, Sgt. Jim Darrall, from Springfield, Pennsylvania; and last, because of Sgt. Russ Brooks, Gooding, Idaho, armament specialist.

These GIs gave the Thunderbolt "Spokane Chief" the magic extra performance that a ground crew can give to a plane, just the way grooms can give extra speed to a thoroughbred.

The day Roberts broke a tie to go into the lead as top ace of the Eighth, he bagged two Jerries. That was a good day for the Thunderbolts—they bagged 21 for the loss of 2. It was on the big Münster raid, October 10.

Look how the whole country shared the celebration for that day's work. The victors came from eleven different states:

Capt. Walter Beckham, from DeFuniak Springs, Florida, got 3 to raise his total to 6—that made him an ace.

Lt. Glen Schlitz, North Camden, Ohio, scored one kill to make his total 5. He was the kid who went on 35 missions and never saw combat; then, on his 36th, he knocked down 3 in one day.

Lt. Robert Johnson, from Lawton, Oklahoma, reached 5 and became an ace that day, too. Since then he has become one of America's leading aces. (See Illus. 119.)

Capt. Gerry John, from Owenton, Kentucky, killed a pair to raise his score to 7.

Lt. C. W. Silsby, from Dothan, Alabama, got two, and Lt. Will Hurst, from Homer, Illinois, bagged one alone, and shared a second kill with Lt. Bill Tanner, Canastota, New York.

Others who made singles on that mission to Münster were: Lt. Phil Larson, Quincy, Illinois; Major Dave Schilling, Detroit, Michigan; Lt. Boy Taylor, Ontario, California; Lt. Jim Jones, Columbia, Louisiana; Lt. Tony Carcione, Bethlehem, Pennsylvania; Lt. Johnny Evans, Edmond, Oklahoma; and Capt. Wally Cook, from Cincinnati.

You'd like to spend a week just talking to those kids, one at a time; but that's impossible. Sometimes, though, you can find one boy in whose story you will find the esentials of all the stories of all the aces. Such a boy is Charley London, Captain, the first ace of the Eighth, with 6 to his credit when I talked to him. (See Illus. 131.)

Charley London looks like the kind of a boy an artist would pick to pose for a recruiting poster for the Air Forces. He comes from Long Beach, California —or at least, that's where he lives when he's at home now. He was born in Oklahoma City.

"My dad was a shoe salesman for a wholesale outfit. We just sort of drifted out to California along about 1925.

"I'm twenty-five—got a brother twenty-eight. He used to fly for commercial airlines—he's in Air Transport now. He's gonna have it on me when he gets out after the war. Gonna have a lot of time in on the big boys, and all I'll know is fighter planes."

In this war Charley London is happy to be the pilot of a Thunderbolt: "Hell, with a fighter, you can shoot back at whoever is shootin' at you. I mean you get the kick out of it, personally. But in a bomber, all the pilot can do is chauffeur his plane and hope the gunners will handle the shootin'. No fun."

Charley grew up in Long Beach; got used to craning his neck to watch planes overhead. He was a good swimmer, and in football he was a blocking back. That's sort of the way the Thunderbolts work with the Fortresses now. "We run interference for them through the German fighters that try to tackle them."

He went into the Air Forces in 1940. For Americans, flying was only remotely connected with fighting in those days; Charley had never even talked to anybody who had crossed bullets with an enemy plane. Charley always wanted to be in fighter planes. He thinks that most boys do when they first get their wings—"Those bombers are too doggone big to feel like you're flying."

That's why all the Fortress pilots love to fly the little Piper Cubs you find around the bomber stations.

Charley was at March Field in California when the Japs hit Pearl Harbor; a bunch of the kids were sitting around the lounge when somebody ran in and yelled: "Hey, the Japs just bombed us!"

Charley remembers very clearly that nobody believed him, thought it was a joke; nobody believed it could happen. And then the news came in over the radio. "Hell broke loose around there. All military personnel was ordered to return to the post. We started dispersing the aircraft and hunting for ammunition. We were flying P-38's then, and we just couldn't find any ammunition anywhere. Somehow, never thought we'd need it quick.

"And then we started flying patrol every day. There were blackouts everywhere. It was war, all right."

But it was a long time before they really got into it; hysteria died, boredom set in. A pilot came back from Java and talked to the boys—he told them how Americans in about 18 P-40's were fighting about 100 Zeros day after day—"Zekes," he called them. That was pretty exciting, and it made all the kids who hadn't already wanted a crack at the Japs, start wanting one.

There is an undeniable difference between the way American kids feel about the Japs and the Germans.

Somehow, the Air Force feels it most deeply. In the first place, the Japs hit Pearl Harbor, by air; and only by air have we been able to strike directly at Japan. Every airman knows and grits his teeth at the memory of what the Japs did to some of the airmen captured on the Tokyo job. And every airman now knows the story of the Australian pilot who was beheaded by a Jap Samurai sword. Even here in England, you would see knots of Eighth Air Force combat crews reading that story in the *Stars and Stripes*. First they would read, and then there would be the same sudden explosion of wrath in every group: "Why, those goddamn lousy sons of bitches. Just wait—just wait—we'll stuff every goddamn one of them head first into a Fortress prop, we'll hang 'em from the wings, we'll—"

There are some vivid plans for dealing with the Japs when the Eighth moves to China bases after the Jerries cry, "Kamerad!"

It's interesting reading the results of polls on American opinion about the Japs and Germans. There was one that got a wide play over here, run by Denver University: It showed that sixty-two per cent of the American people believe that the Japs will always want war; only twenty-two per cent hold the same stern view about the German people. And I'm afraid you'd find the same soft view toward the Germans even over here in England. No wonder, then, that kids like Charley London say, "All of us wanted to get out to Australia to fight the Japs. It wasn't a question of not wanting to fight the Germans because it's tougher. It was just that we really hated the Japs. It was personal."

And then a couple of RAF Wing Commanders visited Charley's outfit, and told them about the Battle of Britain:

"Those RAF fellers were so doggone blah-zay about everything. I mean it

106. Men of the 8th (Chapter 17) meet English girls and marry them . . . sometimes—the GIs more often than the officers. Here's Sgt. John W. Kern, Newcastle, Ind., and bride, former Joyce Samson, 19, of ———, England. They met at the Samson-Hercules Dance Hall.

107. No Man's Land in the heart of London is the dreaded Piccadilly Circus. Walking through the "danger zone" are members of the famous "Shoot Luke" Liberator crew, the outfit with 7 Purple Hearts: (l. to r.) Johnny Murphy, San Diego, Cal., skipper; George Black, Monterey, Cal., co-pilot; top-turret gunner Floyd Mabee, Lafayette, N.J.; and Sgt. Bill Mercer, radio operator and gunner, Zanesville, Ohio.

108. Many were the airmen who brought their troubles to the Red Cross Rainbow Corner in Piccadilly and dumped them on the shoulders of Jo Sippy—and many left more than their troubles with her. (Chapter 18) Does that sound corny? Or like "I Left My Heart at the Stage Door Canteen"? Maybe it does, but one thing that thrives on war is sentiment.

109. The whole crew of the famous "Windy City Challenger" loved Jo Sippy, because their skipper, Johnny Perkins from Chicago, "went steady" with her for 6 months until his last trip. It was one-way . . .

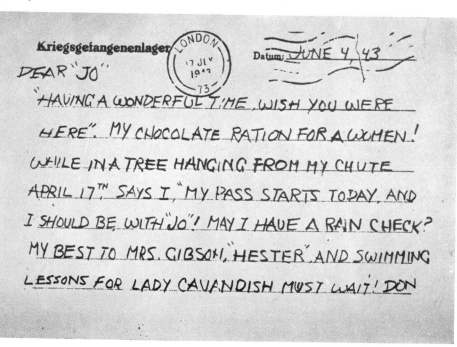

Kriegsgefangenenlager   LONDON   17 JLY 19??   73   Datum: JUNE 4, 43

DEAR "JO"

"HAVING A WONDERFUL TIME, WISH YOU WERE HERE". MY CHOCOLATE RATION FOR A WOMEN! WHILE IN A TREE HANGING FROM MY CHUTE APRIL 17TH SAYS I, "MY PASS STARTS TODAY, AND I SHOULD BE WITH "JO"! MAY I HAVE A RAIN CHECK? MY BEST TO MRS. GIBSON, "HESTER" AND SWIMMING LESSONS FOR LADY CAVANDISH MUST WAIT! DON

110. Kids kept writing to Jo Sippy—especially after they were prisoners of war. Mrs. Harvey Gibson and Lady Cavendish (Adele Astaire) had smiles like Jo's—they worked at Rainbow Corner too. (Chapter 33)

111. Love story: Once upon a time, there was a French boy who flew Thunderbolts in the 8th
Air Force. . . .

112. . . . and he was married to a beautiful Canadian girl, married for two wonderful years. Read their story in Chapter 20.

113. The eyes of GIs and of officers too, follow show-stopper Tris Henderson from the stage-door through London streets. But "that's all, brother," because her heart belongs to "Pappy" Crandall. (Chapter 19)

114. Pete lied about his age by two years to get into the U.S. Army Air Corps. Somebody found out. He could have been smeared for this, but some sympathetic officer eased Pete back into private life with this obituary: "Lack of inherent flying ability." In the Eagle Squadron, which he promptly joined, Pete shot down 6 German planes. (Chapter 21)

115. On the Dieppe job, Pete got shot down, ditched into the Channel. Little Flight "Leff-tennant" Oscar Cohen, now a Major in the 8th, fetched him home in a two-seater. After Pete transferred to the 8th, he was dunked in the drink once more.

116. Clothes don't make a man—but here clothes made an American. (Chapter 21) A young ex-Eagle Flying Officer, Koming Anderson, swapped the blue uniform of RAF for the khaki of the U.S. 8th Air Force at a mass-transfer ceremony. But on his right breast he still wore the wings and crest of the RAF, evidence that he was one of their "first of the few."

117. Not all the Eagles lived to join the 8th. Of the original Squadron (#71), 8 were killed in action, 17 were killed on active service, 3 are missing, 6 are prisoners of war. Above, a dead Eagle's belongings are packed to be shipped to next of kin.

118. "My Comrade" is what the Russian on the side of Zemke's Thunderbolt means. First time Hub's group made contact with the enemy, they got "bounced," lost 3 and got not one of the Jerries. "That was my fault, not the plane's." He's more than evened the score since then—much more. (Chapter 22)

119. Three aces out of 40. Col. Hubert Zemke, center, CO of an 8th Fighter Command Thunderbolt group that now boasts 550 kills and 40 aces. Lt. Robert S. Johnson, Lawton, Okla., left, and Capt. Walker Mahurin, Ft. Wayne, Ind., right.

120. "There's something different about a fighter pilot." You've heard that said. Is it true? We don't know. Test your own perception. On these two facing pages there are 20 airmen of the 8th. Ten of them are pilots of Thunderbolts and ten are the single crew of a Fortress. Which is which? And how did you know? Is it in the clothes they wear? Or do you see it in their faces? One clue: It's easier to make a fighter pilot smile.

121. 100% American are these 2 sky-tilted faces of crew chiefs "sweating out" the return of their Thunderbolts—Sgt. Vincent Novacek from Max, Nebr., and Sgt. Ray Harris, Walled Lake, Mich.

122. Pompetti is his name, Peter G., Flying Officer, aged 22, from Philadelphia. The 2 Jerries he just knocked down brings his total bag to 4.

123. Lightning change in a Thunderbolt. Jack Oberhansly, 24, from Spanish Fork, Utah, took off as a Captain on September 24, 1943, knocked down 2 Jerries, came home and landed, a Major.

124. "Besides the plane, there is something else important about our job," said Hub Zemke. "A good fighter pilot has got to *want* to fight." Hub used to box in college; in England, he once slipped away from his station, came to London and fought in a big boxing show under the name of "Corporal Zemke."

125. "Battle-damaged" Thunderbolt is brought home by Lt. Justus Foster, Junction City, Ky. Bet you when his crew chief saw this wreck, he exploded: "For Chrissakes, Lieutenant, what the hell have you been doing to *my* ship!"

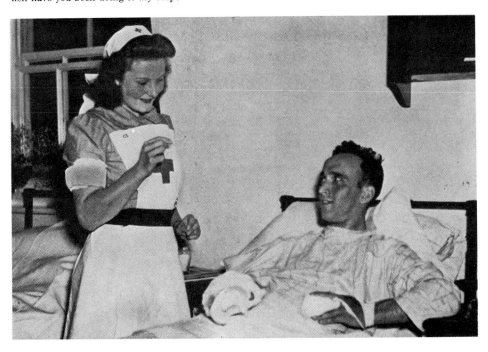

126. Short Thunderbolt story: Lt. August V. de Genaro, of Connecticut, out over enemy territory, disregarded his own safety, went to the aid of an embattled comrade, was himself attacked by a large formation of enemy fighters, shot down one, was wounded, bailed out over the Channel to avoid risk of his fighter crashing on the thickly populated coast. Result—the DSC.

was easy to see they were hot, and we all knew what they had done in the Battle of Britain, but they talked about it like it had been just a pretty rough football game. And they didn't even call the Germans Huns—they called them Jerries."

Newspaper editors thought that the front pages at home had done a good job of telling the story of the Battle of Britain; and writers like Quent Reynolds and broadcasters like Ed Murrow had helped, but somehow, they all failed to leave us with any real hot hate. It was dramatic and exciting—but not horrible enough.

It's a funny thing, about trying to plant an idea in people's minds; you never know what is going to happen. For instance, we shot a lot of color film on the operations of the Eighth Air Force bombing missions—we hoped to show the horror of flak and fighters and blazing Fortresses.

But it didn't work out—people just thought the colors of the skies were "wonderful," and the names of the Fortresses were "cute."

It's a mistake to make war anything but ugly.

"Most of us over here now realize that we've got to lick the Germans before we can get around to the Japs for dessert. Whipping Germany is business; whipping Japan is going to be fun."

Charley came over here with the P-38's; they never did get to go operational; another group did, but even that outfit never tangled with the Jerry. Then they shipped all the Lightnings down to Africa to support the Push.

In February, Charley's bunch got the Thunderbolts; nobody had even seen one before, much less flown one. They all learned the tricks of the new plane without killing anybody. They went on ops on April 1, starting first with fighter sweeps over enemy territory, trying to goad the Jerries into a "reaction."

Charley got his first Jerry the first time they went out on an escort job with the Forts, on May 14th.

"It was a quick kill. They were getting lined up on Our Big Friends—that's what we call the Forts. And I got lined up on them. They seemed sort of surprised to see me up there. That night, we all knew that we had a pretty good airplane. It wasn't anything definite, but we had a feeling we would be okay in the Thunderbolt against anything."

You know how vividly a fighter pilot remembers his kills; Tommy Hitchcock told me once that he remembered minute details of combat twenty-five years ago. Charley's memories are so clear that they are almost wired for sound:

"The Jerry I got was one of a bunch after a straggling Fort. I got lined up on him as he was cocking on the crippled bomber for a tail shot. He went in, blazing away at the Fort, and I was blazing at him, and the Fort was blazing at both of us. He went under the Fort, and I went over it and then dived down in front to get back on the Jerry's tail. I think both the Fort and the Jerry too thought I was another FW. I got on his tail as he was pulling up to come around for another crack at the Fort, and got him just as he turned. About a thirty-degree deflection shot. Must have hit the pilot—he went into an inverted spin and then down, smoking and breaking up. There were about 15 fighters attacking that crippled Fort, like they always do. We had about 4 Thunderbolts trying to protect him. No, we lost. They got the Fort—but that was the only one they got that day."

That was on an Antwerp show. Charley's next kill was on another Antwerp job—the one on which Maj. Gen. "Monk" Hunter, Fighter Command boss, rode as an observer.

"We went down to help out another wounded Fort. The Big Friend fired a flare to make us see he was in trouble. Six Jerries were lined up on him when we piled in. I got one of them and the leader of our second element got another and the rest got th' hell out of there.

"The Big Friend? He got home okay, this one. We flew along with him and he crash-landed down on the south coast of England. We came down beside him and got out of our plane and went over to see if we could help out the Fort's crew, but they were just laughin' like hell. They sure were pretty happy, and they shook us by the hand and said how much they thanked us for helping them home."

On the wall of that Thunderbolt squadron room, there hangs now a scrawled letter from the skipper of that crew of the Fortress "Tough Stuff." It's an eloquent testimony of the way the Forts feel about their Little Pals, the Thunderbolts.

I asked Charley, "Don't the Jerries ever get you on the hip? I mean, do we always have an easy time?"

"Hell, no. Take that time they ambushed us. It was over Ostend. We weren't so smart then. Our leader saw a lone FW stooging along at about 18,000 feet down below us—we were flying at 28,000 that day. It was a trap, but we jumped right into it, peeled off and went down on him, my whole flight of 12 Thunderbolts. I just told my group leader I was going down and down we went.

"The Jerry went down, too, down to about 5,000 feet, where he knew our performance isn't so hot. They always try to pull us down to their best fighting levels. When we got down there, we ran smack into a hornets' nest of about 20 just waiting for us. It was ambush.

"There wasn't any haze or any cloud. They had just been so far below us and they were so well camouflaged against the ground that we didn't see them until we were among them. That single plane had been the bait in the trap and we bit.

"I saw a box of four planes set to bounce us, and turned right down into the middle of them, firing at the right side of the box. The left side got on my tail, and I went right on down on the deck. Wasn't any use in trying to dogfight down there. I just turned my nose for home and tried to tuck my tail under my wings and blared on away."

Thunderbolts go out in groups; each group is split into squadrons, and the squadrons into flights. They try to work in fours, but never less than twos. The trailing wing-man is supposed to protect the tail of his pal until he peels off for an attack.

On June 29, big day for the Thunderbolts, Charley got a double. He piled into a line of three ME109's, got the first one, pulled up and got the second, and was about to nail the third "when doggone if the Forts didn't chew him up right under my nose."

As Charley talked, he was almost unaware that I was there; an occasional question would set him off again. He was playing with a small, black recognition model of a P-47, twisting and turning it and zooming and diving it in play combat.

The June 29th job was a Fortress slug-fest to a target just beyond Paris; it was a big day for the 47's—they got 25 Jerries, Charley's outfit got 16, Major Roberts got a triple.

"We ran into about 100 of the Jerries all over the damn sky. You know, they were sort of surprised to see us there. Didn't think we could go so deep, I reckon. I got lined up on an FW190, slick as a whistle, and doggone if an ME109 wasn't flying right alongside of me, not bothering about what I was doing at all. He musta thought I was another FW. I was scared he would get on my tail when I climbed up on the 109, but I scrunched my shoulders and looked straight ahead and prayed and gave the 109 a squirt in the tail. He broke up and went down."

Lt. Col. McNickle, the new CO, was flying on his third mission that day— Col. Anderson had been shot down and killed weeks before. McNickle was following an FW down through the formation of Forts, and both went down together. The Thunderbolt boys felt pretty bad about it until they found out that McNickle was not dead, but a prisoner of war.

Charley scored a double that day, too. "I climbed back up after the first kill and got my sights on a 109 coming out of a dive down below. I went down on him quick before he even saw me. Must have hit the cannon ammunition in his wings or something, because that Jerry didn't just burn, he flat-ol' blew up. Both wings tore all to pieces and the fuselage went up, too, like he was carrying bombs in it."

When you close in for a kill, you hold it as long as you can, giving him short bursts until he starts to burn. You can see the incendiaries crackling on him in little spurts of flame, and then pretty quick they'll eat into a gas tank or something and then the thing blows up. That's when you are supposed to climb up fast to keep the debris from smacking into your nose.

The routine of a slug-fest bomber escort job runs about like this:

The fighters are generally just about winding up the briefing when they hear the Forts taking off to form overhead. The fighters can wait to take off, because they fly straight to the rendezvous point over the enemy coast; the Forts climb to altitude in formation over England before they cross the Channel.

Then the fighters take off. Circle the field twice. Form up as a Group. The leader gives the call sign; then says, "Setting course." Then there is radio silence. Quickly now, you cross the Dutch coast. Flak opens up down below. One fellow may break radio silence: "Flak left below." The Group starts to weave a little in evasive action.

Then you'll get a few boys calling in: "Can't drop my belly tank. Homing." Then they head over Antwerp. This is a raid into the Ruhr area. There is a huge box of brown flak forming over the city. Col. Stone to Group: "Turn to port—we'll go around."

The Ground Control gets through with this message—the Forts will be about ten minutes late for the rendezvous. Every Thunderbolt pilot hears that message. Ground Control signals that "our Big Friends are being attacked."

Col. Stone makes the decision. Go on in. About forty miles deeper than planned. Very tight on gasoline. Somebody sights bombers ahead: "Big Friends at eleven o'clock low."

Col. Stone: "Wide sweep—come in behind Big Friends." And then in a few minutes: "One squadron down, one follow, one top cover."

Charley's squadron is supposed to stay top cover. Too many Jerries up high to do any good. They go down too, to get in the fight. Charley makes the decision, calls Stone: "Coming down." We were then at about 31,000 feet. Calls the Forts: "Your Friends have arrived, but why don't you bastards ever answer our call?"

In about three seconds, three guys yell: "I got one!" Not much cussing. Except once in a while you hear: "There go the bastards." Col. Stone watches the gas. He is still commander. After they start working lower as they fight, Col. Stone calls: "Everybody out." They are all split up, but everybody takes the same heading for home, and slowly the Group re-forms.

Four Thunderbolts went down in the scuffle. One of the pilots will get home. Half way across the Channel, a cripple starts calling: "May day—May day —May day." Comes from the French SOS, "M'aidez." He says that three times, then goes over to another channel, the special one for Air-Sea Rescue. And then he hits the drink.

A few 47's circle the dunked ship a few times, then head for home. Gas is low. One of the boys in Charley's squadron just barely makes the coast—he strains to miss the beach, because it's mined. He belly-lands in a field.

"When you know you have to belly-land, you keep your wheels up—a P-47 is so damn heavy you can't judge the glide. Doesn't hurt it too much to land on the belly—just put a new skin on her and a new engine and she'll fly again." The one that landed that day is flying now. They're pretty damn tough.

The day they lost their first boss, Col. Arman Peterson, was a rough one:

"We mixed with the red-nosed FW's over Flushing that day. You can go out sometimes on a sweep and the Jerry won't come up and fight you. He's saving himself for the bombers. But over Flushing, those red-nosed bastards always came up at us, and they did again this day.

"One of the boys got hit and called the Colonel to find out if he should bail out. There wasn't any answer, but we didn't think much about that—often your radio conks out like that. The guy stuck to his plane and we went on fighting until our gas got low and then we headed for home. We got 6 Jerries and saw one of our own go down that day.

"But we didn't know until we got back to base and got out of our planes that the one that went down was Col. Pete. We wanted to get back to the Bob Hope show that was going on at the base. But when we found out that the Colonel had been shot down, everybody went and crawled into a plane, and we all went out to search for him. No luck."

Gas is a constant nightmare with the Thunderbolts; time and again they'll get home with about fifteen gallons left—which is just about enough to circle the field once in case you can't get down the first time you come over.

It took Charley about 60 missions to knock down 6 Jerries. During that period, his outfit of about 100 pilots lost 12 men. Pretty happy odds.

Chapter 24

BIG LEAGUE

*"... it was more fun killing Japs, but I'd
rather knock down a German plane ..."*

THERE are a lot of hot Lightning pilots over here who got their bachelor's
degrees fighting the Japs, and then came on into the Battle of Germany to win
their master's. They aren't all in Lightnings. There are three veterans of the
Pacific Front over here in Thunderbolts now. There is Bill Cummings, for
instance. When he comes home from war, he'll need a rest for a while, because
he's battle weary and grey now, quite grey, at thirty-two. (See Illus. 132 and
134.)

Bill comes from Kansas, from Lawrence. Studied geology at the University
of Kansas—left at the end of three years to take a job as a construction engineer
with the State Highway Commission. Like so many others, he just "had to fly,"
so he went into the Air Forces in 1937. When the Japs hit Clark Field in the
Philippines, Bill was Operations Officer of the 24th Pursuit Group. You know
that story.

The Japs didn't get Bill, but malaria did; he was ordered to bed in a Manila
hospital. Then one morning, when his fever was hitting 103, the medicos came
to him and said that the Japs were closing in. "Because you are sick, you must
surrender with the rest of us."

Bill sat up, then stood up: "Hell, I'm sick, but I'm not that sick." He hauled
on his clothes and took command of the evacuation of the hospital. He super-
vised the loading of all the sick and wounded into open boats down by the
docks, and while the job was still half done, the Japs dive-bombed the area.
Bill sweated from the heat, from the fever, and from fear, and maybe that's
what cured him. He got his battered boatloads to Corregidor, and then he
joined the famous Bamboo Fleet of aircraft that fought back against the Japs,

169

carried food and medicine to stranded Yanks in scattered last-ditch stands in the jungles, and finally evacuated all they could before Corregidor fell.

Back in Australia, Bill ran an Operational Training Unit, to get new boys ready to fight the Japs. "They had damn little time in the air before they went into their first fight."

They fought in P-40's and P-39's, behind Allison engines, and their only complaint was: "There are not enough of them." There have been air battles like that on other fronts—in Greece and on Crete and at Dunkirk and in Norway. Each battle made new and glorious stories by the simple process of demanding the impossible, and getting it, from our fighting men.

Bill had been based in New Guinea. It was in places like that that his hair first started turning grey, and it first became hard for him to smile. Bill wears the DFC.

Bill made two great friends out there. One was "Speed" Hubbard. Speed and Bill are both Lieutenant-Colonels now, Bill the boss of a Thunderbolt Group over here, and Speed the air exec. (See Illus. 132 and 135.)

Speed got his name because he talks so slowly. Comes from Fort Worth, Texas, thirty-one years old, not married. He went into the Air Forces in 1938, "was at Clark Field when the Japs hit us on that first day."

"I had just landed my plane from patrol when they hit the field, right in the big goddamn middle, they hit it. They got my plane, strafed it so much it just sort of fell to pieces. We were all set to hit them the next day. Everything we had was being loaded up, but they hit us first. I guess you might say that all my action that day was just divin' for foxholes."

After that, they all joined the infantry and spent their time trying to guard a vital ferry with rifles—no more planes to be had. And after that:

"I was on Guadalcanal after I bossed a fighter squadron on New Caledonia for a while. It was pretty rough on Guadalcanal—couldn't leave a pilot up there for more than about two weeks. The Japs would shell us all night and then strafe and bomb us all day. Only way we could get any rest was to take off and fight. Never got any sleep."

They used Airacobras there, for strafing the landing barges; they left the Jap fighters and bombers to the Marines and their Grummans. For action on Guadalcanal, Speed Hubbard was awarded the Silver Star—it didn't catch up with him until he got to the States. Over here, he felt as most of the Pacific veterans do.

"Hell, I'd like to get back at the Japs. They fought dirty—didn't have any feelings about shooting a feller after he bailed out. It's gonna be different fighting over here—out there, we fought with handfuls, the way the British fought here in 1940. I guess it's different everywhere now. We got real air armies." *

The third of the Three Musketeers was "Dixie" Dix, a Major, also not married, twenty-six, Operations Officer of that Group that Bill bosses. Born in Sullivan, Indiana, Dixie worked his way through Purdue, was intercollegiate lightweight boxing champion. (See Illus. 132 and 136.)

After graduation, he worked for a year with a power company to pay off what he had borrowed for tuition; and then he went into the Air Corps. He was late getting to the Pacific Front. Got to Australia in October, 1942. Soon after, he went along with 32 other fighter pilots on the old *Langley;* destination: Java. Off Java, they were dive-bombed, and sunk. Dixie's left jaw was shattered by bomb fragments; his left arm was shredded.

Here's another case to prove that Destiny marks some airmen for survival, no matter what happens. He and one other pilot were taken with the crew into one lifeboat; the other thirty pilots got into another lifeboat, were picked up by a destroyer, and were never heard of again.

Dixie and his pal were picked up by a second destroyer, and transferred to a tanker. That tanker was bombed and sunk. They were picked up once more by the same destroyer. Two months in a hospital patched him up; and then Dixie went back to combat. Couldn't keep him down on the ground, not even by Presidential order. Dixie got his first Jap on a bomber-escort job. He was flying behind an Allison in an Airacobra.

Then Dixie got sent home—gunnery instruction. That's where he again met the two guys he knew first under fire at Port Moresby—Hubbard and Cummings. They were bound for the Big League with a Group of Thunderbolts. Dixie raised hell until he got a place in their outfit, and here they are.

They would rather kill Japs—because they are typical Americans, and typical Americans want to kill Japs. But they would rather knock down a German plane than a Jap plane—because they are typical airmen, and airmen like to beat the best. They can find the best in the Big League.

Here are three more Lightning stories—about three boys who began flying behind Allisons, and still do.

The first story is about the boss of the Lightning Group—Lt. Col. Barton Russell, from Montana. He knows Hub Zemke, who brought the first Thunder-

* Speed Hubbard was shot down over Bremen in 1944.

bolt outfit over here, and Col. Salters, boss of thé Photo Recon outfit, veteran of the China front: "It's like a college reunion. Looks like they all wind up over here." (See Illus. 133.)

Col. Russell got into the Army Air Forces by going first into the Navy— that's an entry that lots of boys have used, and the Army Air Forces were the winner. When you get a boy who works that hard for a chance to fly, you get a good pilot. He was apologetic about his war record, apologetic and yet a little belligerent:

"I've fought the Battle of America for two years—just sat on my tail out there in California and trained other guys and watched them go off to fight somewhere where I would have given a leg to go."

But finally he made it; and now he's the boss of a P-38 outfit. It is an honor and a challenge. The Lightnings were here before, you know—but they never tangled with the Jerry before they were all sent to Africa. And then, too, in those days the Forts were contemptuous of fighter escort—they were making short runs into France, their losses were low, and though there were clouds of Spits along, the Fortress boys got in the habit of saying: "Nothing can knock us down."

Since then, the Forts have learned that many things can knock them down: flak and fighters and rocket projectiles and fighters and aerial bombs and fighters and collisions and fighters. Over deep penetration targets, when they have to fly straight and level on the bombing run, the fighters pile in on them, and the Forts scarcely live up to their name. That's why Col. Russell reported:

"I've talked to a lot of these Fortress fellers, and they are sure enough glad to see us over here with the Lightnings. Guess it's about the first time I ever did see a bomber outfit glad to see fighters."

This was all before the Lightnings had been out; already, Col. Russell was dreading the "boredom of just flying along as escort and having to stick to the bombers. Hell, we want to fight."

Already he was dreaming of a time when they might be allowed to carry bombs under their own wings. You can't keep a pilot from wanting his plane to do more than it's supposed to do.

One of Col. Russell's squadron commanders is Capt. Andy Anderson. He flew Lightnings up in the Aleutians. General verdict on Andy is: "He's a hot character." He went to school with the first ace of the Eighth, Capt. Charley London.

And another one is Maj. D. B. McGovern, from Providence. He looks a little like a twenty-seven year old Wallace Beery. He went from Mitchel Field on Long Island out to Australia, and fought first at Moresby, then in New Guinea for nine months:

"It took me twenty-eight days to get out there on a boat, and thirty-two hours to get home on a plane. Boy, that taught me more about aviation than all the combat I've had."

Major Mac is a jovial guy, looks a little fat to be a pilot—but that fat hides the nerve tissue he'll need to insulate himself against the test ahead. He flew Airacobras out in the Pacific—knocked down 5 confirmed Japs. He had a lot of fun with the Cobras, finds the Lightning a lot of airplane—"A Link trainer between two P-40's."

War was very different out there. "For instance, one of our guys got shot down and what do you think happened to him? Naw, th' Japs didn't get him. An alligator goddamn near ate his arm off!"

The things that you found on the ground were different and the war itself was not the same: "Hell, this is a gentleman's war over here. But those Japs. Listen, you can say that I get an insane pleasure out of killing Japs." He said it as you might say: "Boy, I sure do get a kick out of seeing Betty Grable in a movie"—not anger, but appetite.

Major Nat Blanton was the one you'd get the most out of talking to—not about planes, maybe. He didn't have very strong opinions about planes. Col. Russell said: "Listen, I'll take the Lightning any day. The Spitfire? Not enough airplane!" (See Illus. 137.)

But somehow, Nat Blanton was more interested in other things. He saw more and remembered more. He looked as though he might have been about thirty, not at all like a fighter pilot—the kind of guy who would have been running a damn good chain of garages if the war hadn't come along. He comes from Oklahoma, drifted out to California and worked in the oilfields for a while, and then went into the Air Corps in 1940.

"When the Japs hit Nichols Field, I was on the ground. I guess that's the maddest a fighter pilot can be, to be down on the ground when bombers are knocking the hell out of his field."

Every time they would move to another field, the Japs would wait until they got all moved in, and then WHAM again. The same thing happened to the RAF when the Jerries moved into Norway. Once they got you on the run, it seemed you could never get started fighting back at them in the air.

After we were driven out of the Philippines, Nat Blanton kept on fighting.

He flew a P-40 from Java against the oncoming Japs: "Reckon I got about 130 combat hours in five weeks. The squadron I was with got 65 confirmed during the seven weeks I was there. Guess it must have been like that in the Battle of Britain—on a bigger scale, but 'bout the same kind of fighting."

A great West Point football player, Bud Sprague, was their CO—he was shot down over Bali. Most of their action was defensive—they got back a lot of the pilots that were shot down, and only lost 11 for keeps while they were there. They knocked down about 3½ Japs for the loss of every American plane. Good hunting.

The famous "Buzz" Wagner had been Nat's CO up in the Philippines. The story is that Buzz and Bud Sprague tossed a coin to see who would get the outfit that went to Java; Bud won the toss, but in the end both lost, because here were two that Destiny had crossed off. Bud got it over Bali; Buzz got it on a routine flight back in the States.

"That Java fighting was rough. I remember one scrap where we had 12 fighters up against 54 Jap bombers and 52 Jap fighters. It was always about like that, the odds. We got up every morning about 4:30, and we were airborne from three to four times before we flopped into the hay at night.

"I was shot down once out there—crashed in the water. But it wasn't so bad, because I got the sonofabitch that shot me down. He didn't swim home from his dive.

"The most planes we ever had was 31. The day we pulled out, we had just 5 fighters left. We had a field that was pretty well hidden, and we had strict orders never to return until all the Japs had left the air. We had to crash-land somewhere else if there were any Japs around.

"It was a little bit rougher on the older boys because the kids they sent us as replacements were so green that we had to fly with them before we could trust them alone. That's why a few of us got in so much time. I got me 4 confirmed in Java and 1 over Darwin. But most of the boys got more than they ever put in claims for. Hell, you couldn't help get more than 5 if you lived, there were so damn many of them to shoot at.

"The damnedest things can screw up war in the air. Take what happened to us on Java. We had a good field. Plenty of gasoline. About as many planes as we had pilots to use them, until along towards the end. We had all kinds of supplies, including ammunition. But one little thing damn near had us down to where all we could do was go up and throw rocks at the Japs.

"You know the links that hold the shells in the feeder belts? Well, they just drop out in the air when your guns fire. Like I said, we had plenty of ammunition, but it all came up in boxes without any links, and we were getting low on the links we had.

"A couple of us went over to a tinsmith on the island and took some of the links along. We asked the old guy if he could make them. He was an old Dutchman, looked like Santa Claus. He took one of the links in his hand and looked at it, then walked into his shop and talked to some other guys, and then came out, grinning, and said sure he could make the links. 'How fast can you make them, Pop?'

"And he said—very proud—that his shop could make as many as a hundred in a week. That was great. You use up a hundred in one short burst from one gun in one plane."

Toward the end of the fighting, when they had only 5 P-40's left, the fighter boys had their backs to the sea—it was 900 miles to Australia, and you can't fly that in a P-40. Not a prayer.

"We hitch-hiked a ride on a B-17. It sure was a load on that beat-up old Fort, 25 of us on board. We took off for a test-hop, but when we got up we figured we might as well go on to Australia, so we did."

Nat got a Silver Star and Cluster, a Purple Heart, and an Air Medal for what he did in the Pacific. Some caught up with him in the States; the Air Medal didn't catch him until he got here.

"One thing about fighting over here, the living is good. Dying may be quick, but it's not so bad when the living is good. That food out in Java gave me blood boils. I had seven of them under one arm. Hurt like hell. Never got 'em lanced because I was scared the doc would make me go to bed. He poked 'em open the last day we were in Java. It was a funny thing about those boils. They never hurt me when I was fighting, only when I was down on the ground. Wonder why that was?"

Chapter 25

"UGLY DUCKLINGS"

". . . it takes a long time to outgrow
a bad reputation . . ."

THIS is a story about the Marauders and the kids who fly and fight in them. The Marauder has had some rough going over here in the Big League. A lot of people had to be sold on it. (See Illus. 142–147.)

Arthur Brisbane once said: "God thought up the best advertisement—the rainbow. And he was smart enough to reserve the best space for it."

Airpower over here in Britain has sold itself in the same space. Day after day and night after night, you hear the roar of bombers and fighters over London, reminding all the men who make decisions in high places that no city is safe from air power. Great advertising.

Air power has sold itself by performance. That's the only way an individual plane, like the Marauder, can sell itself. The Marauder should have had a head start—the name of the maker has been a byword that dates back nearly to Kittyhawk. But it ran into sales resistance none the less.

The bombers Glenn Martin makes are the heroes of this story. The B-26 Martin Marauder, medium bomber, came to this front several months ago. They used them first on low-level stuff. The first job was a sweet one; no losses. Twelve of them hit a power station in Holland early in May. Then they went out once more to hit another target in Holland. But this time they got the hell knocked out of them. They just got shot down. That was all. Period. And it was period, too, for the Marauders.

There were a couple of rough jokes being told on Fortress stations about the plane: "Have you heard about the wire they sent to the Martin plant?

'You've got a fine plane, but we suggest one modification: Put four silver handles on it like a proper coffin should have.'"

Another one was aimed at the Marauder's lack of wing span. They called them the Baltimore vagrants—no visible means of support. And the most cutting crack of all was this one: "The Marauder is a beautiful piece of machinery, but it will never take the place of the airplane."

They had just about buried the Marauders when a stubborn guy named Thatcher, from Maryland, came over with a new group. They tell me he flew the first B-26 off the line. He was convinced the Marauder was a good plane for this theatre, and his was the group that first proved it.

Tactics were shifted; instead of hedge-hopping, they went out at medium altitudes, and bombed in formation like their big-brother Forts. Spits covered their raids, as they had covered the first of the Fortress jobs. The Marauders flew 4,000 sorties—that means that a total of 4,000 planes went out—on a total of 75 raids between the end of May and the end of September. The total loss was only 13—only one shot down by fighters, the rest bagged by flak. The "Ugly Duckling" had lost its label.

Main target of the Marauders was the Nazi airfields in France, the fields from which Nazi fighter planes would fly to stop an invasion. The Marauder tactics were dress rehearsal for the Big Push.

One of the boys who rides the Marauders has linked the Jap and German fronts with his story—Capt. Fred Kappeler, from Alameda, California. He's the Group Navigator for Col. Thatcher's outfit. Before he came here, he was in one of the Mitchells that followed Doolittle to Tokyo. It's tough to make Fred talk about that trip.

"What the hell—I just rode."

But sometimes the kids in the outfit will get him to tell the story, about how it all started:

"They asked for volunteers, but we didn't really have a chance to volunteer. I was out playing golf one afternoon when the order came in. Our CO didn't even ask us if we wanted to go. He just said okay for all of us, and he didn't even know what the job was. But that was fine with us. We would have been sore if he hadn't grabbed the chance. All we knew at first was that it was to be a dangerous and important job somewhere in the Pacific. Most of us that first night guessed where it was and how we would have to do the job, but we didn't have to wait long to find out the whole story. We got told the next day.

"We trained for two months, and then we went to sea, eighteen days at sea before we took off. Guess you saw it in the movies. Pretty bad day, but we had to do it when we did, or miss the chance. There were sixteen different targets, one for each plane.

"Mine was a refinery. We didn't get the one we were supposed to, but we did get another one, with 2,000 pounds of incendiaries.

"We got jumped by 5 fighters—didn't have much firepower on the Mitchell then. Just one gun in the nose and two in the turret, and in the tail we had two black broomsticks to make the Japs think we had a sting. We got 2 of the Japs that came after us and then the others turned back.

"We got over the place where we were supposed to have landed—but it was at eleven o'clock at night. So when we had only about a half hour of gas left, we all bailed out, and that's all there was to it."

It's almost impossible to get any more out of him than that. There is a saying that "every hero winds up a bore." Not this one. But on one point, I did get a rise out of him. I slyly hinted that the Ploesti raid had been a far tougher job:

"Well, maybe so—but we were in the air even longer than the fourteen hours it took the Libs to get to Ploesti and back."

He went on up into China after that job, and fought with Chennault's outfit for a while. The most B-25's we ever got in the air at one time was about 15.

And then he got serious, very serious: "You know the kind of a job I'd like to get? I'd like to get a job planning deals like Ploesti and Tokyo. The kind of jobs that just can't be done, but we figure out a way to do them.

"You know the best way to get a job done in the Air Forces? Just tell the boys it's dangerous and act like you don't think they can pull it off. That's all you got to do."

That's sort of the way the Marauders got started, too. And it must be the right way. Today they've become the foundation of the whole 9th Air Force.

Chapter 26

THE SPITS

"...bloody good sport..."

My boss on the *Mirror* used to say I was a sucker for the British. I never really denied it. I always liked to tell on myself the story I invented and attributed to Freddie Lonsdale, about how he once said: "The trouble with you, Mc-Crary, is that you look down on the English with the profoundest envy."

I don't deny that I'm a sucker for the British. Let me try to tell another story of a day spent with one of them not so long ago, one of the best of them. It begins with sound effects.

"What the bloody hell could be plainer than that, you bloody idiot! I said American Wing Headquarters. Wing!! Yes. Right. Put me through. Priority One. This is Wing Commander Johnson speaking."

His hair was straight and strong and sweaty and flopping in his face, like that of a fighter whose seconds have just slopped a sponge of ice water across his head to cool him out after a tough round. He wore the rough wool battle jacket and faded blue breeches and quarter-length black boots of an RAF fighter pilot. On his jacket were the ribbons of the DSO and the DFC and Bar. His hands were thick, but nervous; his lips thin, but strong. His eyes did not look—they punched holes through what they saw. He sat on a map-littered desk in the canvased caravan into which fed the control wires of a mobile RAF fighter station. The whole station was under canvas. This was dress rehearsal for the push across the Channel.

Johnny Johnson, twenty-seven, one-time civil engineer, veteran of the Battle of Britain, killer of 25 German planes—more over enemy territory than any other fighter pilot—was the boss of this Spitfire wing, a Canadian wing with a boss as British as a dropped-h.

Savagely, he was hammering a scrambler phone, trying to penetrate the tangle of channels to get through and talk to the Commanding Officer of a Group of American Eighth Air Force Marauders, the medium bombers that Johnny's Spits had escorted on some 30 missions in the past six weeks. He wanted to get a couple of them down for the day for "fun and games—practice attacks—get to know the plane—what she can do—"

Americans ought to get to know guys like Johnny Johnson, quite aside from the fact that they and their Spits nursed our Fortresses through their first shallow penetration missions, and now are nursing the Marauders. In the period from April 15 to July 31, 1943, RAF Spitfires flew 8,743 sorties escorting our Marauders, destroyed 123 enemy fighters, and lost 61 Spits. We ought to get to know guys like Johnny, because they are England. The best of England.

"His boys think the sun rises and sets in his hip pocket, and they're not so far wrong."

Speaking was a gangling tall blond boy, about twenty-three—looked like Paul Hartman of the screwball dancing team of the Hartmans. He looked awkward—slightly sissy—but he wore the slant-striped ribbon of the DFC. You don't get that in the RAF for being awkward and sissy. Johnny called him "The Nippler." Treated him like a kid brother:

"Why dammit, I set up the Nippler the other day for a perfect shot at an ME109, and the bloody idiot missed. Last night I set him up for a wizard shot at a bloody wonderful blonde, and the bloody idiot missed again!"

The Nippler went into the Volunteer Reserves with Johnny back when the war broke out; they learned to fly together; were on the station with the American Eagles at one time. The Nippler was shot down once in the Battle of Britain, twice over Malta—got it in the hip out there, was grounded, and now he's supposed to be on a ground job up in Scotland, but:

"I come down here with Johnny and he lets me sneak in a do now and then."

Let's study the Nippler a little more. It gives you more respect for his opinion of Johnny. We were beating through some bushes out beyond the airfield, trying to scare out pigeons or grouse or rabbits, anything to shoot at. I flushed a grey squirrel out of the bush; the Nippler legged him as he raced toward a tall tree. He walked over to where the squirrel was kicking in the dust. He stopped to pick it up; his Adam's apple did nip-ups. He straightened, took careful aim, and wasted a scarce shell to blow the squirrel's head off.

"I never could kill anything with my hands."

We walked on, and I tried to draw him further into talking; wasn't easy.

He talked about the weary weeks he ferried combat planes across Africa after he got shot up over Malta and couldn't fight any more. He talked about the dim future of civil aviation for all the kids in the RAF—conceded the Air Age to America. What about a guy like Johnny? What will he do? Any airline in America would grab such a man.

"No, I don't think Johnny will ever leave the RAF. He's got a good career there. Everybody, all the big shots say that he's the best Wing Commander in the South, and you can't top that, you know. Old Johnny has been on ops longer than anybody else, but if he doesn't watch, the big shots will ground him or the Jerries will, one or the other. He doesn't want either, but one or the other will get him. . . ."

Johnny knew that "the percentages" were after him, too. If he quit flying now and took over a station, like "Sailor" Malan did down at Biggin Hill, nobody could say he had not done his share of fighting. Since he took over this Wing last April, he had lost some 15 planes and "now we're on the last leg of a sweep for the 100th Jerry." That's hot, brother. And all over enemy territory.

Johnny has a wife. Married last October. Picture of the wedding party is on his table in the old farm house by the field where he sleeps. Johnny has had a tempting proposition dangled under his nose—"Want me to go to Canada, maybe hop down to the States for a couple of days. I never did travel outside England before the war. I'd like to, that's why I was flat out for this idea."

There was a "but": he looked out across the field where the iron mats had mashed a runway out of the turf, where brown tents and camouflaged caravans and netted planes made this whole Spitfire field look exactly like dozens of them were to look when the Tactical Air Force pushed across the Channel, the way other airmen moved into Sicily. Johnny Johnson looked at all this, and then came the "but":

"Sure, I'd like to take a trip to Canada and the States, but I don't want to get too far away. I've flown over France so bloody much, when we hop the Ditch, I'd like to be around, flying over France—*from* France——"

First time I ever heard of Johnny was last winter. I wanted to cook up a newsreel that would show how the United Nations worked together in the air—Fortresses being escorted by Spitfire pilots from England and South Africa and Holland and France and Poland and Czechoslovakia and Australia and Canada and Norway. All these airmen who never saw each other, but only saw each other's planes—all these airmen who spoke in many lan-

guages and accents on the ground, but only one language in the air. I wanted
to get pictures of Spitfires of the RAF flying with Forts of the U.S. Eighth Air
Force. The Canadians offered to co-operate, and suggested that Wing Commander Johnson come up to a Fortress Station, talk to the CO, work out the
deal.

Johnny came up; brought his flight and squadron leaders; they met the
Fortress crews, ate and drank and talked and got to know each other. The
Fortress CO said afterwards: "Jesus, why can't there be more of this!"

Johnny had a wonderful time: "Great chaps, your boys. Remember when
they couldn't hit a thing with their guns or their bombs. Ought to see them now.
We know—they clobber their targets proper."

Johnny has "clobbered" a dozen Jerries on the Fortress shows with the
guns of his Spitfire.

"I copped a couple of your .50-calibre guns up there. Actually, they gave
them to me. I wanted to try them out in my kite—wizard trajectory, your guns
get—but the Stress & Strain boys said no go—said my kite couldn't hold the
extra guns."

Johnny's Spit guns have teamed up with the Fortress .50's on some thirty
shows. Maybe more. His first was September 6, 1942, to Amiens. Once, last
spring, when Johnny's Spits were racing to cover a wounded Fort that was
being hammered by a dozen Jerries out over the Channel, they got there a
little too late—they did get two of the Jerries, but the Huns got the Fort,
sent it spinning, blazing, down into the Channel. Johnny felt the loss of that
Fort deeply; he gnawed his thin lower lip and cussed in crackling four-letter
words. And when he got back to base, he bathed and shaved and drove through
the night to find an American general and tell him how the Fortress had gone
down in flames, with the top turret firing until the Channel waters closed over
the guns.

That kind of fighting by Fortress crews makes Johnny Johnson want to
"know more about your guys."

It was late afternoon before we got word through that the Marauders
wouldn't be down for the "fun and games"; they were going out on a mission;
and Johnny's Spits of the Canadian Wing were "laid on" to give top cover
for their cousins. Instantly, there was tension. Men ducked in and out of tents.
Johnny's lips became thinner, his hair straighter, his hands thicker, his eyes
sharper—everything on the field that was strong became suddenly stronger.
Where there had been hospitality, far more than any Englishmen ever got on

a Fortress station, now there was preoccupation. Johnny stuck out his hand:

"Well, old boy, come down again, or we'll come up. Like to meet some of your popsies. Hear the Americans have all the best girls in hand. You know, I'd like to meet some of your chaps who have tangled with the Japs. Any of them over here? Like to talk to them. I'd like to have a crack at the Japs after the Jerries are done in. Bloody good sport that would be—bloody good."

The day before, the King had announced the creation of a new British holiday—"Battle of Britain Day," September 26, a day to remind the people of Britain of what Mr. Churchill once carved into granite, timeless words:

"Never in the field of human conflict has so much been owed by so many to so few."

Our debt to the Spitfires is not quite so old as Britain's, but it's deep. Many a grey-faced, blue-fingered, frozen-eyed American boy has looked back over the tattered tail of a crippled Fort at the Focke-Wulfs queueing up for the kill, and then seen the vultures scatter for home as the pilot's voice shouted into the intercom:

"The Spits! There they come! Hot damn, come-a-buzzin', cousin!"

Three weeks after I saw Johnny down at his station, I met him again in town. The Eighth Air Force was cooking up a decoration, a "gong" for him. I asked him to come up to London and bring his log book with him so we could get the right figures for the citation. We went to Claridge's for lunch—a Canadian Squadron Leader, Buck ——, DFC and Bar, was with Johnny. Buck's face was burned dark, all the part not covered by oxygen mask and goggles. As we walked down Brook Street, his running commentary on the girls we passed made them blush, and even Johnny squirmed. Inside Claridge's both looked around at the cold marble elegance of the place: "What's this?" asked Johnny. Buck whistled.

Johnny is the type of Englishman who has never been in Claridge's. We sat in a corner of the big room; he hauled out his log book; we went through a sparse record that concealed a dozen epics.

From August, 1942 to September, 1943, when they took him off ops and put him into a chairborne planning job, Johnny flew seventy-one escort jobs with the Forts and Marauders, and four supporting sweeps.

On the slug-fests he shot down for certain thirteen enemy fighters; on the supporting umbrellas he got two.*

---

* Johnny Johnson had shot down 27 planes by May 1, 1944. He had been put back on combat again, flying back over his favorite hunting grounds, the coast of France.

Doubt if that score will ever show up in the Lend-Lease accounts; it should, on the credit side for Britain.

Just the night before I had been down at a Marauder station; the CO gave me an interesting note on Anglo-American relations:

"When an RAF pilot drops in here and we take him up to the bar for a drink, we only pay for our own—drinks for the RAF are on the house. Guess that's why all the Spitfires seem to give out of gas over our field. Which is okay with us."

At lunch, Johnny and Buck talked about Topics A and B—Girls and Flying.

It's hard to get these boys talking seriously; the first job is to make them talk at all—to a "paddlefoot." But you can always hook them with this question: "What happens to you after the war?" Buck's answer was quick and typical:

"The guy who pays me the most to do the least work gets me for keeps."

But ten minutes later, he was solemn, his burned forehead was wrinkled in thought, and he was talking like this: "There's no capital in Canada, that's the trouble."

Johnny confirmed what the Nippler had told me. He wanted to stay in the RAF. "It's a good life, Tex. I've thought about going to your country. I want to go, when all you chaps get back and I know somebody there. But I don't think I could take it there. You live too fast in America."

"Johnny, you're more like an American than anybody I ever knew who was born in America—and I've never known any American with half your intensity."

"Would you say that? Really? Hmmmm, you mean I'm high-strung? Would you say that, Buck, about me?"

Buck laughed at Johnny's puzzled face: "Listen, Johnny, you're not high-strung. You're just punchy!"

And we let it go at that. Then we talked politics. Johnny ventured an idea that Arthur Brisbane once wrote a column about: "You know what would be a wonderful idea—can't you find an American to marry Princess Elizabeth?" He was serious, dead serious. We talked on about the Royal Family, about the House of Lords—and at that point, a girl sent over a note, a girl I knew, wife of an RAF pilot. The note read:

"You said you always wanted to see what a Duke looked like. Well, there is one sitting in that corner by the door."

I showed the note to Johnny and Buck—they craned their necks as hard as I craned mine to look at a Duke. He was a boy, about twenty-eight, in an officer's uniform. Sandy-haired, pale. Said Buck: "So that's a Duke."

We talked about Douglas Bader, the great RAF pilot with the two aluminum legs. Johnny was his No. 2 man, was on his wing the day he was shot down over France. He must have been a great leader. The guys in his outfit must have worshipped him.

"It wasn't so much to fly with tin legs," said Johnny. "It wasn't that he flew with tin legs, anyway. It was just that he had so damn much guts. That was it."

And we talked about "Sailor" Malan, the man who shot down thirty-two planes, most of them over England in the Battle of Britain.

"Listen, they gave Malan credit for thirty-two. I bet he shot down fifty. He was fighting in the days when he would come down, flop on his bunk for fifteen minutes' sleep while they checked his kite and got it ready, and then go up again. All day, while there was light to see, he went up and fought. He never checked his kills. Some Intelligence bloke would ask him how many he had for the day and he would say, 'Make it a couple,' and drop off to sleep as if he were slugged. But I bet he got fifty."

After lunch we went by the PX and picked up my ration of cigarettes— which Johnny took and split with Buck. And then, so long:

"If you want to get hold of me before next Sunday, just ring through to Melton Mowbray 500—that's the police station. We haven't a phone in our house. And ask for Mr. Johnson, the constable. He'll take a message. He's my father."

A constable's son. Old Beaverbrook was so right when he said: "Pilots— they are our new nobility. Not dukes or earls or lords, but pilots. Praise them and pray for their glorious survival."

Chapter 27

TED'S TRAVELING CIRCUS

". . . from Norway to Poland to Germany to France to
Italy to Rumania and back to Germany again . . ."

WENDELL WILLKIE, after he had circled the United Nations in a four-engined bomber, dedicated his book to the crew of the Liberator that showed him how air power has made all nations shrink into "one world."

The Libs of the Eighth, more than any other bomber, have helped to shrink Hitler's conquests, too.

The Fortress boys scornfully call the big-bellied Libs "pregnant cows." I saw the first Lib land in England, in the winter of 1941. Went out to a field near London, where they make Mosquitoes now. Lord Beaverbrook, then Minister of Aircraft Production, was putting on a private party for Averell Harriman, Biddle, and our Ambassador, Mr. Winant. All the types of American aircraft that we had sent to the RAF were lined up for inspection; one by one, they took off, buzzed the field, and went back to their own nests. Then we waited. I was standing with Homer Berry, then RCAF Wing Commander and now USAAF Colonel, the veteran soldier of fortune who flew me over here in the Cat. We knew that the first Lib would land in a few minutes. The RAF officers were cracking jokes about the big-bellied ship:

"Doubt if she'll be able to set down here, old boy. They tell me she takes three counties to get down in. Great cargo ship—never do as a bomber."

Skipper Berry got red in the face, turned down-wind, cussed to let off steam, then turned back into the biting gale that swept the field and waited. Five minutes later, the Lib came in, easy as a Cub. The skeptics squirmed, Berry guffawed and rubbed it in.

I got a good picture that day, stole it with a Contax from under my coat—

186

a picture of Mr. Winant fondly fiddling with the controls of the Lib. It was prophetic in a way: Two years later, this shy, deeply impressive man apologized as he asked a personal favor from the Assistant Secretary of War for Air, Robert A. Lovett, in England to inspect the Eighth Air Force:

"Bob—er—my son—that is, I've got a son, you know, and he flies. Yes, he flies a bomber. Do you suppose you could find out, I mean, would you mind finding out for me, just when he is supposed to get to England?"

Lots of Forts and lots of Libs have come to England since that first Lib landed here in 1941, and now these Libs and Forts are not Lease-Lend—they are part of the striking force of the U.S. Eighth Air Force. Their combat crews and their ground crews are Americans.

The first group of bombers that flew in formation across the Atlantic to this aerodrome of democracy were Libs. Their boss was a stocky, sandy-haired guy named Ted Timberlake. Comes from Texas, has a brother who beat him to a General's star as Bomber Commander out in the Middle East. Col. Ted is a West Pointer; his roommate for a couple of years up at the Point was Nick Cladakis, Federal Milk Administrator in New York; shrewd politician. Could have had a good civilian job in some hush-hush line, because he knew Greece. But he went back into the Air Force when we went to war. Last I saw of him he was headed for the Middle East, and last thing he told me was: "Look up Ted Timberlake. He's somewhere in England with a group of Libs. You'll meet the greatest guy in the Air Force—the greatest." (See Illus. 159.)

Five days after I got to England, I took Nick's advice. Arriving by courier about supper time at a mudhole mistakenly called a bomber field, I went into the officers' mess and asked where Col. Timberlake was. "In there." The bar had a great colored map across one wall, the home town of every man in the Group circled in red, signature beneath. A broad-backed man who looked like a cross between Spencer Tracy and Bobby Jones was downing a coke, and talking to a kid Lieutenant Colonel who looked like the winner of a high school tennis championship in California—that was Col. Ted and his Number 2 man, Kay-kay Compton. I had a letter in my pocket from General Eaker, which said something about how I was to see all the things to be seen around the station because I had come to England with a letter from General Arnold, and so on.

The letter was a wrong move, and refrigerated the thing quick. But then I mumbled something about Nick Cladakis and instantly I belonged. We ate dinner, then we sat around and talked long and seriously about bombers.

British weather had these boys on their backs, the weather and the flak and the fighters. But tonight, they were happy, almost hilarious:

"This morning we got orders—yeah, from General Eaker. Verbal. We're getting sent down to Africa. Don't know what we're going to do, but it's sunshine and dry land and eggs and orange juice—hot damn! I hope it's for a year!"

We talked another hour; they were leaving next morning. Somebody came in to report that a gunner was stricken with appendicitis. I asked Col. Ted to let me go in his place. He said: "Can you?" I got on the phone, made discreet inquiries, was flatly squelched. That was the night of December 5, 1942.

Ten weeks later, the Libs came home. I found out they were back through an Intelligence officer they swiped from one of the first Fortress Groups transplanted from the Eighth to the Twelfth Air Force—a guy cut to Timberlake's tastes: Mike Phipps, most famous as a polo player, most fondly remembered as the boy who used to do my homework in architecture ten years ago at Yale. (See Illus. 183.) I took Dave Scherman and Jim Dugan up to their new home to dig out a story on the group that was now named: "Ted's Traveling Circus." Dave and Jim found a bonanza of stories.

First raid the Circus pulled after their African adventure was the job on Vegesack, March 17, when Forts and the Libs hammered the U-boat yards, knocked down fifty-two German fighters, and for the first time really proved the case for daylight bombing. The Circus lost only one plane.

By April, the Circus had fought its way out of the stepchild role, and had earned the right to wisecrack on even terms with the Fortress boys. Col. Ted used to say: "Listen, there's nothing wrong with the Fortress. It's a damn good medium bomber, and they'll go right on doing a good job as long as there are Libs to escort them."

By April, the Circus had fought in four Air Forces: the Third in the United States, where Bill Williams first hooked a headline for Col. Ted's Libs by sinking a sub in the Caribbean—Bill was shot down over Holland on his 25th mission; the Eighth Air Force here; the Twelfth in Northwest Africa; the Ninth in the Middle East; and finally home to the Eighth.

They had flown about 290,000 miles, 35,000 on combat; they had searched the seas for subs off four continents and fifteen countries. They had knocked down thirty-nine enemy fighters for the loss of ten Libs—almost one fighter for each engine of the ten Libs lost. They had dropped 2½ million pounds of bombs, a couple of depth charges, a crate of eggs, a dozen oranges, and a dud practice bomb on enemy targets from Vegesack to Brest to St. Nazaire to Bizerte to Sfax to Naples and Palermo and back again to Wilhelmshaven. The Circus was more than mere legend or publicity. It was morale plus all-American miracle.

Don't know exactly what it was, but something had been transfused into the kids in the Circus. Maybe it came from Col. Ted; maybe it came from their chaplain, Jim Burris from Missouri, who would have given his left leg and right arm to be put on combat. Or maybe it came from crew chiefs like Charlie Chambers, from Pennsylvania, an able joe who kept his ship flying for thirty-two missions, including the African jobs, without a miss, and himself made six missions in her as a gunner. I don't know where it came from or what it was—but something about the Circus was special.

There were kids in the Circus like Capt. "Shine" Shannon, skipper of "Hot Stuff," one of the Libs that worked against the U-boats in the Bay of Biscay while all the men and machines were being pumped into North Africa for the Big Push on Italy. JU88's used to bounce the Biscay Bay patrol bombers, and, of course, most of the bombers ran for home—"nacherly," as Li'l Abner would say, because a bomber's business is not dog-fighting. But Shine's "Hot Stuff" once spotted a Jerry in the clouds, bounced it, and chased it home. After that, "Hot Stuff" was known as a P-24, not a B-24. Dave Scherman took the last picture of Shine. "Make this one for posterity," Shine said, after he finished his combat tour and got assigned to fly General Andrews home, via Iceland. You remember what happened. (See Illus. 161.)

Shine's father is the publisher of the Washington, Iowa, *Evening Journal*. He wrote an editorial about his boy that might give you an idea what kind of boys there were in the Circus, what kind of people they came from. Here it is. It reminds me of the late William Allen White's moving tribute to his daughter Mary.

"Bob was so much a part of this community that a few personal words are perhaps justified. The avalanche of friendly expressions, the sympathy, the kindnesses—all point to the fact that his old home town was deeply and sincerely interested in him. I know that his friends and neighbors share the shock and sorrow of his death, just as they seemed to share our pride in him.

"I still think of him as a little boy. That is probably a common parental experience. We don't like to see these children grow up, and we mentally resist the processes of time which bring them to manhood and womanhood. Little memory pictures of Bob's childhood days crowd in now in panoramic fashion.

The little blue middy suit he wore to school. His peculiar, springy walk. The time he disturbed the bumble-bees' nest and got stung on the leg. They are endless and precious. He had in his makeup an infinitely tender streak. I think of him as he sat on the basement steps holding in his arms a chicken which we had marked for immediate execution. He was crying at the thought and his tears were trickling down on the prospective victim. The chicken didn't taste so good at dinner that night.

"In the home, he was a constant source of entertainment. He early acquired a fine sense of humor and he often worked it to the point of exasperation. He carried that trait to school with him, and his monthly report cards sometimes made us shudder. He was so full of mischief that we knew instinctively, when devilment was afoot in the neighborhood, that Bob was in it somewhere. We scolded, of course, but secretly we were amused. One thing he dreaded above everything else—he thought that somebody might decide he was a 'sissy.' It is reasonably certain that nobody did. There is evidence that he was the despair of some of his teachers, but, in spite of it all, they seemed to like him; and to him this was more important than good grades.

"From that rather irresponsible period of his life, there emerged gradually an engaging personality, a fine character, a love of people, a kindly attitude. Little children in the neighborhood said, 'Hi, Bob,' whenever they met him on the street, thereby paying him high compliment.

"Old people liked him, too, and they pleased his parents tremendously by reporting over and over again how kind and considerate he was. This characteristic became a habit. He found joy and pleasure in kindliness. In the home, he never forgot a birthday or an occasion that might call for a small gift.

"Three hours before the tragic message of his death reached us from the War Department, there was a Mother's Day cablegram in the house, from England. He wrote constantly from his various bases in the war and we wondered how he found the time. But we knew he was simply practicing an art he had developed to a high degree—the art of being kind.

"Into all his letters, he breathed a deep appreciation for his friends back home, his family, his opportunities. We got from him only the pleasant, the delightful things, none of the bad. If he mentioned hardships at all, he made us think he was enjoying them to the fullest, and probably he was.

"In aviation, he found the niche for which he must have been intended. He made an enviable record, and reached the rank of Captain in what we understand—not from him—is a remarkably short time. His citations and decorations were mentioned only casually in his letters, and his last decoration, an Oak Leaf Cluster, wasn't mentioned at all. When this fact was called to his attention, he replied in a letter received Monday night: 'I didn't mention this last award to you because I didn't feel it was important enough. I haven't done anything special in this war except go out in a bomber and come home. We did have a good record all through our combat experience, but it was routine flying and there were no heroics. Please make this plain to my friends. I don't want them to get the wrong impression.'

"I quote the above because it seemed to be his wish. That attitude was typical of Bob.

"He would not complain, I am sure, of his fate on that foggy Iceland shore last Monday. He was where he wanted to be when he died: in a bomber. He had flown nearly 100,000 miles over three continents. He had participated in the greatest adventure of all time. He had played an important part in that adventure and he had enjoyed himself while he was doing it. He had lived dangerously, excitingly, and we believe usefully in his twenty-seven years. He would not have asked for more than that.

"For his family and friends there are heartaches, of course. But down through the ages, mothers and fathers and brothers and sisters and friends have suffered those same heartaches. When the world goes on a mad and bloody spree, sorrow trails inevitably in its wake. There are millions of fathers and mothers in the world today who have learned that fact, and there probably will be millions more before Man finally decides that wars are futile, unnecessary, and not worth the price we pay for them. Until that day, those of us with sons in the service must take our turns at grief.

"If Bob's contribution has any influence at all in the direction of permanent peace, we shall take a measure of comfort from that thought.

"But just now, our own small world seems pretty drab.

"In common with other parents, we have probably been centering our thoughts too much upon a glorious anticipation—the day 'when Bob comes home. . . .' "

You may say that Bob Shannon's story is not unusual, only typical. Maybe you're right. Maybe that's what is so special about the Circus—all the kids in it are so typical; but typical of all the best that Americans have made of themselves and inherited from their ancestors. Under the pressure of war, that best shines forth like fine steel at white heat.

And when I say that the kids in the Circus were Americans, I don't use the term narrowly, as Hitler would speak of Germans. For instance, one of the good Americans in the Circus was a Jap, yes, a Jap. His name was Ben Kuroki. Born in Nebraska, raised in a farming community that respected him, Ben almost had to break into the Army, and finally wound up in the Circus. Before take-off for England, he had to plead with Col. Ted to take him. Once in England, he studied gunnery, mastered that trade, then pestered every pilot until he finally got into Jake Epting's crew on the old "Red Ass" as tail gunner. He finished his tour of duty as engineer and top-turret gunner over Ploesti, and, as reward, made only one request—he wants to go on flying for another 25 missions over Germany, then another 25 if the Circus moves to China to hit Japan. (See Illus. 174 and 177.)

He's a damn fine American—got it from the soil of Nebraska and strengthened it by fighting with the Circus. When gunner Kuroki walks down the streets of London with the rest of the crew of "Red Ass," anybody who even looks at Ben peculiarly is liable to get a shoving around from the other gunners. When you belong to the Circus, you belong. Period.

And there were guys in the Circus with All-American names like Tony Yenalavage, from Pennsylvania, bombardier. (See Illus. 173.) His citation for the DFC tells his story:

"Lt. Yenalavage—for extraordinary achievement while serving as bombardier on a B-24 airplane on combat missions. In the early minutes of the return flight from a successful bombing attack, the pilot was completely disabled and the co-pilot seriously injured by cannon fire from enemy fighter planes. Although he had never flown a bomber, Lt. Yenalavage immediately took his place at the pilot's controls, and, with coaching from the wounded co-pilot, kept the plane in formation until reaching the coast of England. Then, due to bad weather conditions, he broke formation and flew on alone and landed safely at a strange airdrome without further injury to personnel or damage to the airplane. The courage, initiative, and unerring judgment displayed upon this occasion uphold the highest traditions of the Army Air Forces and reflect great credit upon this young officer and upon the armed forces of the United States."

And there was Sgt. Bob Jungbluth, from Arlington, Nebraska—he left his radio on a mission to revive a knocked-out waist gunner whom the others had given up for dead. That job done, Bob grabbed the waist gun and shot down one of a swarm of fighters that were boring in on the spot left open when the regular gunner fell. His citation reads: "He continued to fight heroically until critically wounded by an exploding 20 mm. cannon shell. His right arm was blown off just above the elbow."

Another Circus story: A shell blasted the nose of "Jo-Jo's Special Delivery." Seriously wounded were Bombardier Coy Ellison, from McLean, Texas, and Navigator Jim Gill, Puckett, Mississippi. Into the intercom, Ellison yelled: "Gill is bad hit!" Into the intercom, Gill yelled: "Ellison is hit bad!" Both stuck to their guns and kept hammering the Jerries that were closing in on the bloody-nosed Lib.

Down in Africa, all the special qualities of the Circus got their severest test, came off with highest ratings. They went south hoping to find a hotter war and more sunshine. They found hotter war, but only mud in Northwest Africa with the Twelfth Air Force. They moved to the Middle East with the Ninth—and there they found plenty of war, plenty of sunshine—and sand.

The Circus lived in pup tents, insulated against wind and sand by sheets of metal torn from crashed enemy planes. Most eloquent footnote on the operation comes from Col. Ted: "My whole office was two five-gallon gasoline tins. Jeez, but what a wonderful life, with only ten gallons of room for paper work!"

They pulled missions every other day, 7 in fifteen days, none less than ten hours long. Between missions, they brightened the nights with home-made fireworks—cooked up out of captured German munitions. They played a rugged brand of softball that was half football, half boxing. A jeep scraped a baseball diamond out of the desert by pulling an iron girder across the sand. Capt. Johnny Murphy, skipper of the fabulous "Shoot Luke" (see Illus. 167), described it:

"We dragged the infield on the morning of the 18th, played a few innings, took off to bomb Sousse, got shot up, made an emergency landing on Malta, stayed there two and a half weeks, and when we got back, with seven candidates for the Purple Heart, my God, what a difference in the old place!"

And what was the difference, Johnny? "Hell, they'd finished the outfield!"

Others organized a special Kamel Kore, or "Thirteenth Heavy Dung Disposal Group"—all pilots who had had their Libs borrowed and never returned by Topnotch Brass, were eligible for combat service with the Kamel Kore, whose "dungadeers" were briefed for phony missions designed to open the "dung bay" doors over unpopular targets. Bob Hudspeth, its Air Officer Commanding, was lost during a very real mission against enemy shipping at Brest.

The casualties did not spare special guys like Bob Hudspeth; but always, there seemed to be other joes who had special mad talents for fun, perhaps suppressed all their lives, until they joined the Circus!

I don't think the Chaplain will mind this story—God knows that no sky pilot ever deserved or commanded deeper respect from fighting men than Jim Burris. On New Year's Eve in the desert, the Circus celebrated. A Technical Sergeant reported that "some guy come bustin' into my tent about ten minutes to midnight hollerin' his head off about somebody havin' stole his jug. I give him the stock answer—'Aw, go tell the chaplain.' And he hollered back: 'Dammit, I am the chaplain!'"

The Circus landed in Africa in good American uniforms—which were either inadequate, or quickly worn out in the desert. They were replaced by an odd assortment of British battle dress. A prize picture in the Circus history is of Col. Ted wearing the British battle dress, shaking hands with General Alexander of the British, who was wearing American flying clothes. As Mr. Churchill said, things have got sort of mixed up.

Somehow, the Circus always managed to look different—maybe because circumstances had put them into British battle dress and given them deep tans that they brought home to damp Britain in the winter, but probably because they really were different.

For instance, there was Al Pezzella, from Newton, Mass. He was a bombardier. Busy over his bomb sight, with Naples down below, he looked up just as an ugly hunk of flak whisked by his bottom—but missed. He stuck his left hand out and barked into the intercom: "Ball one!"

Al was a bookworm bombardier, would mark his place in a new novel with a shell clip until the bombs were away, then turn back to his book. A long mission was a "ten-chapter deal" to Al.

Maybe you read about the Fortress crew that brought a donkey home when they shuttled to Africa after plastering Regensburg. Bob Grant of the Circus brought some transportation home from Africa, too, but more practical: British motorcycle. Called down by Col. Ted, Bob, respectful and straight-faced, said: "I got it sent parcel post, sir!" Bob was shot down over Germany with only two missions to go.

You could praise a joe like Johnny Murphy for turning back twice to protect a straggler, both times getting shot up. But Johnny would duck the praise with an alibi: "Hell, I had to get that bastard home—he owed me thirty-one pounds!" That was the Circus.

And of course all crews worship their skipper, but none so much as the

127. Col. Arman Peterson, Flagstaff, Ariz., was the CO of an outfit that trained back home on Tomahawks (P-40s), brought Lightnings (P-38s) to England, had them taken away and sent to Africa, then got Thunderbolts (P-47s) to fight with in the Battle of Germany. Shortly after this picture, taken when the King visited his station, Pete was killed in action with his group. (Chapter 23) The new CO was shot down on his second mission, is now a prisoner of war. In no group has the luck been so tough or the morale so high.

128. "Flagari" was the name of Pete's plane, and these were the names of his ground crew: (l. to r.) Sgt. Arley Lindsey, Ada, Okla.; Col. Pete; Sgt. Johnny Bradshaw, Ft. Worth, Tex.; and S/Sgt. Harry Bahneman, Pittsburgh, Pa. There was a Bob Hope show going on at the station when suddenly, as if by signal, all the pilots who had not flown that day got up and walked out on the show. Later, a worried Bob Hope found out that it wasn't because his show was slipping. They had found out that Col. Pete had not come back, and they had gotten into their planes and gone out to hunt for him.

129. The Lightnings that were first sent to England wound up in Africa, with camels in the background. Pilots like Walt Rivers from Paducah, Ky., proved that they could fight on even terms with the Jerries' best.

130. One of the aces of the Duckpond's outfit is Maj. Roberts from Spokane, with 6 kills to his credit at the end of some 60 missions. Name of his plane is the "Spokane Chief." (Chapter 23)

131. Another ace from the Duckpond is Capt. Charley London—he had 6 kills in 60 missions, too. His crew chief comes from the same town, Long Beach, Cal. "That helps," says Capt. Charley. "We speak the same language."

132. Freshmen in the Battle of Germany, the 3 fighter pilots getting a chalk-talk from a Fortress Colonel are veterans of the air war against Japan. L. to r.: Lt. Col. Bill Cummings, Lawrence, Kans.; Lt. Col. Tom "Speed" Hubbard, Ft. Worth, Tex.; Maj. Gerald "Dixie" Dix, Sullivan, Ind. Talking to them is another Texan, Col. "Put" Putnam—he was the pilot of the first Fortress to drop a bomb on Germany. (Chapter 24)

133. Skipper of the Lightning outfit is Col. Barton Russell. Told that over here some pilots scoff at the Lightning as "just a Link trainer between 2 P-40s," he issued this challenge: "I'll lick anything that flies with a Lightning."

134. The 3 Musketeers: Bill Cummings . . .

135. "Speed" Hubbard . . .

136. . . . and "Dixie" Dix . . . finally got together in The Big League.

137. From the Pacific came two more veterans. Out there they flew Airacobras (P-39s) at low level; in the Battle of Germany they fly Lightnings 5 miles high. Maj. Nat Blanton from Oklahoma got 4 Japs over Java: "It was like the Battle of Britain. You just went up and fought, and then came down, refueled, had your guns checked and loaded and went up and fought again . . ."

138. A new kind of fighting is ahead for Maj. McGovern, from Providence, R.I. He got 5 Japs when they were hammering Port Moresby, Australia. Out there, he was "catching"; over Germany, he'll be "pitching." Lightnings helped the Forts go deeper and deeper. And after the Lightnings, there came other fighters with still more range, like the Mustangs—and finally the super-bomber that needs no escort.

139. Very lonely is the job of a Photo Reconaissance pilot over Germany. Maj. Jim Wright from Cleveland, Ohio, is one of them. He flies a Lockheed Lightning, without guns. Speed and wits are his only defense against the German fighter planes that come up to keep the "Focus Cats" from stealing secrets with a camera.

140. Inside the nose of the Lightning, where 4 guns are usually carried, Sgt. Jim Nolan from Cleveland will mount these mammoth PRU cameras. They get the pictures that tell Intelligence what has been bombed, what must be bombed again.

HAWKER HURRICANE IIc
HAS HUMPED BACK, LARGE
RUDDER, AND THE TAIL SECTION
PROTRUDES BELOW FUSELAGE.

141. No different from other airmen are PRU pilots in their tastes in humor and art—one of them drew this pin-up girl, with apologies to Petty, and the caption was: "Target for Tonight."

142. The Marauders (Chapter 25), like the Libs, were the target for acid wisecracks from the veteran pilots and crews of the glamorous Forts. Favorite joke of the Fortress boys was this one: "The Marauder is a beautiful piece of machinery—but it will never take the place of the airplane." Needless to say, they don't make many cracks like that any more.

143. There were losses, yes, but the Marauders came through their early schooling with a loss percentage far lower than the Forts had when they went to France. There were factors that made the job easier for the Marauders—but still, battle-tests showed that the B-26 was full of fight.

144. Those specks behind the Marauders are the Spitfires that shepherd our mediums through Jerry fighters; the smudges are the flak against which evasive action and tin hats and armored vests AND LUCK are the only defenses. Homeward bound, below, one Marauder with a smoking engine looks in trouble . . . but that one made it back to base. The tiny circled speck in the blur of the prop on the left is another Marauder in trouble; it did not get home, hit the drink instead. All but one of the crew were fished out by Air-Sea Rescue.

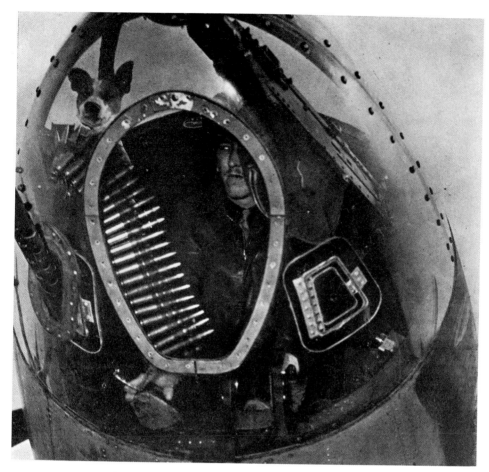

145. Marauders have their mascots, too—just like the Forts and Libs. Peering through the nose of a B-26 with his master, Hugh Fletcher from Cleveland, "Salvo" gets ready to go up for another jump, in his own special and private parachute.

146. The commanding officers of the "first of the many" Marauders were as tough and as colorful as the bosses of the first Forts and Libs and Thunderbolts and Lightnings—they had to be. Flipping their lucky coins to decide who will buy beers are the 4 COs who first battle-tested the Marauders: (l. to r.) Col. Earl Storrie, Denton, Tex. (hometown of the skipper of the famous Fortress "Old Bill"); Col. Lester Maintland, Boerne, Tex.; Col. H. B. Thatcher, Chevy Chase, Md.; and Col. Glenn C. Nye, Raleigh, N.C.

147. But most interesting man in the Marauders is Capt. Fred Kappeler, from Alameda, Cal.—he was navigator in one of the B-25s that went to Tokyo. For that job, what he needed most was either hiking shoes or a bathing suit. In the Battle of Germany, what he needs most is a flak helmet.

148. Captain —— (it is not safe to print the names or show the faces of airmen whose country is occupied by the Nazis) of the Free French Air Force, is given the Air Medal for escorting 8th Air Force bombers on 8 raids with a squadron of Free French Spits. Long and proud is the record of the Fighting French in Spits of the RAF.

149. From Norway came Captain J., pictured with his English bride. For escorting U.S. 8th Air Force bombers to their targets, Capt. J. of the Royal Norwegian Air Force received the American Air Medal from Gen. Eaker. The whole magnificent story of the air forces of the "conquered" nations is told in the RAF official story "Freedom in the Air." (Chapter 26)

150. Because Allied airmen helped the 8th do its job, Gen. Eaker pinned American medals on Englishmen and Poles and Canadians and Frenchmen and Czechs and Norwegians. Above is Flying Officer N. M. O. Jones, a Welshman who is one of the many RAF Photo Recon pilots. His award, the Air Medal.

151. From Canada, Flight Lt. Robert A. Buckham of the RCAF gets the American DFC, "for extraordinary achievement while escorting bombers of the U.S. 8th Air Force on 7 bombing raids." A Canadian Spitfire Wing was high scorer on escort jobs with the Marauders of the 8th Air Force.

152. English airmen have helped the 8th mightily, too, in the job of bombing Germany. Targets like Hamburg were hit by the RAF at night, by the USAAF by day. In gratitude for the work of the RAF bombers, Gen. Eaker awarded the U.S. Silver Star to Wing Commander Richard H. Waterhouse.

153. As Mr. Churchill said, British and Americans are "getting all mixed up." Nowhere is that more true than in the air, and nowhere are the results more profitable to both. Another American Silver Star went to Wing Commander Graeme Harrison, for leading his bombers on 11 raids that helped us.

154. From New Zealand's Royal Air Force comes Warrant Officer Allister Saunders—he got the Air Medal for saving an American fighter pilot.

155. Warrant Officer William Greenfield of the British Royal Air Force got the DFC for his part in 87 Air-Sea Rescues—23 of American airmen.

156. For his part in 13 rescues, Flight Sgt. George Leighton of the RAF got the Air Medal. Leighton is an air gunner—often Air-Sea Rescue has to beat off the Jerries to do its job.

157. Many others were the ways in which the RAF helped us. Flight Lt. George H. T. Hatton got the DFC for flying deep into enemy territory to get weather information.

158. Grounded now, there is only seriousness where always there used to be a grin on the face of Wing Commander Johnny Johnson, RAF veteran fighter pilot. (Chapter 26) Surest way to furrow his brow is to ask: "Johnny, what are you going to do after the war?"

tail gunner of Pat Murphy's outfit, the pilot who once did a loop in his Lib: "Listen, from now on, dey can shove dis combat. Dey done grounded my pilot!"

Promotions came slowly to the boys in the Circus, because they were hopping so much from one Air Force to another that their service records were always screwed up. To the sad second lieutenants of the Circus, "Gold Bar Boy" Morry Elstun, of Ross, Ohio, delivered himself of a metrical lament for the other Gold Bar Boys who fought their way through 25 missions with the Circus without ever getting any silver on their shoulders. The funereal title is: "Dulce et Decorum Est Pro Patria Mori":

At twilight smokes in G.I. Row,
Sit the Gold Bar Boys forlorn,
Amongst their dreams of silvery things
Upon their shoulders worn.

Raid after raid, they flew their crates
Into flak and cannon shell,
And flew them back and patched them up,
While promotions went to hell.

After raid 29, they're beginning to crack,
And all are grown punchy and old.
But with hands still shaking from cannon and flak,
They polish their bars of gold.

Five miles up in the steely sky,
They fought the bloody Hun,
Where flak comes high and splinters fly,
And Gold Bars flash in the sun.

Now the 30th raid is being made,
With the Gold Bar Boys in the rear.
As usual, the flak and the cannon played,
And end was creeping near.

Into a spin, over Berlin,
The whole damn squadron goes—

Four Gold Bars in each cockpit,
Four Gold Bars in each nose!

Shed a tear for the Gold Bar Boys,
Who flew their crates to meet their Fate,
But missed one of war's greatest joys:
Showing their "silver" to a hot blonde date.

Their Gold Bars gleamed in the sun,
They braved the flak and the cold;
They scoffed at the fire of the bloody Hun,
For Country—and for Bars of Gold.

'Tis said that the Hun, by pity softened,
Buried the boys beneath the stars . . .
And to give them what they'd missed so often,
Covered their graves with *silver* bars.

Everybody in the Circus was tough, but not everybody was rough. There was quiet Gerald Ahlquest, son of missionaries in India, who once taught math because he thought it might help to teach himself navigation. He writes poetry—not jingles. The rest of the Circus is awed by the fact that he has written 2,501 letters home.

And though most of the Circus boys somehow look big, some of them aren't. For instance, there was Jack Jones, from Franklinton, Louisiana. Five-foot-six, 118 pounds, but a damn fine pilot.

And though most of the kids in the Circus are the first of their names to be famous, one named Walt Stewart, Utah pilot (see Illus. 181), had a grand-uncle named John M. Browning who used to sit around on the Stewart ranch out near Salt Lake in 1900 and think. He was the man who thought up the Browning machine gun, one of the first gadgets that made aviation dangerous. But Walt is far more famous for a letter he got from his mother than for anything Uncle Browning ever did. His mother once wrote her Lib-piloting son:

"My boy, I'm so glad you're in one of those beautiful big Flying Fortresses." The Circus will not soon forget or forgive a pilot who has so utterly failed to bring up his parents in the faith.

All mothers, think the Circus, are sometimes pretty dumb about bombers; few of the pilots have not had letters from home advising them: Dear Son: Be careful. Fly low, and slow. But Mother Stewart is still the one most in need of missionary work. Incidentally, Walt Stewart was once a Mormon missionary, back in 1938. No kidding, to Scotland.

Most of the crew chiefs in the Circus have the same fierce possessiveness toward their Libs as Charlie Chambers explosively demonstrated the day his boss brought a ship home with 200 holes in her: "Goddamit, Lieutenant, what the hell you been doin' to my ship!"

As a matter of fact, Col. Ted is only a hired hand around the Circus. Two GI's actually own it, Mishmash and Barnhill, Master Sergeants, the two Group Inspectors. With twenty-four years in the Army to lean on, Sgts. Mishmash and Barnhill, real names, are rougher than the Truman Committee when they pull a ship inspection on the crew chiefs.

The Circus feels that it has a proper proprietary interest in all Libs; for instance, Joe Tate got his Lib, "Ball of Fire," shot up on the first mission. He was prowling around some British ferry fields, looking for spare parts of the "Limey Libs." He found a Lib that nobody claimed, flew it home, named it "Ball of Fire Junior." The Senior is now the Circus hospital ship.

I guess the best story about the Circus is the one about Benny Klose, from South Dakota (see Illus. 184), the bombardier in "Boomerang," first Lib I ever pulled a mission in—went with a new crew as turret gunner; the turret was out that day, just plain quit because, the crew chief said, "there was a stranger in her seat."

Benny Klose is another of those special typical Americans, like Shine Shannon. He was captain of his high school football team back in '34. He always wanted to fly—but his family said no. An 83-year old aunt stepped in and backed Benny's ambition—after she went out and paid $5 for a ride in an airplane herself to see if it was safe to fly. Benny washed out as a pilot in primary training; then shifted to bombardier training and made the grade.

He got to be a Group Bombardier for the Circus, the man on whose judgment every Lib in the group releases its bombs. Benny did twenty-eight missions, then was grounded, and sent up to higher headquarters because he was an extra special bombardier. Very.

Benny had more than his share of the nerve-strain of combat: "Up there in the nose, you get to feeling that every Jerry is out to get you personally.

Flying in the lead ship, you always know they want to knock you down to break up the bombing of the whole group. Sometimes, it's pretty hard to keep your eye on the bomb sight."

Certainly Benny had earned the comfort of a chairborne job, but the other day, I asked somebody where Benny is now. I heard he had been made a Major.

"Benny Klose? Why, he's lower than a lieutenant now. A cadet—in flying school back home. Learning to be the pilot of a Lib."

Mr. Brisbane used to say: "Talent does what it can; genius does what it must!"

That's the kids in the Circus.

Chapter 28

OPERATION, "WHOPPER"

"... remember, the Danube ts brown and not blue ..."

THERE have been innumerable severe tests of men in this war—of Americans on Wake Island and Bataan and Corregidor and at times in Tunisia; of the British at Dunkirk, the Russians at Stalingrad. But those were times of "taking it." There is a vast difference between the strains imposed by defensive and offensive battles.

The raid on the refineries at Ploesti was a bold offensive action, in which those who planned it knew that the losses might be as high as 50%. Though the boys who went on the job did not know losses might be so high, they did suspect it. And the way in which they faced it cannot be better described than in this incident before the final briefing.

There was an engineer named Sgt. Fred Anderson, engineer and top-turret gunner, on Packy Roche's Lib. Fred had been on the first Lib raid on a Nazi target in Europe. He had finished his tour of duty, but like so many others in "Timberlake's Traveling Circus," Fred Anderson volunteered to go along on the Ploesti job. He already wore the DFC and the Purple Heart; he wasn't on the job for medals. A lot of big shots had talked to the boys during the last days before the raid. Air Chief Marshal Tedder had told them:

"I came here two and one-half years ago during the reverses in Greece and Crete and North Africa. The Hun had us on the run in those days. But now, the whole position is reversed. You and your boys have messed him up considerably. He is in a mighty uncomfortable position now. Italy is not out yet, but she is wobbling. This blow to the Axis oil will help Italy make up her mind to quit."

General Brereton, Commanding the Ninth Air Force that furnished some of the Liberators to match others from the Eighth for this job, also told the boys that what they were about to do would shorten the war.

But most impressive was what Col. Baker told the Circus outfit in his own private briefing—that was what Fred Anderson will never forget. Baker had succeeded Col. Timberlake as CO of the Circus; he had been the air exec; he was leading the Circus on the job; he was a Circus man, 100%. After the briefing, at questions time, somebody asked what would happen if Col. Baker's ship didn't get to the target.

"Don't you worry about that. Nothing like that is going to happen. I'm going to take you to that target, all the way to the target, even if my plane falls apart."

Fred Anderson will not forget that scene. He remembers how he felt:

"You know, everybody, some time or other, runs smack into something that is big, bigger than anything that has ever happened to him before. This was one of those times for me, for all of us. Ploesti was the biggest thing any of us had ever seen, or ever would see. We knew that. We felt it all over. God-damn it, every man who left that briefing knew that this was one target that had to be destroyed. Not just hit. *Destroyed!* Guess this was the first time any of us really understood how bombing was connected so close with shortening the war and saving lives."

A general had told these boys that it would take many divisions of ground troops a whole year to cross the Mediterranean and fight up through Greece to where they could destroy Ploesti. The Libs were to do the job in fourteen hours.

"Nobody was thinking about himself that day. Hell, the job was so much bigger than any of us, or all of us. We had one idea: take the bombs to the target, to hell with flak and fighters."

It's a fact worth recording that no Eighth Air Force group has ever been beaten back from a target, either by flak or fighters.

"When we walked out of that briefing, each of us knew that coming back was secondary on this job."

That's just another way, a quieter and somehow more impressive way, of repeating a famous line from American history: "Damn the torpedoes! Full speed ahead!"

I had been keenly interested in this job for long weeks before it came off— it was scheduled for some time in August. Actually, it came off on Sunday, August 1. Dave Scherman got the first pictures of the rehearsal for the Ploesti job quite by chance. I had sent Dave and a British Movietone cameraman, Jack Ramsden, up to the Circus station to photograph a practice mission.

They had no trouble getting their pictures, but they complained bitterly because "the damn Libs kept hedge-hopping—you could always see the ground in the pictures, and Libs are supposed to fly four miles high."

A couple of colonels and at least one general blew a valve when they heard that pictures had been taken of a low-level practice mission. That was the tip-off for the job ahead. But they didn't need to bother about Dave and Jack—both of them, of course, caught on that there was a low-level job cooking. They even kept the secret from me, said they "didn't get any pictures—lousy weather." Once you come in contact with the Circus, you catch the spirit. You wouldn't do anything, not even under torture, to hurt them. The Circus secret was safe with Dave and Jack. (See Illus. 166 and 185.)

Shortly after the Circus pulled out for Africa, I got tangled up in their job again. Col. Jake Smart, General Arnold's "special jobs" man, wanted to try an experiment—to put the briefing for the Ploesti job into a sound film. Name of the film was to be *Operation, Whopper*—code name of the mission. I was assigned to work on the job. Worked with an English boy, Wing Commander Lord Forbes. The kids in the Circus called him "Silly-pants"—until they got to know him. He used to write a page in the *Sunday Express*. Had his own plane and flew it all over Europe, writing about the places and things he saw. That's how he got into the RAF. He was out in the Balkans when the war started, used to fly the diplomatic pouch between Belgrade and Warsaw and Bucharest—for fun.

So he was just moved officially into the RAF, made Air Attaché. As a news-paperman trying to write a story about the Jews being smuggled out of Poland through Rumania, he learned a lot about how to slip out of a country. That's how he happened to help a lot of Polish airmen to escape after the Nazis moved in. The Poles do not call Lord Forbes "Silly-pants." They decorated him.

I remember how, on the *Mirror* back in peacetime New York, we used to explain why the British didn't knock out the Rumanian refineries. We had "reliable information that persons high in the British Government have financial interests in those refineries."

Forbes told me the real reason why the job wasn't done by the RAF. They had to decide between using their pitifully few planes to cover withdrawal from Greece, or to knock out the refineries. The choice was hard, but obvious.

We worked on the film in two places—very hush-hush job—very few people in on it. As the job went on, I felt more and more uneasy. I would sit in a little sound-proof studio and talk into a microphone about how "the cables on the barrage balloons are not so heavy as the British or German cables, so you can probably fly right through them." Those words would soon be heard by a bunch of kids I knew down in the desert somewhere, and they would believe what they heard, and they would try to fly their Liberators through those cables so that they could bomb at low level.

We had a lot of interesting arguments during the making of that film, Forbes and I. He worked late at night, and in between parts of the job, we would walk outside the studio and sit on the edge of a great hole in the ground. The hole had been dug to look like the Wadi Gap in the Tunisian Campaign— the British Army Film Unit was shooting cut-in scenes for their sequel to *Desert Victory*, and this hole was one of the props.

The most interesting argument was on whether or not, in the commentary for the briefing film, we should tell the boys how tough the job would be. Forbes would say:

"Well, old boy, if this were being done for the RAF, I would say that we should come right out with it and tell them that half of them might not get back. The British temperament reacts best to the whole truth, but with your boys, well, I don't know—"

Of course I got mad at the implication that our kids couldn't take the truth as well as the British, and when I got mad, I couldn't think straight. But at the end of the argument, I agreed that the best approach was to stress the importance of the job, as an antitoxin against inevitable awareness of the dangers of the job.

And so, at the end of the film, we had a "conclusion" which was like a locker-room fight talk. We flashed on screen pictures of Doolittle's bombers taking off for Tokyo—the pictures of the first Fortress raid on Europe. The commentary said:

"These jobs were big jobs—but this job, the job that you men have been selected to do, this job is the biggest job of the war."

Then we put a picture of President Roosevelt on the screen, saying: *"The Nazis and the Fascists have asked for it, and they are going to get it."*

And then we filled the screen with a picture of a blazing oil tank and my commentary wound up: *"Okay, you know what you've got to do—let's go!"*

Forbes was a little uneasy about winding up with the President like that. "Suppose some of the boys are Republicans." I explained that even to the most rock-ribbed Republicans among those boys, Franklin Delano Roosevelt was Commander-in-Chief.

The most satisfying part of the whole job for me was the day we showed it to the topside people in the RAF; among them, the man with the face of a hawk and the hands of a concert pianist, "Peter" Portal. I had heard people say that, in meetings of the top Army, Navy, and Air men of our two countries, two men always stood out: Marshall and Portal. I understood about Portal that afternoon—his searching questions, his keen criticism and keener interest, and finally his verdict that this method of briefing bomber crews was something that should be further developed. That was his quiet decision after the others had spiked the whole idea with curt condemnation.

I felt much better about the job after that, because Portal had said: "This film will help." That was enough.

The film was a mixture of technical navigation data, moving pictures of the run-up on scale models of each target, comedy tricks to emphasize the "don'ts" of the job, and finally, kindergarten geography.

"You Americans have never learned to read a map that shows anything outside America. Geography is a blind spot with you," Forbes had said. I had never thought of it that way, but it's the truth.

"For instance, all you know about the Danube is that there was a waltz written about it by Strauss or some other foreigner."

So in my commentary, very slowly, so that they would not forget it, because the whole success of this job depended on crossing the Danube in the right place at the right time, I said:

"And remember, the Danube is brown—brown, not blue—"

Among airmen, Commanding Officers like to lead their men on big jobs like those, but Col. Ted Timberlake—he's a general now—Col. Ted was ordered to stay on the ground when his Libs went to Ploesti. He laughed, because he is a good soldier, and made some lame crack about, "Boy, am I relieved to be left off this job!" Everybody knew he was lying; Ted Timberlake would have given his left leg and right arm to go on that job.

It's now American history, what happened on that raid, where fifty-three Libs were lost. But I'd just like to tell you a few special stories. One is about Col. Baker, the CO of the Circus who had said that he would lead his outfit to the target "even if my plane falls apart." (See Illus. 162.)

It was a good day, that Sunday, when the brown-green ships from the Eighth and the sand-pink ships of the Desert Ninth Air Force headed north across the

Mediterranean. As they crossed the Balkans, they saw farmers in the fields even on Sunday, and once they saw naked girls bathing in a river. "Let's bail out here!" was the instant wisecrack that bounced around over the intercoms.

Baker's ship was in the lead as they went into the target. The flak was heavy and accurate.

Some of the boys said there were an awful lot of new guns around there—new earth around the gun emplacements. Baker's ship was hit, hit hard. Joe Tate saw the whole thing:

"Baker was four hundred feet in front of me. He got hit three times: once far out on the wing, then at the roots of the wing, and then finally square in the cockpit. His wing tanks and the bomb bay tank burst into a sheet of yellow flame. The Force was still sixty seconds from the target. The minute he was hit, he jettisoned his bombs—you can tell when the pilot drops them instead of the bombardier—they just dumped. But Baker kept on leading the Force into the target, like he said he would, aiming his ship for the narrow space between the towers of the cracking plants in the heart of the refinery we were headed for. I saw something coming down out of the nosewheel hatch of Baker's ship—it was a man's legs. He dropped clear and came tumbling back over our props as his 'chute caught the air—came so close I could see that his legs were on fire. Baker kept his ship on course.

"But when we got right on top of the target, the devil himself couldn't have held that ship in formation any longer. Baker was flying pilot and Jerstad was co-pilot. The cockpit must have been a blast furnace. We could see the flames through the windows as the ship lost speed and we pulled up with it. The right wing started to crumple and drop off, but not before old Bake had taken us through the target. And then he pulled his ship up into a steep climb. God only knows how anybody inside could have been still alive, but something inside was pulling the ship up and up and out of the path of our Force. Three men fell out the back of her, and then it fell off and crashed into a field.

"Baker could have saved himself if he had wanted to belly-land in a field before we got to the target, when he was first hit. Other ships had made belly landings. But Baker stuck."

Seven of the ten men in Baker's ship had finished their tours of duty; they volunteered for the Ploesti job.

"Coming back was secondary . . ."

There were two Congressional Medals of Honor awarded that day—one to Col. Leon Johnson from Moline, Kansas, CO of another Eighth Air Force outfit; and one to Col. John Riley "Killer" Kane from Louisiana—both of them led their forces into targets where delayed action bombs dropped by other groups were already exploding.

One more story about the attack itself. I don't know the names of the heroes of this story. They were just another crew of another Lib. Its bombs had been dropped early—it was flying on over the target area, it had been hit, was already in flames. On the edge of the target area, there was a still untouched building. Briefing had told the crews that this was a vital power house. That blazing Lib turned from its course, headed straight for the power house, crashed into it—the fuselage came out on the other side, minus wings—and crashed into still another building.

Gunners on that trip said afterwards: "That's the first time we ever really laughed at fighters. They were waiting for us when we came out on the other side, but we were right down on the deck, clipping trees with our bomb bays and catching corn stalks in our wings. The fighters tried to form for frontal attacks, but after flying through the hell we'd just left, we didn't even bother with evasive action. We just plowed right into those fighters and they scattered like ducks. Then they tried to re-form and get on our tails, and a lot of them got tangled up in our prop wash and spun into a crash. I guess they just didn't know how to handle us because, by that time, we were all a little crazy."

Some of the Libs landed in Turkey—some of them got down okay in Rumania—some landed in Malta—some even went on and found freshly conquered fields in Sicily to land on. Capt. Harold Kendall, from Charlton, Iowa, was one of the joes who landed in Sicily.

They found a half-finished fighter field. The crew was still standing by inside the "Lucky" with ears cocked for the bail-out gong when Kendall landed, with all red lights showing on the last drops of gas in the tanks. "Lucky" hit the end of the landing strip, plowed on into a flock of P-40's dispersed beyond the runway, and came to a stop, literally leaning against the sides of a hill. The crew piled out and kissed the ground, and waited to be congratulated by the ground crews on their magnificent emergency landing. Top-turret gunner Jim Goodgion, from Ruston, Louisiana, described a very different welcome from what they expected:

"Them grease monkeys, instead of giving us a glad hand, damn near blew their tops. They had just taken seven cracked-up P-40's and made two good ones out of them and here we come along and mash the hell out of the whole seven of them all over again."

Lt. Kenton D. MacFarland, from Galt, California, flew his Lib home across the Mediterranean with two engines shot out on the same side. General Arnold was still talking about that one when he came to England a month later to visit the Lib outfits at their home stations.

And Ben Kuroki, the Nebraska-born Japanese turret gunner on Jake Epting's ship, the "Red Ass," was along on the Ploesti job. All he had to say after it was over was: "To Tokyo I would like to do the same with Libs."

There was something prophetic in the wisecrack that one of the Circus boys made when they saw a picture of all the leaders in that huddle at Quebec:

"Hmmmmm, see where Churchill and Roosevelt are meeting again. Looks like another job cooking for the Circus."

A couple of days later, I was having lunch with Wing Commander Johnson and Canada's Squadron Leader Buck McNair in Claridge's. Col. Timberlake was there. I walked over and said: "Going to bring you a visitor next week if I can persuade him to take a couple of days off. I want him to meet the Circus."

Col. Ted laughed: "I'll be glad to see you, but I'm afraid you're a little late to see the boys. They're gone again."

Chapter 29

ADVENTURE'S BEST ENDING

". . . the Spitfires that rise from that field now to give
air cover for an Allied invasion,
rustle the grass on his grave with their prop wash . . ."

HE was one of those who fought in the "thin blue line" of the RAF to beat back the Luftwaffe in the Battle of Britain.

He was an American. The first American to join the RAF. The first American to die in the RAF. Very few, too few Americans know his name. On the Roll of Honor in Westminster Abbey that lists 375 airmen who died in the Battle of Britain, you will find it.

That Roll is symbolic of that Battle. The first name is an English one—Pilot Officer Hugh Charles Adams. Born, raised, shot down, and buried in an English village.

The last name on the list is a Polish one—Pilot Officer Aleksy Zukowski, from Vilna, Poland. Zukowski was a giant of a man. Oddly enough, he was raised in Japan, and became a skiing champion out there. But when the Huns slashed into Poland, Zukowski was in the air against them. When the Huns slashed into France, Zukowski was in the air against them again. And when they tried to smash into Britain, Zukowski died to stop them.

This first American's name is on still another scroll in England, in St. Paul's Cathedral. Below the tablet that bears his name is a glass case with his RAF wings in it. Some friend had saved them from his tunic and sent them along to the Dean of St. Paul's. The inscription on the tablet reads like this:

PILOT OFFICER WILLIAM MEADE LINDSEY FISKE, RAF

AN AMERICAN CITIZEN WHO DIED THAT ENGLAND MIGHT LIVE.

His name lives in one other place in England; in a rambling little house that rises off an alleyway between the two places Americans know best in London, Grosvenor and Berkeley Squares. It was a famous house in the last war. The fabulous Canadian, Mike Edgar, lived there.

Rose Fiske lives there now—Mrs. William Fiske. American officers know 125B Mount Street well, on Thanksgiving and Christmas and New Year's Day, and in the late afternoon when work is done. And "Fisky" watches, and approves, from a picture frame. (See Illus. 190.)

Americans who never knew Fisky get a warm picture of him from Rose. Amazing girl, tall, lean, erect, dark, tremendous strength in her face, determination in her walk. She was certainly beautiful at twenty. At thirty, distinguished. Her dark hair is streaked with grey. She likes to talk about Fisky.

"We lived in a house by the field. He came home to lunch one day, furious with me. It seems that he had been up at dawn that morning, got on the tail of a Heinkel out over the Channel and herded it right across our house so I could watch him shoot it down. He was in a rage because I wouldn't get out of bed to look. He couldn't understand why I couldn't tell *his* Hurricane from all the others, just by the sound of it."

I suppose a first essential of understanding the story of Fisky's brief three weeks of ops with the RAF is to know his story from the beginning. He was born in Chicago, but he was raised all over Europe. His father was the European representative of a great investment banking firm, Dillon-Read, Wall Street. As a boy he had brief schooling at a private ranch school in California. Then to England.

At fifteen, he spent a year on a sheep ranch in the Argentine. At seventeen he went to Cambridge. Spent his vacations in Switzerland, became a great skier, racing driver, set records on the bobsled and Cresta runs.

Out of Cambridge, he went twice around the world, once with the elder Douglas Fairbanks. And then he took a fat inheritance to Hollywood, collected a cast and a crew, sailed for Tahiti, and settled down to make a picture about the islands. His stars spent more time in splints than on sets, more time putting liniment on sore muscles than Max Factor makeup on wrinkles and double chins. Fisky had invented a game of riding bamboo rafts through rapids on a river. The movie was a flop.

And so he went to Paris and worked in a bank for almost a year. A bank was a cage. He went back to Hollywood, formed a small company, made shorts and Westerns, good ones, profitable. That was typical of Fisky. First he did a thing wildly, then well.

Then he went back to banking in London. That was 1937. The year he married Rose, once Countess of Warwick, but never really happy until she was Mrs. Fiske. And all his friends were young Englishmen. They were all wealthy—call them playboys. Perhaps they were. But not the nightclub brand. They drove fast cars, skied, flew fast planes, lived as dangerously as their money could permit.

Most of Billy Fiske's best friends belonged to an RAF Volunteer Reserve Squadron—601, the City of London Squadron. Whitney Straight and Billy Clyde and Roger Bushell and Willie Rhodes-Moorhouse and Beaverbrook's tough son, little Max Aitken. Fisky flew, too—had about 90 hours to his credit. But he wasn't in 601. He was American, remember. But as the meaning of Munich grew clearer, he told these friends of his: "If war comes, count me in."

In August, 1939, Fisky was living and working in New York. Hated it. Billy Clyde was working in America, too. Clyde got a cable from London, calling him into active service with 601. Fisky phoned a friend in London. "Is this it? Yes. I'll be there."

Rose booked passage on every boat that sailed during the following week as Fisky scrambled to settle his affairs. War seemed imminent—he didn't want to get caught in America by the Neutrality Act. On September 3, when England went into the war, Fisky was on the "Aquitania," one day at sea.

Rose followed as soon as she could. They took a house close to the station where he got his secondary training. And on bad-weather days, the house was full of eighteen-year-old kids from Australia and Canada and South Africa.

"They were such babies. They all looked up to Fisky, told him all their troubles, everything from their debts to their blind dates. You must understand that everybody loved Fisky. I mean that literally. I never really understood it until he died. And then the cables and letters came from all around the world, from all kinds of people. They all loved Fisky."

Fisky was posted to 601 when he finished his training. That was in July, just about three weeks before he was shot down.

"The day Fisky got his first Hun, he was so happy. Never before had he been half so happy as when he was in 601. He never could have been again."

They fought all day, went up again and again, the pilots of the Spits and hump-backed Hurricanes, as our own boys fought in the Pacific in the beginning.

"There were such wonderful guys in 601. They wore red linings in their tunics and mink linings in their overcoats. They were arrogant and they looked terrific, and probably the other Squadrons hated their guts. But by God they did fight. Look at the records. None better. And they always did everything without any apparent effort. They had always been like that at everything, all their lives."

She told me a lot of all this about Fisky one night after we went to a play called *Flare Path* together. There was a scene where three RAF wives, living in an inn on the edge of a bomber field, looked out and saw a Wellington crash and burn.

"Fisky was killed in August. I had gone up to London that morning. His field was in the south of England. I phoned him about lunch time—we weren't supposed to call the field, but you know how it was.

"I called him again right after lunch. I couldn't get any information except that I could hear over the phone that the field was being bombed. I called back again in fifteen minutes. They told me that Fisky was being taken to a hospital.

"I drove down as fast as I could, and all the time I told myself that this was so lucky because surely he had done no more than perhaps to break an arm or a leg and that would keep him out of the war for a while and maybe he would get through the whole war all right. Over and over, I said that—"

At about that time, Fisky was lying in an ambulance, quizzing the doctor that rode with him: "Listen, I'm not going to die, am I? Tell me."

Not frightened, just worried. Maybe he knew. They took him to a new hospital. A military hospital, built for such things. By the time Rose got there, Fisky had been to the operating room. They had covered his legs and arms and most of his face and head with black goo. He was burnt to cinders.

"He was conscious for a little while. He didn't die until next morning. And when he was delirious, all he would talk about was his plane. He wanted me to go and see if it was all right. They told me afterwards that he could never have walked again if he had lived, and he would have hated that."

He landed his plane. Didn't crash. It was blazing. His will power, or maybe it was instinct, made him get out. He walked a few steps, and then he fell.

Fisky was buried in a country churchyard near a corner of the field from which he flew. When Spitfires take off now to give air cover for our invading troops, they fly across Fisky's grave.

There are a lot of things you can write at the end of a story like Fisky's. Lady Patsy Ward wrote up his story and at the end she put a poem that had been written about another dead boy in another war:

> "Because of you we will be glad and gay,
>   Remembering you, we will be brave and strong;
>   And hail the advent of each dangerous day,
>   And meet the last adventure with a song . . ."

That fits Fisky. And so does this story: Old Mosey King, boxing coach at Yale, sat in a corner and gnawed the edge of a towel. He was watching a kid named Van Munson being chopped to ribbons by a real slugger. Van's eye was cut. He was walking into everything, taking it, and staggering on and on to take more. And still he kept fighting. Afterwards as we worked to stop the bleeding, slapped the boy's face to clear his head, Mosey looked at me, and quietly said:

"You know, it's a funny thing about the way a young gentleman fights. Even when knocked out, he just don't seem to know how to lie down."

Chapter 30

PELLEGRINI, BOMBARDIER

"...there are only two kinds of missions ...
those you come back from alive ... and the other kind ..."

THERE is a film prepared by the Office of War Information that every dough-boy who came to Britain for the Big Push was supposed to see. Called *Welcome to Britain.*

I wrote one sequence in the film, just about five minutes long. In it General Eaker is inspecting the crew of a Fortress. He's talking to the bombardier. Suddenly, two Spitfires buzz the field, swoop low, and bank for a landing. The bombardier says:

"The Spits come in here pretty often. When they do, we always give each pilot a carton of American cigarettes before he leaves. We're always plenty glad to see the Spitfires, especially in combat when we're in trouble."

Then Captain Burgess Meredith, one-time Hollywood star, narrator of the film, tells the doughboys:

"That's Joe Pellegrini. (See Illus. 192.) He was the leading bombardier of his group on the big Schweinfurt raid where we lost 60 Fortresses. Going into the target, they run into pretty heavy flak and rocket-firing fighters and they're pretty badly shot up. And Joe says to the pilot, listen, if we get knocked off our bombing run, we're gonna go around again and make another run. The pilot says, are you crazy, Joe? There's only two planes left in our whole damn group. And Joe says, okay, if there's only two of us left, all the more reason to go around again and get it right."

If the story of Joe Pellegrini, bombardier, is the only story of the Eighth that the doughboys ever hear about, they couldn't get a better idea of what the Eighth has done to make the doughboy's job easier.

In the two raids on Schweinfurt's ball-bearing factories, we lost thirty-six Forts on the first one, and sixty on the second. A total loss of ninety-six. Ten men to a Fort, 960 men.

But they knocked the hell out of those factories. Every pulling or turning weapon in the German armed forces felt the impact of those two raids. The results are showing up now. Doughboys, be grateful to airmen like Joe Pellegrini.

To me, Joe's story is one of the great ones of this war. It's the story of an Italian-American, a boy who has always aspired to be the best that Americans are permitted to be. He's just one of those "foreigners" who believe in men like Abraham Lincoln and Thomas A. Edison and Sgt. York. He believes in hard work. He believes in courage. He believes in everything that is fine and strong about America.

Joe was born in South Philadelphia—the Italian district. His father comes from Italy, from a little town right on the toe of the boot, one of the first to be freed from the Nazis by the Allied invaders. Joe's mother comes from Italy, too. Joe has eleven brothers and two sisters. "All Italians have big families, even in Italy. But in America, where there is a chance for your children to be somebody, well, I guess we sort of let ourselves go."

Yes, Joe is married. To a home town girl. Married her while he was in his final phase of training out in Idaho. No, he's not a father yet. He was a little cautious. He wanted to wait until he was sure he would get home to help give his kid a start. And then he told me something that he said he didn't want me to write about, until I explained to him that long before this ever gets published, his wife will know what's happened to him, one way or the other.

"I've never let her know, but ever since I got back from my first mission, I made up my mind I would never again think about whether or not I would get home from the next target alive. A man is no damn good as a bombardier once he starts figuring the percentages on getting home in one piece.

"Some fellows need a little fight-talk to get over their nerves. I don't want to sound like any flag-waver. I hate that kind of stuff. But you got to have a reason for fighting this war. I mean it. When I check in the new bombardiers to our squadron, I look for the suicide boys. I don't mean like the Japs or the Nazis, all of that let's-die-for-the-Fatherland stuff. What I mean is I like to find boys who are willing to get killed just to get this damn war over with so somebody can get home to America and make things all happy again.

"We get letters from the kids in the prison camps over there in Germany. I want to find bombardiers who are fighting to get those boys out of the prison camps and back home.

"The story of Schweinfurt is one that I tell all the new boys. All the men that went down on the big Schweinfurt deal, they knew what they were fighting for, and by God, they didn't turn back. Every time a Fort went down, it was still pointing its nose at the target. Somebody or something inside her was still trying to get to the target."

Joe tightens his fist until his knuckles are like white bone, and he pushes his black brows together in one thick and angry line when he talks like this. Terrific intensity.

Joe Pellegrini's feelings about America have probably had a lot of kicking around. Most of the kids in Joe's neighborhood felt Mussolini was doing things in Italy. They were sort of proud of him. The feeling lingered even after Italy went into the war on the wrong side.

Joe joined the Army in June, 1941. There were a lot of jokes about the Italians even then, and the jokes got rougher and rougher. Maybe those jokes had something to do with Joe's conception of what courage means to an American.

"Sure, I've heard a lot of people talking about how the Italians haven't got any guts. And they say the same things about the Jewish boys. Well, we've got some Jewish boys up in our squadron, and they've got just as much guts as anybody I ever knew. Being brave hasn't got anything to do with your race or your religion or your color. It's all in you, yourself, and in the way you were brought up. Being brought up in America gives a fellow a head start."

I didn't question that statement. The usual reporter's tricks just don't work with Joe. A reporter is supposed to be tough and skeptical of the kind of statements Joe makes about Americans being something special. A reporter is supposed to look for the "angle" and then puncture it. But Joe doesn't puncture. For instance, if you try to trap him with a question about how he would have felt if he had been ordered to drop a bomb on Italians fighting on the side of the Germans, Joe just answers, slowly:

"I wouldn't have any feelings about it. Dropping bombs on Italians would be just like dropping bombs on Germans. They are both wrong. It's like in the Civil War. Both sides were American, but one was wrong, so there had to be killing until the right side won."

Joe always wanted combat. First flying job he got was as a photographer-gunner with a Liberator outfit doing patrol work off the West Coast. He passed his flying cadet exams, but washed out because he couldn't land a plane. Then he wanted to be a navigator, but somebody talked him into being a bombardier. He came to England in March, with a replacement crew, and went through a month's training before his first mission:

"I knew about half of what I needed to know to make my first mission when I got here. The first night, there was a gunner slept in the bunk next to me at the training school. He had a big scar across his face where the fragments of a 20 mm. had cut him up. I thought his scars were wonderful. Somehow, I didn't connect them up with blood or getting hurt or anything.

"He didn't mean any harm by it, but he tried to scare me about what I was getting into. Guess that's just human nature, though."

Joe's first raid was on April 17, Bremen. The first Bremen show. They were briefed for "about a hundred flak guns in the target area that day." Joe can remember that a hundred flak guns didn't mean a thing to him when he heard the number. But over the target, he found out what the veterans meant when they reported that "flak was so damn thick, you could step out and lie down in it."

That was the first raid for Joe, first for his crew, first for the plane. The plane got the whole left stabilizer shot away. She had 128 holes in her from nose to tail. The tail gunner that day—who finally got it on the 18th raid— got a 20 mm. through the heel of his boot, right up through the sleeve of his leather coat—exploded just over his head and never drew blood. No Purple Heart.

"The German fighters, they just sort of fascinated me at first. You would see them coming in and you'd just look at them and not realize they were mad at us and trying to knock us down."

That was before the fighters chewed half the tail off his Fortress. Then Joe knew he was playing for keeps. That's when he started figuring things out. "I talked to everybody who'd listen and answer questions. I drew pictures of our formations, and figured out the best way to concentrate firepower. I studied gunnery as hard as I had ever studied bombardiering back in the States, where we never really thought we'd have to use our guns.

"But about using guns, I learned something too. I learned it from a captain who'd finished his tour of duty as a bombardier over here. He was talking to a bunch of us one day, telling us we ought never to fool around with our guns on the bombing runs. No matter how much we were being attacked, forget the guns until your bombs are away. I said that was suicide, and he ate me out plenty. I'll never forget that. And ever since then the first thing I try to teach a bombardier is he's got just one job to do up there: Get those bombs on the target. Forget the flak and the fighters until your bombs are away. Then you can shoot back. If you don't get your bombs on the target, you've wasted the trip, I don't care how many fighters you shoot down."

Probably Joe made a nuisance of himself in his Group with his ideas about bombardiers. He got into trouble with his squadron CO by going to the Group CO and asking permission to get in extra time with practice bombs whenever weather permitted and there was no mission. That made trouble in the beginning. But today, in Joe's outfit, whenever any bombardier wants to go up and try out a new idea with practice or with live bombs, he gets a plane, and no quibbling from Group Operations.

"Always before, everything had been pilots, pilots, pilots. Nobody paid much attention to the bombardier. If the pilot is flying the plane instead of the bombardier, going into the bombing run, the pilot can mess up the job.

"Anybody who understands mathematics can figure out what will happen if the pilot jockeys the plane even five degrees during the bombing run. He will lay the bombs maybe 700 feet off the target. It's better to be 200 feet out of the formation and to fly parallel, than to try to turn the plane back into the formation during the bombing run. And if the pilot monkeys with the throttles during the bombing run, changes the speed, he'll throw the bombing off. A change of five miles per hour at 25,000 feet altitude might put your bombs 400 feet beyond the Aiming Point. These things never get pointed out to pilots, unless a bombardier sounds off about it."

Joe's best job of bombing was on the second Schweinfurt deal. Schweinfurt is a target that is damn nearly as important as the oil refineries at Ploesti. The Eighth was prepared to spend a lot of bombers to smash those ball-bearing factories. All the kids felt the importance of the job. It put a chill across the small of their backs. Not in fear. But just the way you feel when you face something so important.

The show began on the afternoon of October 13. Take-off was set for 7 A. M.

There were no stars in the sky when the combat crews shuffled through the night to the briefing; they sat huddled on benches until the curtain was jerked back from the maps and they all saw what the target was. There was instant whistling and nervous laughter and wise-cracking. Solemnly, one Captain performed a ceremony that was reserved for tough targets: He took out a roll of toilet paper, tore off ten squares for each man, passed them out.

At the end of the briefing, when it had been decided that Joe would be the Group Bombardier for the day, he got up and asked a question:

"Sir, seeing that this is such an important target and it is a bad day and we are liable to have clouds over the target, could I have your permission to take the group around again if we can't see the Aiming Point on the first run?"

There was electric silence. Every boy looked first at Joe and then at the CO. Hell, it was suicide to make two runs over a target so deep inside Germany. That's how everybody felt and they were right. But Joe just stood there and asked his question a second time. And then the CO answered. As he spoke, the others caught the spirit and there was no disagreement:

"Yes, Pellegrini—you can go around a second time, and a third and a fourth today. This is one target you must hit."

Quietly Joe said: "Thank you, sir." And then more than ever this Group realized the importance of what was ahead of them. But all of them were confident that there would be no mission—not today. The field was closed in solid with a thick ground fog at Stations Time.

"We all felt sure that it would be scrubbed before take-off, or recalled before rendezvous. Oh sure, we knew we'd have to do it later if we didn't do it today.

"And that's what made me so goddam mad. We had to go the second time anyway. If the bombing had been better the first time, we wouldn't have had to go back again. We could have done the whole job for the cost of those thirty-six bombers we lost on the first deal. You can't find any better proof than this Schweinfurt job of the importance of bombardiers."

They took off though they could not see the end of the runway, and they were not recalled before rendezvous. They climbed through the overcast, assembled, and went on to the target. The first fighter attacks hit them while they were still over water; but Thunderbolts drove off the Jerries. No more attacks until the mission pressed on beyond the range of Thunderbolt cover.

"Then they piled in again. We were still a hundred miles from the target. The attacks were heavy and persistent that day, like they knew where we were going. They drove every attack home. The Jerries were carrying belly tanks so they could stay up and keep hammering at us.

"First, the single-engined fighters hit us. And then the twin-engined rocket planes queued up and lobbed their flamers at us. I was busy with my bomb sight. I kept my eyes on my job and my hands off my guns. And then our tail gunner, who's supposed to let the leader know what's happening to the rest of the group started calling out the B-17's going down behind us, another and another.

"It was worse than I'd ever seen it. Our whole low squadron was gone. And then the twins started boring in on our nose. I had to use my guns then. Before we had reached the AP, both the navigator and I had used up all the ammo in the nose. The waist gunner sent up seventy-five rounds. And then I could see the AP ahead, best visibility I had ever seen.

"The officer-gunner in the tail reported that there were only three more ships left in our group besides us. Then, as we reached the AP, he called out that one more had gone down in flames.

"I watched the lead group go into its AP. They had a different one from us. As we turned into our run, two projectiles hit the cockpit. The radio and the Automatic Flying Control were shot out. The pilot regained manual control of the ship. I was talking to him now. He was debating whether to try to make the run or give it up and join another group for protection.

"I said that if we get knocked off the run we've got to go around again. Maybe we did have only three ships left in the group. All the more reason to do with our few bombs what the whole group was supposed to do.

"I told him, by God, Major, I can see the target in my bomb sight. I can see what we came all this way to hit. I said I knew I could hit it, but he didn't think we could hold it on the run. The tail gunner called up that we had only one other plane with us now, just two planes out of the whole damn group left.

"Looking in the sight, I could see we were drifting off the course. I knew we had given up the run. We pulled in by another group. I sighted on the old AP even though we were with another group. The pilot told me to drop on their bombs. I held mine for seven seconds and then dropped. The pictures show that we hit the target.

"When my bombs were gone, I just stood up and cried. I couldn't talk to anybody. I thought the Major didn't have any guts, but of course I was wrong. He just didn't think we could have gotten to the target at all alone, and maybe he was right.

"When we got back to base and landed, just the other ship and us, the ground crews all flocked around us and asked where the other planes were. How did we get separated?

"We told them the others had been shot down. They thought we were kidding. They couldn't believe it. All but two shot down."

Interrogation was grim and ghostly; the tin shacks where some 20 crews usually packed the place were now almost empty, with only the two crews that got home from Schweinfurt. At interrogation, Joe went over to the CO. His lips were trembling, his fists tight-closed, his eyes full of anger:

"Sir, I'd like to say something. Please, I want to go on flying and bombing. I want to go on past 25 and 30 and 40. I want to keep going."

The CO saw that Joe was in pretty bad shape. He slapped him on the back. "Sure, sure, Joe, anything you say. You better get some coffee in you and then go hit the hay. You look pretty tired."

Next day Joe went to the Boss again: "Sir, I don't want you to think I was out of my head yesterday and didn't know what I was saying. I meant it."

About a month later I got a letter from Joe. It was young and awkward; the phrasing was that of a boy whose family spoke a different language. I remembered that Joe had told me, "I was sort of the black sheep. I was the first one that wouldn't speak Italian around the house."

In his letter he told me: "I finished up yesterday on Emden. And I am happy to tell you that I had the big satisfaction of seeing my incendiaries go right onto the target. As I say, I have finished my tour of duty, but I am staying on here. I want the Germans to get to know me better."

Most boys are ready to quit when they get home from Mission X. They figure they've used up their luck. Joe is different:

"I hear the boys all the time talking about percentages and odds. There's only one odds—50-50. You come back or you don't. And the odds are the same for the 25th mission or the first or the 50th. Maybe not in your imagination, but in mathematics. A bomb sight teaches you to believe in mathematics. It's bad for bombardiers to start believing in luck."

Chapter 31

EYE-WITNESS

*"... I agree with the Jerries ... it was the
best bloody bombing I ever did see ..."*

THIS is the story of a man who saw Eighth Air Force bombs smash a German
target from a ringside seat. He's a little Scotsman, named Corporal James
McLoughlin, from Broughty Ferry, Dundee. He used to work for a shipping
line that ran an importing business on the side. He was a salesman in one of
their retail stores. (See Illus. 191.)

Over his counter went oranges and bananas and dates and olives and pine-
apples and dozens of other things that came from far places, places to which
"Chipper" McLoughlin had never been. As a matter of fact, Chipper had
never been anywhere, not even to London, not even out of Scotland, until the
war. And then he crossed the Channel with the short-lived British Expedi-
tionary Force.

He was soldier and stretcher bearer and surgeon and grave-digger before
the end, and the end came quickly and brutally. They were driven back to the
cliffs at St. Valéry, right to the edge of the Channel. They flopped over the
edge and made a last stand on the ledges above the surf. The Huns pushed on;
their machine guns clawed the top of the cliffs, and shredded any man who
stuck his head into line of fire.

Chipper got his tin hat knocked off and the top of his head creased. He
was always letting curiosity outargue discretion. But finally they had to surrender, and the conquering division was Rommel's Number One Panzer outfit.
Rommel himself was on hand. And as the Tommies came up over the edge of
the cliff to surrender, a German officer stood on the nose of a steaming tank,
and shouted in good English:

"So, you are beaten, Britishers! Look behind you now. There across the Channel lies your England. Look at it for the last time. Because within seven days, *we* shall be there, and it will be ours!"

You know the old saying that "all Englishmen live upon an island, and each Englishman is an island unto himself." There never was a better proof of that than Chipper McLoughlin, Scotsman.

He looked up at the German officer, grinned, and said, quite loud enough for all to hear: "Bollocks, Jerry!"

And the German officer had a pretty good idea what Chipper meant. He barked an order, another German slugged Chipper with the butt of a Luger. Chipper went down, and out, but grinning.

He was marched into Germany, a prisoner of war—but still and forever "an island unto himself." That march was torture. But we have it from a buddy of Chipper's that never once, even in sleep and sickness, did that grin go from Chipper's face.

It must have been hell for the Huns, seeing that grin always there. I have it from lots of prisoners of war that the only people inside Germany who ever smile are the dead and the prisoners.

Well, they tried pretty hard to wipe that grin off the face of Chipper McLoughlin. They told him that Britain was beaten, that Hitler had decided to give the bombers of the Luftwaffe the pleasure and the honour of winding up the job, now that the ground troops had had the supreme satisfaction of beating the British in the field of battle. And Chipper could hear the bombers roaring out toward Britain from one of the early prisons where they kept him. But still, he did not believe that Britain was beaten or even badly bent. And still the grin was there.

But in the fall, in the days of the Blitz, they gave the prisoners American newspapers, and our headlines did make it seem as though Britain would not, could not, last long. And so Chipper's smile was a little strained going into December, and sometimes when the lights were down, so was his smile. And that's when he began to cook the plan that got him the Truth, every night, direct from London.

With packets of Red Cross food, and cigarettes, he bribed a guard to get the "loan" of all the keys to the prison—not the keys that would get him outside, but only the keys to the inside doors, so that he could move around inside the prison. From these keys impressions were made in candle tallow; and from these impressions, rough keys were made that gave Chipper the run of his prison. And that's how Chipper got to listen to the British news broadcasts every night in the officers' club while the guards slept.

And, as Chipper learned to speak German, he told his prison keepers each day how the war was really going, long before they got it from their phony communiqués. And now Chipper's smile was rampant, belligerent, again. Maddening to all Nazis who saw it.

Over the prison radio, Chipper heard Christmas services from Home—by far the most beautiful he had ever heard. From that day on, Chipper was an "island of cheer" in the prison. And always his audacity fed on his conviction that the Huns were losing the war.

For instance, toward the end of his stay in prison, he robbed the Huns of the services of a couple of regiments of Italians. It happened like this. After Italy checked out of the war, the Germans made prisoners of their former allies. Droves of them came into the same prison camp where Chipper and his outfit were cooped up.

They were a sad lot. Everything possible had been done to make them miserable, in body and in spirit. They were stripped of their Italian uniforms and dressed like clowns in old uniforms dug out of some ancient storeroom, uniforms that the Italians and the French wore in World War I. Everybody laughed at them. They were given all the dirtiest jobs.

One of them got shot—a young Italian who was put to picking up papers around the yards. As in all prison camps, there was a double barbed-wire fence around this one, and a sharpshooter's tower at every corner, machine guns ready. This young Italian, quite innocently, poked his arm through the inner wire to reach for a piece of paper that had blown just outside. The guard saw him, levelled his gun, and without warning chopped the young Italian to pieces.

Everybody saw it. Everybody was very quiet as two stretcher bearers came out, picked up the crumpled form, dumped it into a blanket, carried it away.

Next day, a bigshot Nazi general arrived at the camp, and all the Italians were lined up in parade formations to listen to the bigshot make a speech, full of promises to all the gallant, brave, and unfortunate Italians who had been betrayed into this criminal alliance with the butcher nations of England and America. Just sign up with the German army, the mighty conquering German army, and your uniforms and new weapons and new equipment will be restored to you, so that you can go to the Russian front and fight to save Europe from Bolshevism.

Now the Italians did not care particularly whether or not Europe was saved from Bolshevism, but they did want new uniforms, and they didn't like being prisoners. They were all about to sign up on the first dotted line that was poked at them.

At that moment Chipper McLoughlin went into action. With a pal, he rushed back to the morgue, got the dead Italian soldier, put him on a stretcher, covered the body with a blanket, then raced out across the enclosure where all the Italians were gathered. Nobody stopped them—it looked like an emergency case.

Just as they passed the front of the packed Italians, Chipper neatly planted one foot on a corner of the blanket. The dead boy was uncovered for all his comrades to see. There was a whisper through the crowd, then a murmur, and then a growl. And so the Nazi general got no recruits that day for the Russian Front.

Chipper never saw the Russian Front, but he knows a lot about it. He became a medical orderly in the German hospital. Lots of the British prisoners worked at such jobs. He got to talk to many of the Germans who had been wounded on the Russian Front. There were dozens of cases of boys with feet so badly frost-bitten that they had to be amputated.

And Chipper knew how many of these men deliberately poured water into their boots to guarantee frostbite. Anything was preferable to staying at the Russian Front and losing your life. As a soldier, Chipper knew what has to happen to an army before men will pour water in their boots.

But all this was *indirect* evidence of limping, waning German morale. Chipper McLoughlin was human; he longed for the sight of Germans being killed, and then one day he got what he wanted. It was a Saturday.

Everybody had been told that Sunday would be a big day; all the prisoners were to be taken to the nearby assembly plant for Focke-Wulf fighter planes, just outside the Northeast German city of Marienburg to see Hermann Goering dedicate a magnificent new runway, the runway that was to be used for testing the new Focke-Wulfs before they went up into the Battle of Germany against the Forts and Libs of the Eighth Air Force.

But Goering got scooped on his opening. At seven minutes to noon on Saturday, a cloud of Fortresses flew over the prison. All the prisoners whipped off their shirts and waved and yelled, and almost as if in response to the waving shirts, bomb bays opened, and down came the tumbling compact pattern of bombs.

There had not been such accurate bombing anywhere in the Battle of Germany as this special show for the boys at Marienburg Prison Camp. They were all called into service to clear away the wreckage of the plant and haul out the dead Germans. Chipper cannot remember when he had more fun, poking and pulling at the delightful wreckage of another German factory. "It was every bit as bloody good fun as opening Christmas parcels."

Chipper's home now, a repatriated prisoner. He's had his thirty-day leave. He has a new wife, and a new son on the way whom he expects to be born on a new Armistice Day.

Chapter 32

CRUSADE'S REWARD

". . . you know, it's the greatest game
ever devised by man . . ."

A FEW years ago, the directors of the Meadowbrook Club on Long Island tried to figure out a way to make more people come to their polo games. Their motives were mixed—partly financial, partly an understandable pride in their game. The boss of the directors asked my advice. He was the president of a great shipping line, knew nothing about mass publicity.

I tried to explain to him, from a newspaperman's point of view, what it would take to build up a great polo player like Tommy Hitchcock into a great popular figure like Babe Ruth, a figure that would attract crowds to polo the way the Bambino did to baseball. (See Illus. 189.)

I didn't accomplish quite that. But after that experience I became keenly and increasingly curious about Tommy Hitchcock—not as a polo player, but just as a hell-of-a-man. I took dozens of pictures of him with a telephoto lens between the periods of the games at Meadowbrook; I dug into his story as a fighter pilot in the last war, about how he was shot in the hip, crashed behind enemy lines, and was captured; and about how he jumped out of a prison train and escaped through Switzerland.

Tommy Hitchcock's people were wealthy, solid, established. His father was one of the men who supported the game of polo in America for their own pleasure. His mother was a great horsewoman—she died after a bad fall in the field, riding to hounds, at sixty-eight. She had lifted Tommy onto his first pony when he was three, taught him to swing a polo mallet when he was five. She raised many of the present crop of great players of the game—Stewart Iglehart, Mike Phipps, Pete Bostwick, Jock and Sonny Whitney.

225

At sixteen, Tommy won his place on the Meadowbrook Club polo team. At seventeen, president of his class at St. Paul's School, he did what he had to do: get into the war, in the air.

He passed every test except one—age. So he went to France, and got into the Lafayette Escadrille.

He got his first promotion the hard way. Reward for shooting down one German plane: Corporal Hitchcock. He hit the jackpot with his next kill, two Huns. Reward: the cash pool of his corps, the Croix de Guerre with two palms, promotion to 2nd Lieutenant.

And then in March, 1918, he tangled with two more Huns, then with a third —one too many. Pilots in the last war often sat on stove lids in combat, or crude armor plating. Tommy didn't; he got shot through the thigh, and was forced to land behind the German lines.

For five months, he was a prisoner of war. While his wounds healed, he planned escape. His chance came on a prison train in Southern Germany. Others were to have escaped with him, but only Tommy moved swiftly and surely enough to make his break. He jumped out of the train window, raced for tall timber. He had a map in his pocket. Like most of the things he did, his escape was planned for success, for completion. He walked 80 miles to the Swiss border, got home, and immediately transferred to the American Air Service.

The story of Tommy Hitchcock's polo is too well known to need more than summary here. He was the greatest player in the game for twenty years. For sixteen of them he was rated at 10 goals—the top.

Tommy was almost killed in the East-West matches in Chicago in 1933. Never in the history of the game had polo been so ballyhooed as for that series. Sports writers billed the matches as a contest between the effete East vs. the wild and woolly Westerners. The game was given stiff doses of newspaper publicity. Feelings were tuned tight. In one mêlée of men and ponies, there was a terrific collision. Tommy went down and out of the game with a serious concussion.

Doctors told him that if he played again, he might spend the rest of his life cutting out paper dolls. But Tommy played and rode hell-for-leather anyway. Though his game was off, and his handicap dropped to nine, still he played the only way he knew—all out. In 1935, he was put back up to 10 goals, and stayed there until he quit the game in 1940.

159. From Ted Timberlake (Col., now Brig. Gen. Edward J. Timberlake), born in San Antonio, Tex., educated at West Point, the "Traveling Circus" got more than its nickname. (Chapter 27)

160. Pregnant Cows was the derisive name that the Fortress Crews gave the big-bellied Libs, and the Lib boys said, "Hell, we got nothing against the Fort. It's a damn good medium bomber!" The Lib crews (below) looked just like the Fortress crews. Col. Timberlake always said, though, that there was a difference. "In our outfit, we're just a bunch of carefree joes."

161. Typical of the best of Americans, typical of the kids in the Circus was Capt. Robert ("Shine") Shannon, from Washington, Iowa, killed when the Lib in which he was flying Gen. Andrews home crashed in soupy weather over Iceland.

162. To "Bake" (Lt. Col. Addison E. Baker, Akron, Ohio, successor to Colonel Ted as CO of the Circus) went the honor of leading his outfit on its greatest job. He was last seen aiming his flaming Liberator into an oil-storage tank at Ploesti.

163. "The Jerk"—Maj. John Jerstad from Davenport, Iowa—operations officer of the Circus, was worshipped by young pilots of new crews. "Tough as a mule-skinner and tender as your grandmother, that was Jerk." Jerk didn't come back from Ploesti either, to get his CMH.

164. M/Sgt. Peter Ververis, Norwich, Conn., Operations NCO.

165. Airmen who knew Gen. Andrews, and loved him, always said: "The weather was like a game of poker to the Old Man. I guess there never was a living thing without wings that so belonged in the air."

166. The Libs flew lower than the Forts in the Battle of Germany. The Forts used to say, "The Libs make our best escort. When they're along, the Jerries throw everything at them and leave us alone."

167. The Circus is . . . the jobs it's done: Chalking up another bull's-eye for the famous Lib "Shoot Luke."

168. The Circus is . . . the fun it's had. Giving the British a little Wild West between missions.

169. Capt. Lee Hall, St. Louis, Circus Flight Surgeon.

170. M/Sgt. Charles Chambers, Mechanicsburg, Pa., Crew Chief, kept his plane in shape for 32 missions, flew as gunner on 6 of them.

171. Lt. "Babe" Emmons.

172. Maj. W. S. Cowart.

173. Lt. Anthony C. Yenalavage, Kingston, Pa., bombardier with a DFC.

174. Capt. Jacob C. Epting, Tupelo, Miss., veteran pilot of the Circus.

175. Everybody outranked him. PFC Douglas Alexander, only private in the Circus' first desert expedition. Bomb loader with one mission as a gunner.

176. Glamor for the Circus arrives later in the person of Hollywood's Jimmy Stewart (now a Lt. Col.), veteran of more than 15 B-24 missions, second in command to Ted Timberlake.

177. T/Sgt. Ben Kuroki, Nebraska-born Japanese-American, engineer in Tupelo Lass. Has volunteered for another tour of combat duty although retired. Wants to bomb Tokyo.

178. Squadron Leader, Lt. Col. Kenneth O. Dessert.

179. Lt. Col. Joseph S. Tate, Jr., St. Augustine, Fla. and West Point '41. Squadron Leader.

180. Maj. John R. "Packy" Roche, Davenport, Iowa. Squadron Leader.

181. Lt. Walter Stewart, Benjamin, Utah. Veteran pilot, ex-Mormon missionary to Scotland.

182. Lt. Col. Ramsay D. Potts, Jr., Memphis, Tenn. Squadron Leader, ex-economics instructor at Memphis College.

183. Noted poloist, Capt. Michael G. Phipps, Westbury, L.I. Intelligence Officer.

184. Capt. Benny Klose, Circus bombardier.

185. "Rumania looked like England a helluva lot," said returning pilots. This shot was made over England, during long Ploesti rehearsal period. Dress rehearsals (below) were held over mock targets on the sands of the Libyan desert. (Chapter 28)

186. It was hell, that's all, hell. The Libs over Ploesti—one of the epics of this or any other war.

187. Stripped to the waist, these airmen of the 8th are grimly intent at the briefing for the Ploesti job. At the briefing they saw a movie—but no Mickey Mouse.

188. The faces that came home from Ploesti. That day's battle is written here in tired eyes that have looked into the face of Death.

189. Tommy Hitchcock, Lt. Col., USAAF. He hated to be chair-borne. As the world's greatest polo player, he stuck to the saddle far beyond the age when men must quit the game; as a pilot, he stuck to the cockpit far, far beyond the age when all men must quit combat. His chair-borne crusade for the Mustang won him a new chance to get into the air. He died as he had lived—in action. (Chapter 32)

190. Fisky—Yank in the RAF. "Never in the field of human conflict—" (Chapters 21 and 29)

191. Chipper McLoughlin eyewitnessed American bombing accuracy from the ground, at a German prison camp. (Chapter 31)

192. Bombardier Joe Pellegrini, born and raised in Philadelphia's Italian district, has finished his tour of duty in the Battle of Germany—but he will go on flying "until the Germans get to know me better." (Chapter 30)

193. Think our guys are young? Two airmen of the 8th discuss the war with a couple of Russian GIs—veterans—at an unnamed base in the Ukraine after the memorable shuttle mission of June, 1944. (Chapter 34)

194. Russian children shyly accepted gum. But no Russian would accept any gifts without giving something in return. It was embarrassing for the Yanks—whatever they looked at, Russians insisted on giving them as souvenirs.

195. Yanks got on well with Russian girls. Crew chiefs found them skilled around engines. And, "Jeepers, they sure can dance good."

196. "Parachutes were seen to open." That report at interrogation is the slim hope to which the friends of a missing crew cling, until letters come through to end the guessing about how many 'chutes did open and, if there were fewer than 10, who got out and who didn't. Of the 10 men of "Invasion II," all got down safely. Here are two of Harry "Little Horror" Goldstein's P.O.W. letters, and one from Ben Borostowski. (Chapters 2 and 33)

MAY 4, 1943

Dear Mrs. Buckley,

Your little horror won't annoy you once more. There are several things to be attended to in London. I wonder if you would ask Bill Lancaster or one of the boys to take care of it for me. They are (1) See Jim Regan in our Zone office and ask him to get my films from Jim Ryton and tell them for me. Also ask him to write me. (2) See the governor of the cave and tell him I send my regards (3) Send a telegram to the families of my crew (4) Peggy has a house at Chit House that somebody can have (5) To all the boys and girls our regards and tell them we would like to hear from them.

This camp isn't so bad for waiting around until the war ends. There are a nice bunch of fellows here and they are taking good care of us. We do our own cooking and washing but have nothing else to do. The Canadian and British Red Cross are doing a great job. Their food packages supplement our German ration. We are also well supplied with books and athletic equipment with which we spend most of our spare time. Kindest regards, Harry

Kriegsgefangenenlager

LONDON 5 JNE 1943 73

Dear Colleen,

Arrived here by [...] safe. Thompson, Frank[...] with me. Tell Jo not anymore. Ask Lee to [...] boys and myself send [...]

Kriegsgefangenenlager   Datum:

LONDON 19 JNE 1943 79

Dear Coline; — I guess it will be quite some time before I visit the R.C., and see you all again. If you don't know who I actually am; when you see the rebels' "Lee", or "Kirk" ask them. Also tell them I said "hello". That goes for "B. Lancaster", Carter, and the others. Give them my address, and tell them to write me. We're all okay. Tell "Peggy" "I'm sorry, I won't be at the christening".

sincerly — "Ben"

Stewart Iglehart and Mike Phipps and Pete Bostwick had been talking about him one afternoon, after a game. One phrase stuck in my memory. I don't recall who used it, but it stuck: "Christ, he's a cold fish."

I believed that about him until one afternoon in his office, when I drew him out, got him on the subject of flying in the last war, got him to dreaming out loud about the future of aviation. He was talking about airlines. That was the greater game for him then. There was something in the way he said it that made me know that the other teams were in for a tough time in this new game of Tommy's. There was nothing "cold," nothing "fish" about him then.

Next time I saw Tommy was in Washington, in 1942. I had gone down there to see a bunch of charts that General Arnold had drawn up to prove to his critics that it was not easy to pick a "best" fighter plane. He showed me all the performance curves, and one of them was clearly better than the others in speed and range and rate of climb—the three things we so desperately needed to give the Forts and Libs fighter-cover over targets in Germany.

The plane was the P-51, the Mustang. The British were using the same airframe with another engine; but these curves foretold its performance with an engine not then perfected. This was "it." General Arnold laughed long and loud, and a big grin kept echoing his pleasure. Here was an all-American fighter plane that would confound all the critics.

Later that day I saw Tommy, in Laurence Stallings' office. He looked tired, beat out, ten years older. Afterward, Stallings told me some of the story of his crusade. It is one of the great stories of this war, one of the greatest.

Mr. Lovett once said at the end of a rasping day: "You know, when the history of this war is finally written, the real history, it will be shown how every great victory was won by some obscure man who got mad and stayed mad and didn't mind being called names, until finally he pushed through one little idea that he had fought and sweated and bled for."

Tommy's story is like that. Let's pick up the high spots of it. He came over here to be an assistant military attaché in 1942. He tackled one job because he felt that it was one thing he knew something about: fighter planes.

He immediately approached the problem from a new angle. In those days you would kill any idea if you said to Americans:

"British operational experience has shown," etc.

Somehow, if a thing was British, two strikes were already chalked up against it in America. Tommy reversed the formula. If an idea has been tested and okayed in Britain's battle-lab, then Hitchcock called it right. He knew that over here was the toughest air fighting in the world. Anything that survived had to be good.

When the Airacobra was sent over for a run-through at the Duckpond, a British experimental station, Tommy sat in on the tests. And during those tests, they gave another American plane the same going-over—the Mustang, an "orphan" built only for British order and then powered with an Allison engine, good at that time only for low altitudes. That's how they discovered that, for some mysterious reason, the Mustang airframe was the "cleanest and sweetest thing in the air." Topped the Spitfire. Given an engine of equal horsepower, it would be better than the Spit.

That's how Tommy's crusade was born. It is impossible, unwise, and unnecessary to detail the rounds of that crusade; but the tenacity, the sincerity, and the sheer butt-headedness of Hitchcock pushed that plane through the ranks of all its critics until it became the fighter that is today the answer to many of the problems of the Eighth Air Force.

Remember, this plane was then being built only for British order; it was an American plane that had never been through Wright Field. It was bought only by the British, and hence was "foreign."

After the British order ran out, General Arnold kept the basic design alive by ordering dive bombers adapted from the same airframe. But the pressure steamed up by Tommy's quiet crusade kept demanding fighters. Ambassador Winant, Air Chief Marshal Portal, Mr. Lovett, and finally even Mrs. Roosevelt joined the campaign for the Mustang.

That's the technical end of this story. I include it here because for airmen there is always a great story in aircraft design. Once a shipping man told me that "you cannot see in the blue prints the qualities that make a great ship, but those qualities are there if the designer understands ships, if he understands that what makes a great ship is the *plus* that a captain will find when he calls for it in a crisis, the plus that is above and beyond specifications." It's the same way with planes.

In the meantime, back to the other part of Tommy's story: A few months ago I called him up at the Embassy and was told that he was "away at school." I found that he had gone to the RAF Central Gunnery School for a complete course.

This is the school to which the RAF sends the absolute cream of its fighter pilots, takes them right off combat, pulls them in there, analyzes their special genius as killers, and then polishes and standardizes it so that they can go out and teach it to others. It is a post-post-graduate school. Only the best attend; and only the best of the best get through.

Tommy got through. And with top marks in one most important course.

A few weeks later, I called Tommy again. Gone again: "Away at school." This time at the RAF "school for leaders," where they teach the tactics of air war.

Staff pilots in striped planes are "the enemy." Twice a day the student pilots go out on "missions"—everything from low level and high altitude "sweeps" to bomber escort jobs. It's great fun, thorough as hell. Again, few got through. Tommy did.

Finally, a few weeks later, I met him in the War Room at Headquarters. He was listening to the day's report, but not really listening—he was daydreaming, and almost whistling. And a big grin, like a kid's, pushed unfamiliar wrinkles back to his ears. And later that day, I got the answer.

The planes, the P-51's were coming to England, to fly with the Eighth. Now at last, the Forts and Libs would have fighter cover during those vital twenty seconds of the bombing run over the deepest targets. This was it—victory for Tommy's crusade.

That morning, Tommy had gone in to see the Boss. That shock of rebel hair was in his face as usual. With his speech all prepared, all his reasons, all his pleading, he put the proposition: he wanted to take command of one of the groups of the new Super-X's.

And before he even had time to say a first "please," the Old Man looked up and gave Tommy one of those quiet, quick answers that come from his instinct for knowing what will turn out all right.

"Yes, Tommy, you can have it. Of course we could use you with one of the Thunderbolt outfits, but I know how you feel about your plane. I know what it is to believe in something. You'll get your group. . . ."

And the next evening, after work, I went by and listened to Tommy talk about this crusade of his.

"You know, there is a place for an older man in combat. Age and altitude don't have much to do with blacking-out or greying-out. That isn't why men like me don't get a chance. It's just that when you get older, it's harder to learn a new game, and fighter tactics change all the time.

"Of course skill and stamina do play a large part; but luck is such an important factor. Fully seventy-five per cent of all kills are made by surprise attacks. There is no more dog-fighting.

"If you get up on a man and get him in your sights before he sees you, it doesn't take any skill to get him. You could fly on in straight and level and just stick your guns right down his neck.

"But it is also true that calculation and concentration and experience are responsible for most surprise attacks. Some of these boys will see the enemy planes long before I will, when they are only tiny specks in the sky. They will watch those specks get behind them, and go into the sun. And though they might be on an escort job, and hence unable to leave their positions, they know the danger that is getting cocked above them—they are ready to meet it when it comes slicing down out of the sun.

"The General made me promise not to go out on combat too often, and I won't. But I will go out. I will lead my group. You know, it's the greatest game that man has ever devised."

The sun had set and the moon was out and the night bombers of the RAF would be going out again soon. On dozens of fields, the Forts and Libs of the Eighth were resting from their deepest daylight thrust into Germany—beyond Berlin. Now, when our daylight bombers hit Berlin, the bombardiers in the noses of Forts and Libs know that for those precious seconds before the cross hairs of their bomb sights split the Aiming Point, it's safe to fly straight and level, because there are American fighters over the target to hold the Jerries at bay.

Official records may give to many men the credit for that new fighter with its range to beyond-Berlin; or official records may wink and call in an "immaculate conception." But the story I've told you is the real story—the story of a stubborn guy with a private crusade.

*　　*　　*　　*　　*

When they found Tommy Hitchcock where he fell when his plane broke up in the air, his parachute was half opened.

It was not the way he would have wanted to die. He had worked and schemed so hard for combat. They did give him a group back in the States, because General Eaker had backed him. But then they took it away from him, and broke it up into replacements before he could take it into combat.

In England, General Pete Quesada of the 9th Air Force Fighter Command gave Tommy a job, at least a chance to work at the ringside. Eventually Tommy would have found a way to get into the fight. He usually did.

Some young pilot will remember the day Tommy tried to check out in an AT-6 at Bolling Field at the beginning of this war. He wore wings, and his medals of the last war, so the young pilot wasn't too worried at first. Tommy was a new major then, beginning his quiet way back toward a chance to fly and fight again. They took off, did easy stuff, then Tommy tried to bring the AT-6 in for a landing. He had done quite a little flying between the wars, but none in a plane with half the horsepower of the trainer. The landing was bad and bumpy. The young pilot, half-anxiously, said, "Want to take it around again, sir?"

They did. Once more Tommy tried a landing. This time he came down as though he were strafing the field. He overshot, jammed her down, almost crashed into a line of parked P-40's. Finally he stopped, turned around toward the young pilot, gave him his Will Rogers grin, pushed the hair out of his eyes, and said: "Shall we take her around again?"

The young lieutenant was already out of the plane, safe on the good earth, shaking his head and mopping his brow, stammering, "No sir, not me—no more. . . ."

Next day, Tommy tried to walk down the steps of his house in Washington and almost fell down. To a friend he explained, "You know, my legs are so stiff and sore I can hardly stand up. I was so scared yesterday they were knocking together. I was paralyzed with fear."

But he went around again—and again. He was always scared, but he flew with one purpose: to get into combat. He'd often say, "Fighting in a Mustang ought to be like playing polo—but with pistols."

They buried him very quietly in Brookwood Cemetery, outside London. Ten other Americans were buried the same day, young airmen who had died on the day Tommy was killed.

Chapter 33

P.O.W.—POSTSCRIPT

". . . parachutes were seen to open . . ."

Lt. Douglas Adoue McCrary
Torpedo Squadron X, Aircraft Carrier Y
% Postmaster, San Francisco:

DEAR DOUGLAS:

The other day, Lord "Stuffy" Dowding, who was boss of RAF Fighter Command during the Battle of Britain, made a remarkable speech in Christ Church. "Survival" was his text—more sermon than speech. Flatly, he expressed his belief in life after death. Vigorously, he argued that "we pass on to our next life practically without any break in consciousness at all. Some people who pass on after a long and painful illness require a period of sleep and rest before they regain consciousness.

"But for these men and boys killed in battle, the transition comes instantaneously, rapidly. I have a very large number of messages now from men who have passed over in this war, and the fact that I want to stress is that the tone of these messages is: 'We are okay.'

"There is a great organization of Air Force men over the other side, and I receive frequent messages from them. The tone of those messages almost without exception is happiness, joy, and relief that all the black fears of death are unfounded."

It is good to believe in that kind of "survival," if you can. But I'm afraid that most of the kids in the Forts seem to come from Missouri. And you can't give them much proof.

But among those first listed as missing in action it's different. At the interrogation after a mission, the one scrap of information that Intelligence

232

Officers poke and pull at longest is the one that begins with the words "para-chutes were seen to open."

That is the beginning of the proof of survival; final proof may come like this. Jim Dugan heard about a wonderful woman named Mrs. Colleen Buck-ley, a volunteer worker down at the Red Cross Rainbow Corner in London's Times Square. She gets letters from lots of the kids who wind up as Prisoners of War, somewhere in Germany.

"Listen, Mrs. Buckley, my name is Jim Dugan and there used to be a guy named Harry Goldstein who was a top-turret gunner on a Fortress that went down over Bremen. He was a good friend of mine—lent me a copy of *War and Peace* last time he was in town. Have you ever heard any word from him? Maybe you knew him."

"You mean The Little Horror? You bet I knew him! Like he was my own son! Knew his whole outfit. Sure I've heard from him, and he talked about you. Wait, I'll get you his cards—and there was a letter, too." (See Illus. 196.)

"Invasion II" went down on April 17; Harry's first card was dated April 28; it was received in London on June 5, fresh as paint:

"Dear Colleen:

"Arrived here by parachute. All my crew are safe. Thompson and Frank-lin and several others are here with me. Tell Jo not to wish anybody 'luck' any more. Ask Lee to send some food parcels. The boys and myself send fondest regards.

HARRY (Little Horror)."

And there was another one from Benny Borostowski, the silent ball-turret gunner. He had always called her "Mrs. Buckley," but now his shyness was safely on the other side of the Channel, so he began his letter, "Dear Colleen," too.

"I guess it will be quite some time before I visit the Red Cross and see you all again. If you don't know who I actually am, when you see the rebels Lee or Kirk, ask them. Also tell them I said hello. That goes for B. Lancaster, Carter, and the others. Give them my address and tell them to write me please. We're all okay. Tell Peggy I'm sorry I won't be at the christening. Sincerely,

BEN."

And then there was a longer letter on May 4 from Harry:

"Dear Colleen:

"Your Little Horror must annoy you once more. There are several things to be attended to in London. I wonder if you would ask Bill Lancaster or one of the boys to take care of them for me. They are (1) See Jim Dugan and ask him to get my films and hold them for me. Also ask him to write me. (2) See the Governor of The Cave and tell him I send my regards. (3) Send cablegrams to the families of my crew. (4) Pappy has a blouse at Phil Harris' that somebody can have. (5) Give all the boys and girls our regards and tell them we would like to hear from them.

"This camp isn't so bad for waiting around until the war ends. There are a nice bunch of fellows here and they are taking good care of us. We do our own cooking and washing but have nothing else to do. The Canadian and British Red Cross are doing a great job. Their food packages supplement German ration. We are also well supplied with books and athletic equipment, with which we spend most of our spare time. Fondest regards and thanks.

HARRY."

The "Governor of The Cave" is the boss of a joint where all the gunners used to eat and drink when they came to town on a "forty-eight." Jim went around to see him: "Have you heard the news, Governor?"

"I bloody well have, and Gor bless me, it was just what I bloody well expected."

Those who knew The Invaders best had most faith in their survival.

I've always been afraid that if I had to bail out of a Fort, I'd be so damn scared that I wouldn't be able to find the rip cord, or if I did, I would pull it before I was clear of the ship. But that guy Carmichael, the navigator—remember, I told you what a cool customer he was—well, he wrote to say that he had made a delayed jump, didn't pull his rip cord until he was a few hundred feet from the ground. He had it all figured out—maybe if he held his 'chute until the last, he would go down so fast that nobody would notice him and then he might get out into the country and work south toward France. So he held the rip cord, but did not pull it until the last—he held it while he tumbled through space—he held it, resisted the insistent curiosity and pressing fear that it would not open when he did pull it, held it because he was determined to escape if he could.

But he must have spent all his luck, because he broke his ankle when he landed, and a couple of farmers caught him and handed him over to the cops.

And Jim heard that Jack Gaffney, who took care of No. 3 engine, had had a card from another of "Invasion II's" crew—Don King, the kid waist gunner from Texas. It was the best of all.

"Dear Jack:

"It wasn't your fault. The old ship still wanted to fly, but we had to leave her. See Smitty and get my ration card and send me some cigarettes."

If we can knock Germany out of the war before Christmas I'll bet "Invasion II's" crew will be back on combat by September, in a Fortress named "Invasion III." What's more, they'll be racing your flat-top to Tokyo.

Yours,

TEX

Chapter 34

P.P.S. RING AROUND THE
NAZIS

"...airmen make good ambassadors..."

THE buzz-bombs had just started coming over England. I was sitting out in a movie lab, near London, cutting three films—*Battle for Italy*, the story of six months' operations of the Mediterranean Allied Air Forces under Eaker; *French Air Force*, the story of what French airmen had built in the Mediterranean out of memories and promises and hopes; and *Missions for Moscow*, the story of the 15th Air Force's shuttle mission to Ukraine bases early in June, 1944.

Funny thing about the buzz-bombs. I had stood in the streets of London a few nights before and watched the people when the sound of a buzzer vibrated the sky. There was not a hurried footstep to seek shelter; the only people who hurried were those who wanted to get to a street corner to watch the buzzer bite.

The buzzers bothered me, because every time the alert sounded, all the girls in the lab, working on my film, had to go downstairs to shelter. They didn't want to. They wanted to go on the roof and watch the buzzers come over.

I sat and sorted my film, tried to piece it together into a story of American airmen flying to Russian bases, a story that would capture all the excitement and significance of the mission.

These were not the first Allied airmen to operate from Russian bases. Hub Zemke knew well the RAF boys who flew from Russian soil. And Eve Curie, in the commentary of the film about the French Air Force, paid tribute to the Normandie Squadrons that flew with the Red Air Force.

But there was historic importance to this mission of American airmen, Fortresses and Mustangs of the 15th Air Force, to Russian bases. Certainly, they were a part of the story of the "first of the many."

One of the groups that made the trip was the old 97th—the group that Gen. Eaker flew with on the first mission from British bases against a German target, on August 17, 1942. Gen. Eaker flew to Russia with this same outfit, in a plane with the same name as the first that carried him on an attack against the Hun—"Yankee Doodle."

This mission marked the closing of the circle around the Hun by day-bombers that carried the star of the U.S. Army Air Force. What had begun as a beach-head had achieved encirclement. Ring around the Nazis.

As I cut the film, I found so many traces of the story of the "first." The American commander of the Russian bases, Col. (now Gen.) Kessler, was on his first mission—and he took it in Red Cliburn's "Bad Penny." I was along as cameraman. It was Red's last mission.

One of the American nurses at the bases in Russia, 2nd Lt. Helene Lieb from Minneapolis, was engaged to Red Morgan, the second man in the 8th to win the Congressional Medal of Honor. Red went down on the first mission to Berlin.

One of the kids who worked at the hospital at the main Russian base, S/Sgt. Dick McAllister from Patterson, Missouri, was the boy who took Jack Mathis out of the nose of the "Duchess," dead. "It was just one little piece of flak that went through his left arm and then through his chest. Gee, he was a good guy. Another couple of inches off for that flak and he woulda been okay . . ."

Built around the CO of the 97th was a great story that was all tangled up in the story of The Invaders. His name was Col. Frankie Allen, from Chicago, born in Oklahoma. He went into the army as a mechanic because he thought a pilot ought to know everything about a plane, including the engine.

He flew hundreds of hours before the war for United Airlines. They didn't want to give him a job with United because he was only 5 feet 5. Frankie said: "Listen, Ham Lee, the best pilot you've got, with 23,000 hours, is shorter than I am." He got the job.

When he became CO of the 97th, it was still Somewhere in Africa. He moved his outfit three times, finally wound up in Italy, one of the first heavy bomber groups to be based on the continent of Europe.

Frankie said to himself when he started: "I'm going to fly more missions than anybody else in the Air Forces down here." And he did. Because he thought the Boss should.

After he had had 62 missions, they decided to give the job to another man and send Frankie home for a rest. The man who got the job was a tall, strong-faced, blond colonel named Jake Smart. He was the man who planned the low-level raids on Ploesti.

He came to the 97th and he lived up to the tradition set by Frankie Allen. He flew on every tough mission. After he had had 27, Gen. Eaker and Gen. Twining of the 15th ordered him to stop. He took one more, and he didn't come back. Posthumously, he was awarded the DSC:

"Jacob E. Smart, Colonel, Air Corps, United States Army. (Missing in Action.) For extraordinary achievement while leading his group against a vitally important and heavily defended aircraft production center, Col. Smart remained with a ship damaged by a direct hit until he was assured that his group would accurately bomb the target. Leaving the protective formation to return the crippled ship to its base, Col. Smart displayed great courage, in remaining with the ship when its condition would have warranted abandonment. Col. Smart's courage, determination and resourcefulness led to his selection to lead another attack on a target in the same area on 10 May, 1944. With the skill and courage that he had displayed on 27 missions, Col. Smart again was successful in bringing his group through unusually severe weather conditions and augmented enemy aircraft defenses, to the beginning of the bomb run, when his ship was seen to explode from a direct hit. The gallant, intrepid leadership displayed by Col. Smart in accomplishing his assignment regardless of hazard or opposition, upholds the highest tradition of military service of the United States of America. Residence at appointment: Jessup, Georgia."

When Jake Smart went down, they called Frankie Allen back to take over his group again, and Frankie was pretty happy about it. He didn't really want to quit. He had it figured out a long time ago—the Jerries didn't have his number.

His outfit loved him. You felt it that night at the briefing for the Russian show when he told them: "Listen, boys. We got to get some good pictures to show these Russian fellows. They are hot. Plenty hot. Look at the headlines. We got to get some good pictures of our bombing to show them that we do all right, too. And you know me, boys—if we don't hit that target, you don't get credit for a mission. No target, no mission. That's the rule, and I pay off on the pictures."

Going over the mountains of Yugoslavia, I could look out the nose of our ship and see Frankie's Fort riding just ahead—"The Big Chief." Somewhere back in the group, Gen. Eaker was flying in the "Yankee Doodle II." Going into the target we got crossed up on our approach. Frankie swung the whole outfit around in a 360 and we made another run. Bombs away. On the target. The pictures would pay off on this job. The tail gunner croaked into the intercom, calm and unemotional as the guy who announces the trains in Grand Central:

"B-17 just blew up behind us. . . ."

I grabbed for the list that had the numbers of the ships in the group . . . which was the Old Man's? I couldn't find the list. The navigator was calmly scribbling in his log, "one B-17 down, seen to explode over the target, cause not certain . . ."

I knew "Yankee Doodle" was a new ship. Was this a new ship? I scribbled the note, passed it to the bombardier—my intercom was out now. No, it was an old ship. My stomach fell away from my belt. Real relief.

I thought of that now as I cut together a film sequence showing General Eaker received a huge bunch of flowers from a Russian girl—and another sequence in which Cathy Harriman jokingly hung around his neck a German Iron Cross—one of the ones that had been struck by the Germans to be awarded to the troops who first entered Moscow, but never did.

The Moscow correspondents did a helluva fine job on the story. It was fun to watch them go on talking to the combat crews, far more than they had to to get a story. The way Ed Angly put it: "Hell, we've been out here so long we just like to hear an American talking again."

But I can add these sidelights to the official accounts of the mission—the kind of stories that newspapers don't have room to print and histories forget. One was about the prettiest nurse over there. She reminded me of all the girls I ever wanted to fall in love with. Her name was Thelma "Cokie" Coughenour from New Bethlehem, Pa. The important thing about Cokie was this:

"I never went anywhere much or ever thought I would, but now, I just want to keep going. I want to go to the Pacific from here. None of us knew where we were going when we volunteered for this job—sure, girls like to volunteer as much as boys. The only time I get homesick is at Christmas, but the rest of the time, I just want to keep traveling. I guess a lot of kids feel like that now."

The next is about the wonderful old General with the bad wounds who showed us through the huge exhibition of captured German war equipment in the Park of Culture and Rest in Moscow. He took great delight in showing us the paper underwear the Germans wore on the Russian front that first winter. And then he came to a big glass-top case, the kind you see in a butcher shop. Inside, on the left, was a replica of the edible parts of a horse. On the right, were the bones of a horse. Said the General:

"On the left, you see what the Germans in Rumania ate last winter. On the right you see what they left for the Rumanians—the bones."

The next: Every other night at the main base, the Russians would put on a show for us. The drummer in the orchestra—we got a good sequence of him in the film—was hot as a hep cat. Through an interpreter later, I asked him where he learned his tricks. His answer: "I see a movie about Gene Krupa . . ."

They had an amusing way of announcing these shows, number by number, to the assembled audience of GIs and Russians. First a Russian would come out and explain everything in Russian, at great length. And next, another Russian would come out, and translate—with a very heavy accent. For instance, the first would explain in great detail what the next dance represented. Then the translation:

"Andt now comes dancink—not seemple, ex-zentrick. You'll see."

And then we would get a good round of tap dancing from a Russian boy who was once in the Ballet Russe—only he had seen a Fred Astaire movie.

The greatest single scene we shot in the whole film on the Russian missions was of a Russian kid of eight, chewing his first stick of American gum, watching the show.

The Russian lieutenant who did the translations for the show used to be a school teacher; he's thirty-one, has fought for four years, been wounded three times. Everybody who speaks any English has been sought out in the Red Army and brought to the American bases. I asked him what he would do after the war:

"I do not know. When fighting is done, there must be much building. When building is done, then comes teaching again . . ."

But the thing I shall never forget, never, though I got no pictures of it on film:

As we crossed over the front lines on the way into the Ukraine, the earth was already plowed, great black strips scraped into the green carpet that Hitler had coveted and held and lost.